An Honest Profit

Raymond Baumhart, s.j.

AN HONEST PROFIT

What Businessmen Say About
Ethics in Business

HOLT, RINEHART AND WINSTON

New York   Chicago   San Francisco

To my parents,
Emil and Florence Baumhart,
who taught me that
love is proved by ethical deeds.

ACKNOWLEDGMENTS Cooperation from many persons is indispensable to the satisfactory completion of a book. The cooperation given me was both generous and intelligent; for this I am deeply grateful.

The necessary data were willingly supplied by 1,800 businessmen, who revealed their experiences and views, and who remain anonymous.

Financial support for research expenditures was provided through the John W. Hill Fellowship by Hill and Knowlton, Incorporated, and by the editors of the *Harvard Business Review*. The time and facilities for writing were provided by the Cambridge Center for Social Studies, assisted by a grant from the John W. Hill Foundation.

Most helpful in aiding me to clarify and unify my thinking were Vincent Burns, S.J., Joseph Cunneen, G. Donald Fitzpatrick, S.J., Thomas Garrett, S.J., Thomas McMahon, C.S.V., and Lewis Ward.

Constructive criticism was provided by Kenneth Andrews, David Ashton, Robert Austin, Lawrence Bloomgarden, William Brown, S.J., Philip Carey, S.J., John Clark, S.J., A. Richard Dooley, Joseph Fichter, S.J., William Gies, Rabbi Albert Gordon, Roger Hall, John Herbes, Herbert Johnston, Lawrence Lavengood, Benjamin Masse, S.J., Robert O'Brien, Raymond Pelissier, Theodore Purcell, S.J., George A. Smith, Jr., Reverend Alexander Stewart, John Thomas, S.J., Harold and Dorothy Unger, and Robert Valtz.

Technical assistance was given by John Fitzgerald, S.J., Robert Hetler, John and Elaine Morrow, and Renato Tagiuri.

Dolores Zappala capably handled the necessary secretarial details.

To all these, and to many others who offered encouragement and suggestions, go my thanks.

RAYMOND BAUMHART, s.j.

Cambridge, Massachusetts
January 1968

Contents

List of Tables

Introduction

Ours is a business-centered society. No group in America is more influential than businessmen. Their influence, for good or evil, enters every life and every home many times each day. If this influence is good, the nation is strengthened; if it is evil, the nation is weakened. The United States is a republic, and "republics live by virtue. Monarchies and empires may rely on physical force, or on the wisdom and goodness of the one or the few. Republics are ruled by the many, and the virtue of the people is the life of the nation."[1] Obviously, the myriad decisions of businessmen will significantly determine our national health, ethical as well as economic. Many, especially the impressionable young, imitate the mores and manners of successful businessmen.

One reason for thinking that democracy is superior to totalitarian forms of government is its respect for the worth and dignity of the individual human being. Through personnel management, customer relations, treatment of suppliers, advertising, and other daily actions, businessmen reinforce or weaken human dignity, a cornerstone of our way of life.

In this age of international commerce, the decisions of American businessmen also influence persons outside our borders. Many regard the corporation as the characteristic institution of our society. As Henry Ford II observed: "Around the world we are often described as a corporate society. If that is so, and if it is judged that the corporations are corrupt, then it will be assumed that the society itself is corrupt."[2] Neutral nations watch our managers for examples of the free enterprise system in action, and Communist countries search for evidence of corruption. Consequently, un-

---

[1] John Ireland, *The Church and Modern Society* (New York: D. H. McBride, 1903), Vol. 1, pp. 195–196.

[2] Henry Ford II, quoted in *New York Times*, April 21, 1961, p. 16.

ethical behavior on the part of businessmen at home or abroad can have international repercussions.

In view of the importance of ethical business behavior, it is not surprising that books and articles have been written about the subject. It is surprising, however, that few of these were written by businessmen. Fewer authors have treated this topic empirically, using data acquired systematically from a sizable cross section of businessmen. Virtually no one has bothered to ask businessmen what they think about ethics in business. So I asked them, in three research projects which provide the data for this book. More than 1,800 businessmen replied, 1,612 completing lengthy questionnaires and the rest giving information in interviews.[3] Their views, and my reflections on their views, make up the bulk of this study. It seemed important that a large sample of businessmen be quizzed about a subject they know more about than do most of their critics. The effort of the respondents to be objective is clear from their answers, which are quoted at length. The replies also demonstrate the desire of businessmen to do what is right, the difficulty they sometimes encounter in acting ethically, and the complexity of some of their ethical dilemmas.

No study of this topic could be exhaustive, and no sampling of businessmen's opinions that is financially feasible would provide conclusions beyond dispute. The evidence for my findings, which are summarized in Chapter 1, is not always such as to compel assent, and there is unavoidable imprecision in the use of questionnaires and interview responses to learn about human behavior. However, I have made every effort to be objective, to indicate my methodology, and to let the 1,800 businessmen speak for themselves.

While serving as a United States Navy supply officer during World War II, I learned the importance of business for America's well-being. Since then, as consumer, employee, teacher, and business school dean, I have associated with businessmen. Gradually I became aware of a discrepancy between their business behavior as I knew it and the cynical image of that behavior held by many persons. Because of the significance of the businessman's decisions, the discrepancy demanded investigation. That is why I undertook the research which resulted in this book.

[3] Profiles of the businessmen participating in these projects can be found in Chapter 1. Contents of the questionnaires and the interview schedule are in Appendices A and B. The systematic data-gathering for the three projects was completed in 1962; the interviewing of businessmen, in 1966.

An Honest Profit

1 The Setting, the Findings, and the Profile

The Little Miami River meanders through southern Ohio. In spring the water rages and swirls along, tearing away shrubbery and trees. In summer the water trickles along, barely covering the river bed. Popular interest in the ethics of businessmen is like the water in the Little Miami River. High water in the river usually follows heavy precipitation; wide public interest in business ethics results from unethical practices and widespread coverage by communications media.

In 1959, unsuspecting television audiences heard about the fixing of quiz programs and Charles Van Doren's spectacular hypocrisy. Then came the discovery that disc jockeys were surreptitiously accepting pay for promoting rock 'n' roll records; our language had a new word, payola. Next the president of the Chrysler Corporation resigned and returned $450,000 to the company when a stockholder-lawyer discovered that the president had been using his position for personal gain, to the detriment of the stockholders.

At the beginning of 1961 came news of a price-fixing scandal involving twenty-nine electrical manufacturers, including gigantic Westinghouse and General Electric. Seven high-ranking executives were jailed for 30 days; the companies were fined $1,787,000.

In 1962, a west Texas financial manipulator, Billie Sol Estes, came to the public's attention. He drove many competitors out of business by selling ammonia fertilizer below cost. Then he defrauded finance companies of millions of dollars by selling them mortgages on nonexistent fertilizer storage tanks.

The following year saw the conviction of Gerard A. Re and his son, Gerard F. Re, securities specialists on the American Stock Exchange. They served five months in jail for conspiring to sell unregistered shares of stock to the public and for conspiring to rig the price of an oil stock.

For several years Senator Philip A. Hart led an investigation of fraud in the packing and labeling of food. Although his proposed "truth-in-packaging" bill won widespread consumer support, it was defeated in Congress in 1964 and 1965. The bill finally passed in 1966.

Also championing the consumer's cause, former Senator Paul Douglas advocated a "truth-in-lending" bill, requiring that potential borrowers be informed in advance of the exact dollar and percentage cost of consumer credit. Thus far the bill has lacked sufficient Congressional support.

Management's responsibility to owners of stock in the Texas Gulf Sulphur Company became a central issue in 1965. The Securities and Exchange Commission charged that thirteen company officers, directors, and key employees had illegally used inside information about a giant Canadian ore discovery. A federal judge upheld the SEC's charges on only two of the defendants.

Anthony DeAngelis was sentenced to a twenty-year federal prison term in 1965 after master-minding a $150 million swindle based on salad oil; among the consequences were heavy losses to twenty banks and the collapse of two brokerage houses.

In 1965 Ralph Nader wrote *Unsafe At Any Speed*, an indictment of the automobile industry for sacrificing safety to design and thus causing unnecessary highway accidents. The resulting national discussion led to the unanimous passage of the highway safety act of 1966 by Congress.

During the last three years, price collusion and price fixing have been the leading categories of unethical business in the news. In 1965, among the industries whose members were fined for illegal pricing practices were glass, fiber products, flour, hydraulic hose, steel, and oil. Also fined were managers of steel and oil companies. In 1966, the industries whose members were indicted included thirty-six companies making concrete pipe, matches, and liquid asphalt.

Public opinion about ethics in business is not taken lightly by businessmen. This was evident in the wake of the 1961 electrical industry convictions, when the American Management Association, planning a New York meeting on ethics in business, could not find a business leader to speak on the topic. Thirty executives declined the invitation. Later in the year, Luther Hodges, Secretary of Commerce, felt the need to form a Business Ethics Advisory Council.[1] The council, composed mostly of businessmen, but including clergymen, educators, and civic leaders, investigated ways to assure ethical conduct in business affairs.

The scandals, Congressional investigations, and antitrust prosecutions of the last decade have revealed widespread confusion about ethics in business. This confusion extends to both what *is* being done by businessmen and what *should* be done. There have been substantial differences of opinion about the applicability of traditional ethical standards to current business practices. There has also been disagreement about the extent of the responsibility of educational and religious institutions for the business behavior of their graduates or members. These differences demonstrate the need for serious thought and discussion about business ethics.

Unfortunately, business ethics is a topic so vast and varied that generalization about it is hazardous. The businessman who has personally experienced and become acquainted with a segment of business behavior usually thinks, "This is how the whole thing is." Accordingly, one manager is sure that business practice is nearly flawless and cannot believe reports to the contrary, while another sees the business world as a jungle or rat race. Part of the difference in the views of the two managers is attributable to their subjective outlook, but probably more of the difference stems from their varied experiences. Men generalize from what they know. The accuracy of their generalization is proportional to the breadth and depth of their knowledge. Experience is, of course, not the sole source of knowledge, but most businessmen find little time for reading and study.

This survey affords the reader the opportunity to take a wide-lens look at business ethics. It does not give the whole picture, as little is said about social responsibilities of business in matters such as racial equality, air pollution, or conservation of natural resources. The emphasis throughout is on the person, more than on a larger social unit. When I speak of a company or industry or occupation, it is usually to discuss its ethical impact on the individual manager.

[1] An account of the formation and actions of the Business Ethics Advisory Council is contained in Luther H. Hodges, *The Business Conscience* (Englewood Cliffs, N.J.: Prentice-Hall, 1963), pp. 22–30.

HIGHLIGHTS OF FINDINGS

Here are some of the highlights of my findings, which I propose with varying degrees of assurance:

Most businessmen believe: I am more ethical than the average businessman, and extensions of myself (my department, company, industry, and country) are more ethical than their counterparts.

The popular image of businessmen's ethics, especially that held by students, seems prejudiced; it probably gives insufficient weight to the many responsible decisions made by managers.

The ethical dilemmas of deepest concern to businessmen are personnel problems; more frequent, however, are unfair competitive practices such as price discrimination or collusion, bribery, and dishonesty in advertising or contracts.

Businessmen believe that good ethics is good business in the long run, especially in employee and customer relations.

Most businessmen think that they have the same ethical standards at home and at work but that it is more difficult to live by these standards at work because of the pressures of competition.

* The golden rule, though useful as a starting point, is inadequate as a norm for solving most ethical problems in business.

Managers typically become more ethical as they grow older, partly because of financial security.

It is easier to be ethical in jobs involving fiduciary relationships, such as the accountant's or engineer's, than in those jobs involving competitive relationships, such as the salesman's or purchasing agent's.

In many cases, a company is "the lengthened shadow of one man," the chief executive, whose values most subordinates eventually accept.

Competition is the factor of greatest influence on ethical behavior in business. Unethical practices result from both too little and too much competition in an industry.

Managers of multinational companies, as their handling of culture-related differences reveals, disagree about what constitutes ethical behavior abroad.

Though most businessmen oppose increased governmental involvement in business, many acknowledge that governmental regulation has improved United States business practice.

Although formal education usually makes a person more sensitive and articulate about ethical issues, it influences his business decisions much less than does the personal conviction that he should act ethically, which is typically developed before adolescence, chiefly through parental influence.

A written code of ethical practices is regarded by a majority of businessmen as useful for improving business practices in their industry.

Businessmen not affiliated with a church or synagogue have attitudes as ethical as those of church-affiliated managers.

Although the churches and synagogues have provided some objective standards for business behavior, clergymen on the whole have failed to provide competent counseling for many current business problems.

PROFILES OF OUR RESPONDENTS

The foregoing conclusions were drawn from three research projects. The first used twenty unstructured interviews, plus a standardized questionnaire containing 37 questions which were answered by 100 businessmen whose profile is sketched in Table 1.1.[2] The sample of 100 men was chosen from a population of 216 businessmen who were temporarily residing in Boston while attending one or the other of two executive development programs at Harvard. As Table 1.1 reveals, the sample included a large representation from giant corporations. This is typical of participants in university programs for executive development, as is the relative youth and amount of formal education of the men.

The second project, built upon the first, used a thoroughly revised questionnaire, which was mailed to a systematic sample of 5,000 subscribers to the *Harvard Business Review*. A copy of this questionnaire can be found in Appendix A. As could be expected of subscribers to the *Harvard Business Review*, the respondents were well above average in position, income, and formal education. This six-page, 29-question form was completed by 1,710 persons. The returns of 1,512 of these people are utilized in this book; more than half of the other 197 came from nonbusinessmen, and the rest were

[2] This project was a joint venture of six graduate students attending the Harvard Business School in 1961. The other five were the Reverend Alexander D. Stewart and Messrs. William J. Gies, Roger L. Hall, Robert J. Russell, and Robert C. Valtz. The result was an unpublished report, "Ethics and the Businessman."

incomplete. Table 1.2 profiles the businessmen-respondents whose replies were supplemented by interviews with academicians and business leaders.

Table 1.1
Profile of 100 Businessmen In Project One

Title or Position   *Age*

President, chairman of board, general manager	6	Under 35 years	39
Assistant to the above	6	35–39	19
Vice-president, controller, plant manager	15	40–44	17
Assistant to the above	10	45–49	16
Branch manager, department head, product		50–54	9
manager	37		
Assistant to the above	17		
Specialist	2		
No answer	7		

Formal education   *Number of employees in company*

High school or less	4	1–499	14
Up to four years of college	46	500–999	7
More than four years of college	50	1,000–9,999	39
		10,000 and over	40

Industry

Manufacturing, metals	17	Mining, oil	7
Electronics, electrical mfg.	12	Wood products	6
Transportation, public util.	12	Construction	4
Chemicals, pharmaceuticals	9	Other industries	21
Banks, investments, insurance	7	No answer	5

Table 1.2
Profile of 1,512 Businessmen in Project Two

Title or Position

Top management—chairman of the board, board member, president; vice-president; treasurer; controller; secretary (to the corporation); general manager; general superintendent; administrative director; and assistants thereto   **47%**

Middle management—functional department head (e.g., sales, production, personnel, engineering, brand manager)   **28**

Lower management—assistant to functional department head; district manager; branch manager; section manager; and the like   **12**

Nonmanagement personnel—consultant, CPA, and all others employed in
   business   13

Age		Residence	
Under 30 years	6%	New England	10%
30–34	12	Middle Atlantic	21
35–39	17	South Atlantic	10
40–44	17	East North Central	25
45–49	17	West North Central	5
50–54	13	South Central	8
55–59	10	Pacific & Mountain	21
Over 59	8		

Number of Employees in Company		Formal Education	
1–49	15%	High school	5%
50–249	18	Some college	20
250–999	19	Bachelor's degree	38
1,000–9,999	25	Graduate school	37
10,000–19,999	7		
20,000 or more	16		

Religious Affiliation		Income Group	
Protestant	69%	Under $10,000	11%
Catholic	15	$10,000–$19,999	45
Jewish	7	$20,000–$29,999	24
Unaffiliated	8	$30,000–$39,999	9
Other	1	$40,000 and over	11

Industry

Construction	2%	Manufacturing industrial goods	26
Consumer services	3	Transportation, public utilities	5
Mining or extraction, oil	3	Engineering, research and	
Retail or wholesale trade	8	development	6
Advertising, media, publishing	4	Management consulting,	
Banking, investment, insurance	11	business services	6
Manufacturing consumer goods	17	Other	9

Building upon both previous projects, the third consisted of
personal, focused interviews with 100 businessmen. A type of quota
sample was used, with a special effort made to secure both breadth
and depth of business experience. In selecting the quota, I took into
account all bases for stratification that Projects One and Two, plus
expert opinion, indicated were relevant. Table 1.3 provides informa-

tion about these interviewees, whose experience and opinions are of central importance to this study.[3]

After the data from these three projects had been tabulated and analyzed, their meaning was discussed in interviews with many

Table 1.3
Profile of 100 Businessmen Interviewed in Project Three

Title or Position

Chairman of board, partner	10
President, chief executive	26
Vice-president, general manager, treasurer	18
Plant superintendent, operations manager	8
Department manager, principal	22
Lower level of management	9
Specialist, e.g., broker, company counsel	7

Age		Residence	
Under 35 years	19	New England	18
35–39	25	Middle Atlantic	24
40–44	16	South Atlantic	7
45–49	11	East North Central	25
50–54	7	West North Central	5
55–59	10	South Central	3
60 and over	12	Pacific & Mountain	5
		U.S. Possessions & Foreign	13

[3] Appendix B contains the questions asked in each interview. The objective of the interviews was to acquire insight and depth of understanding. So I used a purposive sample, choosing men and women who represented a broad spectrum of experience. Variety of background among the interviewees was assured by selecting a small number from each of several different groups: the Young Presidents' Organization, a middle-management class, and a program for top management. A handful of the interviewees were nationally prominent figures, selected because of their public utterances or writings about business. Fourteen of the men were known previously by the interviewers, and were selected because they would reveal the unvarnished truth, which would be used to measure the veracity of the others. To secure the 100 interviews, I had to contact about 125 businessmen. No effort was made to determine the reasons for refusal to cooperate. It may be that the interviewees in Project Three are, because of the way they were chosen, above average in their business standards and practice, or in the importance they attach to ethical behavior. Even if this is so, it should not detract from a study which is interested in factors conducive to responsible decisions rather than in the pathology of business.

Religious Preference

Protestant	57
Catholic	24
Jewish	9
Unaffiliated theist, deist	7
Agnostic	3

Industry

Hotels, restaurant, food	9
Advertising, communications	3
Manufacturing consumer goods	10
Manufacturing industrial goods	28
Banking, insurance, investment	13
Transportation, public utilities	8
Retail, wholesale, consumer service	6
Management consulting, public relations	14
Other	9

Number of Employees in Company

1–199	16
200–999	27
1,000–14,999	28
15,000 and over	29

Formal Education

High school or less	6
Some college	17
Bachelor's degree	31
Some graduate study	11
Graduate degree	35

business executives, singly and in groups, as well as with faculty members of several schools of business administration.

The distinctive characteristics of the sample of businessmen who provided the data for this empirical study call for comment. These men and women are better educated, more affluent, and of a higher managerial level than would have been true of a random sample. Concentration on the upper levels of management is advantageous for our purposes because these persons, having climbed the corporate ladder, have a rich reservoir of experience from which to draw their views.

The respondents were able to provide accurate information. Did they? As will be seen in Appendix C, the answer depends on the quality of the written questionnaires and the interview questions, on the willingness of the businessmen to reply honestly, and on the abilities of the interviewers. Obviously, I have confidence that the planning and methodology of this study have made it possible to secure reliable data.

2 The Many Meanings of
"Businessman" and "Ethics"

It is difficult to talk or write about business ethics. One reason is the variety of meanings attached to the words *businessman* and *ethics*. They mean different things to different people.[1] *Businessman* is a term predicated with equal propriety of a corporation president responsible for 100,000 employees and a billion dollars in assets, and of a neighborhood merchant with no employees and $1,000 in assets. Common usage, including the practice of the participants in our research projects, prompts this definition: A businessman is anyone who takes part in planning, organizing, or directing work with the objective of providing service or goods for profit. Since the businessman usually manages people and makes administrative decisions, I shall use *manager* and *decision-maker* as synonyms for *businessman*. *Executive* will be employed solely to designate a member of top management.

When we encounter confusion in speaking about businessmen, we can often clarify the matter by describing in concrete terms the position or kind of activity we mean, or by naming or pointing to a businessman. Ethics, however, labors under the additional handicap of being an abstract word. We cannot point to someone and say, "That's ethics." However, our difficulty goes beyond semantics, since we know that when someone describes an action as ethical or unethical, he may get an argument. Why? Because to describe an action as ethical requires a comparison of the action with a norm of

[1] For a development of this idea, see Leo V. Ryan, C.S.V., "The Many Meanings of Business," *Catholic Business Education Review*, Fall 1963, pp. 5–9; Robert C. Stone, "Who Are The Businessmen?" *Arizona Review*, November 1962, pp. 8–17.

conduct, and there are honest differences of opinion about what this norm is and what principles are derived from this norm. Another source of disagreement is the relevance of a certain principle to a specific action.

HOW BUSINESSMEN USE ETHICAL

To help clarify these problems, the interviewees were asked what they meant by *ethical*.[2] The definition was sought in two ways, the first by an open-end query: "Will you please try to tell me what you mean when you say that an action is ethical? In other words, what does *ethical* mean to you?" After the interviewee had replied, he was handed a card containing a forced-choice version of the same question. The card contained nine definitions or descriptions of *ethical* culled from those proposed by philosophers, theologians, and businessmen.[3]

Many men found the open-end version of the question difficult. One executive commented: "I find defining *ethical* very hard. I have never had to do this before." Seven gave no answer; others lapsed into a long silence which the interviewer finally broke. One manager from a foreign country said:

Before coming to the interview, to make sure that I knew what we would talk about, I looked up *ethics* in my [bilingual] dictionary. I read it and can't understand it. I don't know what the concept means even in my own language.

Another stated, "Really, I never use the word *ethical*, so I haven't bothered to define it."

A useful basis for analysis of the 93 open-end replies is to divide them into three kinds: objective; subjective; objective and subjective. *Objective* here means a reply that refers to something external to the individual replying; *subjective* means something that is internal or personal to him. Here are representative replies fitting each of these three categories.

[2] This question was the last one asked, because of the difficulties it caused in the pilot study. We found that interviews flowed more smoothly when this question was delayed. When a man defined *ethical* early in an interview, he tried to use the word only and always in that sense throughout the interview. This hampered the natural and spontaneous conversation we desired.

[3] For the contents of this question, cf. question 14B on the interview schedule in Appendix B.

Objective:

    In keeping with standards of good behavior.

    Meets criteria of all great religious texts.

    What society considers to be fair and honest.

    In line with the Ten Commandments.

Subjective:

    What is honest in my own mind.

    Consistent with my view of self, the self I want to be.

    That which best serves my interests without harming others.

Objective and Subjective:

    My feelings about what is right and wrong, stemming from my religious beliefs.

    Exercising your free will about the golden rule.

    Satisfies me or my conscience and also satisfies a moral code, usually religious.

Most of the twenty replies which do not fit this scheme of categories are brief synonyms of *ethical*, e.g., "the right thing to do," "fair or honest," "not injuring another."

The 73 categorized answers are divided into objective, 33; subjective, 27; objective and subjective, 13. The objective guides favored by the repliers were religious standards, the golden rule, and society's standards. The phrases most often used in subjective-type responses were "conscience" and "my own code."

Several interviewees mentioned the inadequacy of conceiving ethics as solely subjective:

> *Ethical* is what my feelings tell me is right. But this is not a fixed standard, and that makes problems.

> *Ethical* means accepted standards in terms of your personal and social welfare; what you believe is right. But what confuses me . . . is the possibility that I have been misguided, or that somebody else has been poorly educated. Maybe each of us thinks he knows what is ethical, but we differ. How can you tell who is right then?

Because of the form in which the question was asked, it would be presumptuous to think that men who answered only in subjective terms do not also think of ethics in objective terms, and vice versa. But the answers probably reveal which of the two elements the men weigh more heavily.

The interviewee had to opt for either objective or subjective in the multiple-choice part of this question. As Table 2.1 shows, the first choices were evenly split: 51 subjective, 49 objective. More

Table 2.1
What Ethical Means **(N = 100)**

	First Choice	Second Choice
What my feelings tell me is right.	50	8
In accord with my religious beliefs.	25	14
Conforms to "the golden rule."	18	15
What does the most good for the most people.	3	7
Customary behavior in our society.	3	6
Corresponds to my self-interest.	1	1
About the same as what is legal.	0	2
Contributes most to personal liberty.	0	1
What I want in that particular situation.	0	1

than half of the interviewees gave a second choice, although it was not requested. Apparently these men wanted to give a complete statement of their concept of ethical. This is an indication of the careful attention displayed by these businessmen throughout the interviews.

While these replies say nothing about the behavior of businessmen, they do reveal something about their attitude toward ethics. Senator Fulbright once deplored that "among so many influential people, morality has become identical with legality,"[4] but those interviewed gave almost no support to the answer, "About the same as what is legal" (see Table 2.1).

By far the most popular answer was "What my feelings tell me is right"; second was, "In accord with religious beliefs." It is important to note that the first answer was subjected to qualifications; many associated it with conscience, e.g.:

I choose "what my feelings tell me is right," but what I mean by feelings is conscience, not emotions. There is apt to be some confusion with these words.

"What my feelings tell me is right," plus mind and belief.

WHAT ABOUT THE GOLDEN RULE?

The third most frequent response was "Conforms to 'the golden rule' "—which itself has religious origins—but some interviewees

[4] Eugene J. McCarthy, "An Inquiry into Political Morality," *New York Times*, July 1, 1962, p. 7.

took a dim view of it. Before analyzing some of their replies, however, let us briefly consider three companies whose chief executives publicly claim that the golden rule is a keystone of their administrative philosophy.

The Texas Refinery Company of Fort Worth indicates that its willingness to live by the golden rule is proved by its practice of hiring men over 40 years of age, and by a profit-sharing retirement fund which is financed entirely by the company. Management has won this accolade from an employee, "Since I went to work for these Texans, I've felt like a gentleman and not like some cog in the machinery."[5]

The golden rule is the official corporate philosophy of Denver's Samsonite Corporation, largest manufacturers of luggage in the world. Its officers and salesmen carry a marble encircled by a gold band on which the golden rule is printed; they are supposed to read it for inspiration when they have a decision to make. Cited as an application of the golden rule is Samsonite's treatment of its 15,000 retailers, who are (1) required to sell Samsonite at list prices, which include a 40 per cent markup; (2) told by company salesmen what luggage to buy and how to display it, and are compensated if the advice proves erroneous; (3) aided in training their clerks.[6]

The founder and chairman of the Wrap-On Company, a successful Chicago manufacturing firm, says: "The maximum satisfaction life can offer, as well as the maximum financial rewards, will come almost automatically to those who best serve their fellow men . . . profit is a by-product of service. . . . There are no evil people in this world. There are, unfortunately, a great many who are misguided or misinformed. . . ."[7] He distinguishes selfish selfishness from enlightened selfishness, which is "Nothing but the golden rule with a new label. . . . It pays to have faith in the golden rule."[8]

Though the golden rule is useful in relatively simple ethical dilemmas, it seems to some of our interviewees to be inadequate for most business decisions. Of what help is the injunction, "Do unto others as you would have them do unto you," when the "others" are two or more parties whose interests are opposed? After all, this is the typical business problem. For instance, who deserves preference when there is one job available for two unemployed

[5] Frank X. Tolbert, "Age Is in the Mind," *Petroleum Today*, Fall 1965, p. 25.

[6] *Time*, June 25, 1965, p. 90.

[7] *Northwestern University Alumni News*, July 1965, pp. 1 and 3.

[8] *Ibid.*, September 1965, pp. 1–2.

men, or when there is a conflict of interests between one man and the rest of his department, or between shareholders and employees?

There is additional skepticism because many profess the golden rule but do not practice it. After hearing the phrase frequently, I began to press interviewees: "Have you found it adequate as a help in making decisions?" From the responses I conclude that for many men the golden rule has a profound meaning and represents values dear to them. On the other hand, I feel that some men who have little regard for ethics find it useful to speak about the golden rule when wanting to impress people. Perhaps a reaction to this shallowness accounts for what one man dubbed "the secular ethic: Do unto him lest he do unto you."

OUR DEFINITIONS

Faced by the variety of opinions, I decided to use the following definitions throughout this book. (This is not to say that respondents, when quoted, use the words in the same way.)

Ethical: conforming to principles of human conduct; according to common usage, the following terms are more or less synonymous with ethical: moral, good, right, just, honest.

Ethical standards: principles or ideals of human conduct.

Ethics: the study of the morality of human actions; hence, the standards for these actions.

Morality: the property of an action by means of which it conforms to a norm of human conduct.

Here and there in this book I evaluate statements about business as well as typical business situations, offering reasons for each evaluation. It seems to me that being ethical means acting according to reason, and that an unethical action can be shown to be unreasonable.[9]

It is helpful to bear in mind the distinction between (1) what one knows or believes to be ethical, i.e., his standards, ideals, or code; and (2) what one does, i.e., his actions. There is often a disparity between one's standards and his behavior; usually the former are higher. If our respondents seem at times unrealistic, it

---

[9] If the reader wishes to know more about the norms I use in evaluating a business action as ethical or unethical, he can consult Johannes Messner, *Social Ethics: Natural Law in the Western World* (St. Louis: B. Herder, revised edition, 1965), pp. 12–77.

may be that they are talking about their standards, and the reader thinks they are referring to their actions.

Some of the men in our survey questioned whether there is such a thing as *business* ethics. "Ethics is ethics," they said, "and the businessman is no different from anybody else. He must observe the same principles everybody else does, no more and no less." But this is merely to say that the businessman, like every human being, must do good and avoid evil, and that certain general ethical norms are applicable to business activities. There are certain actions, however, which are the unique or special concern of business, and the specific problems and opportunities confronting the businessman differ from those faced by the politician, for example, or the physician. As a consequence of these differences, questions arise about *applications* of ethical principles. This is especially true when a new economic situation arises or when two or more principles seem to apply to a specific case. For example, in deciding whether or not to move a plant from one city to another—a business problem that is relatively recent—several principles must be considered, and they seem to conflict; private property and the rights of stockholders are involved, as are the company's obligations to loyal employees and to the local community.

There are, then, actions of businessmen in business situations which are not found in other areas of life. The study of the object, intention, circumstances, and outcome of these actions, of their rightness or wrongness, is the domain of business ethics. The number and importance of these actions justify the existence of the special field of study called business ethics.

3   The Image of the Businessman

People tend to think in images. When the name of a company or an occupational group is mentioned, the mind flashes a construct which summarizes all of the person's impressions about the company or the group. Every thinking person has an image of the businessman, built from a variety of experiences and pieces of information.[1] In this chapter, we will consider the popular image of the businessman in the United States, especially that held by students, and then take a look at the businessman's self-image.

The popular image of the businessman includes the notion that he is relatively unethical. For instance, the most frequent rejoinder to the statement that one is engaged in research about the ethics of businessmen is: Do they have any? In a supplementary study of 99 nonbusinessmen, I discovered noteworthy skepticism about the businessman's integrity. For example, 65 per cent of these nonbusinessmen said that they would not use confidential information for personal financial gain to the detriment of others who have no access to the information; but only 8 per cent thought that the average businessman would resist the same temptation. A survey made by Louis Harris and Associates, based on 2,000 interviews, revealed that 42 per cent felt that "most businessmen will do anything, honest or not, for a buck," and 77 per cent regarded business as a "dog-eat-dog proposition."[2]

What are the sources of the popular image of the businessman?

[1] For instance, cf. M. Joseph Hendrickson, "The Corroding Image of Business," *Carroll Business Bulletin*, Fall 1965, pp. 3–8.

[2] *Newsweek*, "What Americans Really Think of Business," May 2, 1966, p. 84.

Personal experience of course, but also communications media, novels, plays, movies, and political speeches. News is an important category for television, radio, daily papers, and weekly magazines. What is news? The unusual, the atypical, the unexpected. Wrongdoing is usually news. One businessman who absconds with $10,000 gets more news coverage in a single day than 10,000 businessmen who are scrupulously honest all their lives.

This is not to deny the important role of the press in calling attention to the shortcomings of business and in arousing the popular conscience to bring pressure to correct that wrongdoing. However, the fact remains that good news is no news most of the time. Since the average reader of newspapers and the ordinary television viewer do not advert to the selection process employed by editors and producers, the popular image of the businessman may well be distorted.

In short, with the important exception of personal experience, the content of the average person's image of the businessman probably comes from sources that select information according to criteria which are likely to make the businessman appear somewhat unethical.

STUDENTS FROWN ON BUSINESSMEN

While the average adult's opinion of the American businessman's ethics is not flattering, the student's is even less favorable. This is significant because many students choose their lifetime occupation largely on the basis of the image they have formed of it. In an opinion panel conducted by Purdue University, one-quarter of the participating teen-agers agreed that "most business concerns are out to make all the money they can, no matter who gets hurt."[3] Executive Philip Sporn has stated: "The judgment of some of our best young talent is affected by a sense of distrust of business as a way of life, particularly as it may not permit a concordance between the ethical standards of business and the ethics of living."[4] Peter Drucker adds: "What shocks the young graduates is that the top executives do not feel entitled, let alone compelled, to act according to their consciences. . . ."[5]

[3] *Purchasing Week*, July 3, 1961, p. 10.

[4] Committee for Economic Development, *Educating Tomorrow's Managers* (New York, October 1964), p. 41.

[5] "Is Business Letting Young People Down?" *Harvard Business Review*, November–December 1965, p. 54.

At Dartmouth, Boston College, and Loyola University, 156 students completed part of the same questionnaire employed in our Project Two. The pattern of the replies was unmistakable: these collegians have a low opinion of the ethical practices and standards of businessmen. To cite a representative example: For a salesman who earns $10,000 a year to pad his expense account by $500 was regarded as unacceptable behavior by 85 per cent of our 1,512 businessmen respondents, but only 17 per cent of the students thought that the typical businessman would regard such padding as wrong.

Business is partly to blame for these opinions. Witness this comment of a student dropped from college for academic deficiency: "My boss [at a Chicago brokerage house] told me not to bother much with the courses because I wouldn't use much of what I learned anyway. He said that what's important in the brokerage business is a quick tongue."

Student attitudes toward business ethics are also influenced by counselors, especially in high school. These counselors, who typically know little about careers in business, seldom encourage and sometimes discourage student interest in education for business. One wonders if the counselors, and therefore the students, are not influenced by vocational or interest tests, e.g., the Strong Vocational Test and the Allport-Vernon-Lindzey Values Test. Some of these tests imply that social concern is inimical or alien to business success. For example, a student who shows unusual interest in serving others is usually advised not to go into business. The contents of these tests and the interpretations given their results by counselors may be leading students to conclude that businessmen are less interested in socially responsible behavior than are persons in other occupations. Of course, counselors' evaluations of these tests may be based on replies given to the questions by persons who are successful in various occupations, i.e., the profile for businessmen may have been drawn from the answers of successful managers and merchants. In this event, businessmen themselves must share the blame for the asocial image conveyed.

On the one hand, collegians strongly disapprove of what they perceive as the businessman's lack of integrity. On the other hand, many college students occasionally cheat on examinations. One wonders how collegians explain this apparent inconsistency. Are their temptations more severe than the businessman's? Do they regard it as less reprehensible to be unethical in academic matters than in economic? If so, why?

THE BUSINESSMAN'S SELF-IMAGE

Having spoken of the popular image of business ethics, we turn to the businessman's own view of the subject. A 1960 study by Joseph McGuire, with information provided by 189 bankers, concluded:

A not very flattering image of business executives emerges from the bankers' responses to this survey. . . . They conceive of the business system as a dominating, materialistically oriented organization of activities . . . individuals are expendable to the goals of the system, and for a man to rise it is necessary that he repress his emotions and his personality. . . .[6]

Though our survey sheds no light on McGuire's findings, it indicates that the typical businessman thinks himself more ethical than other businessmen.

There is often a discrepancy between what a man *says* he thinks or does and what he *actually* thinks or does. This discrepancy is likely to be present in answers to questions about ethical choices. These answers may correspond more closely to the image which the respondent would like others to have of him than to the real him. It is human to try to picture oneself in the most favorable way. Wanting to learn if this bias were present in our survey, we asked several questions in two different ways. In four case situations, one-half of our respondents were asked, "What would *you* do?" The other half were asked, "What would the *average* businessman do?" Table 3.1 reveals that the differences in the replies of the two groups are remarkable. Since care was taken to prevent the sampling method from influencing the replies, the differences clearly reflect the view that "I'm more ethical than he."[7]

Table 3.1
"I'm More Ethical Than He" (N = 1,512)

CASE 1
Imagine that you are a member of the Board of Directors of a large corporation. At a board meeting you learn of an impending merger with a smaller

[6] Joseph W. McGuire, "Bankers, Books, and Businessmen," *Harvard Business Review*, July–August 1960, p. 73.

[7] The mailing list for the questionnaire was split randomly, and the returns of the two halves of the sample match demographically. Also, all respondents were asked twenty-five other questions which were identical, and the replies of the two halves are virtually identical.

company which has had an unprofitable year, and whose stock is presently selling at a price so low that you are certain it will rise when news of the merger becomes public knowledge.

	What I Would Do	What the Average Executive Would Do
Buy some for self?	43%	61%
Tell a good friend?	15	46
Tell broker?	2	10
Do none of the above?	55	30

Note: The figures do not add to 100 per cent since the questions are not mutually exclusive.

CASE 2

As president of a company manufacturing consumer goods, you are considering new ideas for increasing sales. Your marketing department has presented two programs, each of which would achieve the desired increase in sales. One program employs an advertising theme portraying ownership of your product as a symbol of the purchaser's superiority, while the other program uses an advertising theme emphasizing the quality of your product.

	What I Would Do	What the Average Executive Would Do
Emphasize product quality	65%	52%
Emphasize purchaser superiority	12	32
No reason to make a choice here	23	16

CASE 3

An executive earning $10,000 a year has been padding his expense account by about $500 a year.

	What I Think of This	What the Average Businessman Thinks of This
Acceptable if other executives in the company do the same thing	6%	25%
Acceptable if the executive's superior knows about it and says nothing	12	28
Unacceptable regardless of the circumstances	85	62

Note: The figures do not add to 100 per cent since the questions are not mutually exclusive.

CASE 4

Imagine that you are the president of a company in a highly competitive industry. You learn that a competitor has made an important scientific discovery which will give him an advantage that will substantially reduce, but not eliminate, the profits of your company for about a year. If there were some hope of hiring one of the competitor's employees who knew the details of the discovery, would you try to hire him?

	What I Would Do	What the Average Executive Would Do
Probably would hire him	49%	69%
Probably would not hire him	51	31

This attitude received corroboration during a case discussion at the Harvard Business School. Professor Lewis Ward was directing the discussion for managers drawn from thirty companies, all in the same industry. A focal point in the case was selling practices, which were described at length. A dozen managers commented on these selling practices, agreeing that they were unethical and that they were in fact common in their industry. But every speaker avowed that these actions were not practiced by his company's salesmen. Noting many affirmative nods to these declarations, Ward pointed out how unlikely it was that, if these unethical practices were common, not one of the thirty companies present was guilty of indulging in the practices. These managers were saying, "My company is more ethical than the average in our industry."

This same attitude was evident in the way our 100 interviewees handled the two written questions displayed in Exhibits 3.1 and 3.2.

By marking an "X" somewhere on the line below, please rate the ethical climate of your *industry.*

Absolutely   Absolutely
Unethical   Ethical

Exhibit 3.1

By marking an "X" somewhere on the line below, please rate the ethical practices of your *company.*

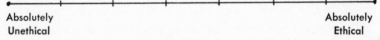

Absolutely   Absolutely
Unethical   Ethical

Exhibit 3.2

I was less interested in a man's answer to either question than in comparing his two answers. The results are shown in Table 3.2.

Table 3.2.
"My Company Is More Ethical Than the Average" (N = 100)

Answer	Number Giving This Answer
Own company rated more ethical than industry average	67
Own company rated less ethical than industry average	10
Own company and industry average rated the same	21
No answer	2

The ethical climate of an industry is made up of the practices of all the companies in the industry. Two-thirds of the men rated the practices of their company more ethical than the climate in their industry. Surely this is another way of saying, "I'm more ethical than he."

The interviews provided other evidence of the existence of this attitude. Thirteen men had experience or extensive knowledge of dealings with foreign businessmen and were willing to compare business practices in their countries with those in other nations. Ten men said that their country's practices were more ethical, one said they were less, and two saw no difference. The majority felt that "businessmen in my country are more ethical than businessmen in other countries."

In answers to a request for the difference in ethical practices between large and small companies, managers' views were related to the size of the company by which they were employed. Employees of large companies believed that the practices of large companies were more ethical than those of small companies; men employed by small companies thought them more honest than the large ones.

One possible explanation of the belief that "I'm more ethical than he" is that our panelists and interviewees *are* more ethical than the average businessman. However, there is not sufficient evidence to justify such a judgment.

The attitude that "I'm more ethical than he" is a psychological phenomenon worth investigating. Perhaps it is related to the tendency of economic competition, whether between companies or between individuals within a company, to push business practice to the lowest common ethical denominator of the competitors. When this happens and the lowest common denominator is the standard for an industry or a company, no one will be below the standard. Given such a situation, it is not hard to see why many managers would feel that they were more ethical than their counterparts. The attitude seems related to the Freudian notion of the psychopathology of everyday life, and probably includes some *projection*, which is a process, usually following the repression of impulses regarded as improper, whereby a man projects his own impulses onto other men.

DISTRUST OF COMPETITORS

Clearly, our respondents distrust competitors. One-half of the respondents agreed with this paraphrase of an observation of Rabbi Louis Finkelstein: The American business executive tends to ignore the great ethical laws as they apply immediately to his work; he is preoccupied chiefly with gain.[8] Five of every nine added that businessmen "would violate a written code of ethics whenever they thought they could avoid detection."

Would such distrust of their fellows be true of physicians, lawyers, or professors? Apparently there is a different relationship between businessmen than between members of the various professions. Could business competition be the cause of this difference? Does competition generate a different, less cooperative, climate in industry than is found in medicine, law, or education? If most persons are reluctant to call business a profession, one of the underlying reasons may be the kind of economic competition present in business, which seems to be different, at least quantitatively, from that found in the acknowledged professions.

FAVORING FRIENDS

Also present in our data is an indication that some managers apply one standard to friends and another to strangers. Table 3.1 indicates that many men who would tell a friend confidential news of a forthcoming merger would not tell their broker, and answers about practices of pricing, hiring, and rebidding on contracts reveal the existence of a special niche for friends. Favoring friends can be an expression of gratitude, which is praiseworthy, unless the grati-

[8] "The Businessman's Moral Failure," *Fortune*, September 1958, p. 116.

tude is displayed at some third party's expense, which is an injustice.

We also discovered that some of the same businessmen who stretch their standards of honesty to favor a friend often go beyond common sense in their trust in company personnel. Coexisting with a distrust of people who aren't affiliated with the company, such as competitors or suppliers, is a naïve trust which manifests itself in failure to set up ordinary internal controls, unwittingly providing temptations too enticing for some employees. In other words, there is a common tendency among businessmen to identify self (including extensions of self, e.g., my department or company or industry or country) with that which is ethical, and to suspect as unethical that which is nonself or other.

Given the choice of naming and discussing "one industry that you think is very ethical, or one that you think is unethical," five of every eight interviewees favored the latter. Given the choice of naming and discussing "one kind of work that you think is very ethical, or one that you think is unethical," they favored the latter 63 per cent to 37 per cent. Asked to recall "an occasion when you rewarded some person in your company for ethical behavior or when you penalized someone for unethical behavior," four of every five chose to speak of the latter.

How interpret this statistical evidence? One way is to say that, since businessmen ordinarily give and receive ethical treatment, they recall the unethical more readily because it is unusual. Another interpretation is that some respondents prefer to talk about unethical actions of others because it makes them feel superior, and somehow salves a personal feeling of guilt. Some managers see other businessmen primarily as a threat; perhaps they are predisposed to look for actions which might be economically harmful. However the evidence be interpreted, the businessman's preference for speaking about unethical business behavior is one of the factors contributing to the popular image of the businessman as unethical.

The rest of this book, by providing a mass of objective information about business ethics, should prompt the reader to ask himself whether his own image of the businessman is true to life.

4 Pressures That Disturb Businessmen

Find out what hurts a man and you learn something about his character. So I tried, through two questions requiring essay answers, to discover which business decisions hurt managers. Such information, it was thought, might reveal the areas in which businessmen would welcome help. The matter was approached first through role conflicts, i.e., the problems confronting a man who is required to fill simultaneously two roles which present inconsistent or contradictory expectations. The question was:

Probably there have been times when you have experienced a conflict between what was expected of you as an efficient, profit-conscious businessman and what was expected of you as an ethical person. Please describe the situation which has been for you the source of deepest concern because of such a conflict.

A breakdown of the answers is given in Table 4.1.

Table 4.1
Role Conflicts Experienced (N = 610)[a]

Type of Conflict	Per Cent Specifying
No such conflict	31.7
Personnel problems, e.g., firing and layoffs	23.9
Dishonesty, e.g., ads, contracts, and promises	17.7
Pricing problems, e.g., collusion, discrimination	13.0
Buying business, e.g., bribes, entertainment	10.9
Other	2.8

[a] There were 902 respondents who did not answer this essay-type question.

The respondents were also asked: "In every industry there are some generally accepted business practices. In your industry are there any such practices which you regard as unethical?" Table 4.2 summarizes the replies.

Table 4.2
Are There Generally Accepted Unethical Practices? (N = 1,459)

Answer	Per Cent Giving This Answer
Yes, many	10.0
Yes, a few	59.6
No	18.1
Don't know	12.3

Of the yea-sayers this request was made: "Please describe the *one* unethical practice which you would *most* like to see eliminated." Their responses are categorized in Table 4.3.

Table 4.3
"The One Practice I Would Most Like to See Eliminated" (N = 791)[a]

Unethical Practice	Per Cent Specifying This Practice
Price discrimination, unfair pricing, price collusion	25.6
Bribes, excessive gifts and favors, call girls	22.5
Dishonest advertising	14.4
Unfair competitive practices, e.g., pirating employees or ideas	13.2
Cheating customers, overselling, unfair credit practices	8.8
Dishonesty in making or fulfilling contracts	7.0
Other	8.5

[a] There were 721 respondents who did not answer this essay-type question.

The questions which called forth the answers in Tables 4.1 and 4.3 are similar. How account for the difference in the replies? Table 4.1 is about a personal problem of "deepest concern," while Table 4.3 refers to an industry practice. The former certainly involved the respondent, and may have happened only once; the latter may occur frequently and need not involve the respondent as participant, in which case it will be of less concern to him. Table 4.1 reveals that intracompany personnel problems cause the deepest concern to most managers. However, Table 4.3 reveals unfairness to and by competitors or customers as the area which managers want most to see improved in their industry.

ROLE CONFLICTS

The 193 managers who wrote that they had experienced no role conflict surprised us, since seven of every ten men in our survey —as Table 4.2 shows—acknowledged the existence of generally accepted industry practices which are unethical. Can a decision-maker go for even a year without being tempted (I do not say yield) to cheat, lie or take unfair advantage? All such situations contain role conflicts. Perhaps many businessmen do not recognize them as such. More about this later.

To obtain a better idea of the role conflicts which bother businessmen, let us hear how they describe these situations. Here are examples of pricing dilemmas:

The president of a small southern company mentions "the use of extreme pressure by competition to force me to collude with them to fix prices."

A sales manager is annoyed by "price differentials extended to 'price buyers' but not to loyal customers—a rotten practice."

The treasurer of a small retailing firm puts a perennial problem in the form of a question: "What is a *fair* profit at retail level for installment purchases?"

The problem of honest communication is another source of concern. How does one tell the truth in advertising, making and fulfilling contracts, tax and accounting reports, and making claims about product quality or delivery dates?

A vice president is disturbed by "requests by customers for false billings to avoid taxes or to help in their depreciation schedules."

A sales representative writes of "not being able to reveal the true facts of a situation to a customer (e.g., in times of acute shortage). To save face for the company it is sometimes necessary to distort the truth."

An insurance manager frets that "companies are constantly presented with claims not covered by the policies issued. The claimant— and frequently the agent—will twist the facts to bring the claim under coverage. The one who reports dishonestly is often unjustly enriched at the ultimate expense of the honest man."

An engineer deplores "cheating in the make-up of reports caused by demanding improvement in index numbers."

Attempts to "buy business" through payola, kickbacks, bribes, excessive gifts or entertainment, or the use of call girls—this is a significant category of role conflict. Managers describe such attempts in these terms:

A western sales manager is bothered by "the excessive entertainment which some buyers seem to feel it is our duty to supply. I feel a buyer who can be bought for entertainment is not a moral person fundamentally, and I don't trust him."

The head of a consulting firm notes a conflict with a happy ending: "As manager of a business, I was asked for a kick-back by the buyer of an important customer; I refused the request and lost the customer. For months after, I was not sure I was right from a business angle. Now, years later, I know I was right, for they came to me for management counsel."

DISMISSALS AND LAYOFFS

Ranking first in the category of personnel problems is internal conflict arising out of firing and layoffs. Of the more than 100 managers who described this kind of problem, here are the words of four:

A training supervisor: "When it is necessary to reduce the work force, the decision of separating the older, less efficient employees or the younger employees, with greater technical skills and vigor, is a real tough problem."

A vice president is anxious about "employees with long, good records, and whose work becomes inefficient. How long can I carry them on the payroll? What is the measure of my loyalty to a man who helped build my business?"

A product supervisor is especially aware of: "treatment of clerical-level, salaried employees during periods of economic recession. This group seems always to take the brunt of any work-force reductions."

A southern personnel director observes: "It has concerned me that the industry's regular [periodic] reductions in work force should always bear so heavily on the 'little people'—particularly when adversity has not always been equally shared by stockholders and top management."

That final quotation deserves some reflection. No doubt most dismissals and layoffs are ethical. And probably the conflicts cited by some of these managers occurred between their head and their heart, rather than between economic efficiency and ethical behavior. But justice can, at times, demand that the brunt of a recession be borne by stockholders and managers, rather than by the little people. It is useful to note here that 83 per cent of our respondents agreed that "for corporation executives to act in the interest of shareholders alone, and not also in the interest of employees and consumers, is unethical." But it takes a secure and courageous administrator to stand up and advocate reducing prices or dividends instead of reducing the number of wage earners.

It also takes courage to fire workers when the common good demands it. Not all decision-makers have the courage. The president of a small company admits that when facing a situation requiring "discharge of ethical but incompetent employees, I can't do it." However, one of our interviewees stressed "the ethic of competence," saying, "Dismissal should follow incompetence, at least if it is the result of a failure to try."

It is reassuring to learn that many managers are keenly concerned with the problem of unemployment. A director of labor relations tells of his efforts:

> We have an in-plant security force of twenty men. We found that we could contract this job to an outside firm and it would result in less salary cost and less adminstrative expense. But I refused to lay off these twenty men, both for business reasons and ethics. These are older men who have been with us for several years. If they were released it would cause bad public relations with the townspeople.

A plant personnel manager tells a similar story:

> I've often battled with equals and superiors about their attitude that we are in business to produce, not to worry about workers. For instance, there is a man on our payroll—three times production men have wanted to fire him. We have no union and they could have fired him because he is only semiskilled, is a miserable guy and a troublemaker. But he's been with us for a while and has eight kids and a sick wife. I insisted that we keep him because of his personal situation. In cases like his, I think that a company should bend over backward.

While the two decision-makers just quoted acted in a responsible manner, the same can hardly be said of the board of directors which tried to hire a management consultant's services for one purpose: "We want to fire our president, with or without evidence." The consultant refused to act as hatchet man.

We heard a number of examples in which top management used ingenuity to prevent firings or to reduce the harmful economic and psychological effects of unemployment. What struck me as a creative decision was made by a West Coast manufacturer, whose vice-president said:

I am bothered when I have to fire men. When a government program was cancelled, we got word on Thursday afternoon that nothing more was to be done, and that all future costs would be disallowed. We begged for more time and got 48 hours. Over the weekend we had to figure out what to do. We had to fire 5,000 men on Monday and 2,000 more on Wednesday. So we decided to contact all the companies in the U.S. who might possibly hire our 7,000 men. We phoned companies over the weekend, told them what had happened, and suggested that they send a man to our plant on Monday morning to hire such talent as they could use. Thirty-one companies responded. We had a regular tent-city set up for them when they arrived. As our employees arrived, we notified them of the government cancellation and suggested the different companies present which were interested in their skills. Within one week we had placed more than two-thirds of the people we had to fire.

Why do men go to great lengths to prevent unemployment? Partly because they have experienced the anguish of joblessness. Partly because they know personally the victims of a layoff, and often know their families. Underlying the thoughtful efforts of many administrators is the feeling expressed by one: "We have a moral responsibility for our employees. Not only because they are our employees but because they are members of a community in which our business is located."

Instances were offered also in which men dismissed personal friends, in one case for the morale of a department, in another for the purpose of shocking the friend into responsible behavior. In both cases, the friendship endured the strain successfully, which is a tribute to the objectivity of the four men.

Closing a plant, which can depress an entire community in the same way that laying off one man depresses his family, can be a heart-rending experience for a decision-maker. Nevertheless, one vice-president, whose company closed several plants after buying out the former owners, felt that in this situation there was no alternative, that what was unethical was the inefficiency and weakness of the previous management. Their mistakes made closing inevitable, but they escaped public wrath by selling the company to the present owners who had to execute the shutdown.

Banking was also criticized by interviewees for its role in closing the doors of companies. Although foreclosures, like shutdowns, are often ethical, there is a natural sympathy for the underdog that makes the average man critical of those who make the decisions.

Similarly, we sometimes encountered a feeling of guilt in interviewees who fired people. Here is how they described it:

After many talks and threats had no result, I fired a woman alcoholic. There were plenty of reasons: absenteeism, disrupting morale of department, etc. But after releasing her, I find I'm busy adding up all the reasons for firing her.

I feel obliged to keep the company going because of the young people I hired. But the good of many may require us to lay off people. It did when our management committee turned down a thirty-million-dollar order from the Polish government for patriotic reasons, even though we were looking for work. When I lay off someone, it hurts. So I rationalize: it is for the good of many. It's not really rationalization, but the layoff bothers me.

This decision to turn down a large contract from an Iron Curtain country illustrates an interesting dilemma. The manager quoted made this decision, despite its harmful effect on the company's idle employees. Was it a matter of ethics or of patriotism, or of both, or of neither? This is a moot question, to which we will return in Chapter 14.

The manager's feeling after dismissing employees is much like the distress felt by a professor who fails a likable student, or a parent who punishes a misbehaving child. The failing grade and the punishment are just and deserved; they are for the good of the individual or for the common good. Yet the person who assigns the failing grade or administers the punishment may be ill at ease afterward. Is this feeling trustworthy, is it a sign from a well-formed conscience? Probably not, if the decision-maker has done his best to weigh the facts and judge justly. The problem probably arises because the good of an individual is frequently clear, near at hand, and tangible, while the common good is vague and often remote.

Every successful decision-maker must have the courage to say "No" when it is right to do so. In the words of a consultant: "I'm consulting now for a company where they may have to let 3,000 men go. If the economic situation requires it, my conscience will not bleed." Or as a general counsel put it:

> Our company is ethical. But the industry is overcapitalized and overproduced. For the good of the industry and the country, capital has to be withdrawn and production capacity shrunk. Hence people must be turned out of work. We're not like many others in the industry; when there is no market, we shut down.

Of course the problem of dismissing one man or closing a plant may be symptomatic of bigger problems. Two respondents looked at unemployment on the macroeconomic level: One was critical, the other philosophic. An Eastern plant manager was distressed that:

> There is no provision in our society for providing useful work for well-meaning, moral, hard-working individuals who just can't make the grade in the occupations they have chosen, and must be dismissed for efficiency reasons. This is a most serious problem for me, and I have fired many persons for this reason.

A Midwestern vice-president said:

> There is something wrong with our economic system when there is widespread unemployment. After all, this is a land of equal opportunity and if you don't have an equal opportunity to work, something unfair has happened to you.

These two men are not overawed by the success of the free enterprise system, and are ready to strengthen it if possible.

Juxtaposing the last four quotations enables one to see two ethical levels in the problem of discharging or laying off workers. At the first level, one assumes the basic justice of the economic system in which the decision is made, and the question is simply whether a specific decision is moral. Questions at the second, and deeper, level ask whether the problem is a result of the economic system; they probe the ethical basis of the system itself. Questions at both levels should be asked about discharge decisions in every economic system, from the free enterprise to the Communistic.

SANCTIONS FOR UNETHICAL BEHAVIOR

Intracompany personnel problems, particularly dismissals, were also illuminated by answers to this query:

> Please try to recall an occasion when you rewarded some person in your company for ethical behavior (for instance, by promotion, pay raise, or congratulations), or when you penalized someone for unethical behavior (for instance, by dismissal, demotion, or reprimand). Would you mind describing the occasion?

Two-thirds of the interviewees recalled penalizing or punishing subordinates (Table 4.4).

Family and community were often mentioned as factors complicating or motivating a dismissal:

> It wasn't so much that I fired him . . . we sat down and talked about the mess he was in and agreed that he would have to leave our company and the community.

Table 4.4
Types of Sanctions for Unethical Behavior (N = 65)

Dismissals for unethical *business* behavior	25
Reprimands	16
Dismissals for unethical *private* behavior	8
Transfers to position with fewer temptations	3
Raises withheld	2
Other	11

I had an assistant who was falsifying expense accounts. Four times I warned him. He did it a fifth time, so I reported him and he was fired. When his pregnant wife heard that I intended to write up the report, she came to me and begged me to give him another chance. I had given him four chances, so I told her No. It made me sick to my stomach to do it.

I fired my secretary recently. She belonged to an association of secretaries, and every four months they have a banquet and are expected to bring their boss. My secretary asked me and I said No. She made some comments to me and about me, so I fired her. It's a stupid idea. I should go to a banquet with my secretary! What would my wife think?

Our company provides housing for the Bantu who work for us [in Africa]. The compound manager was guilty of demanding and accepting money from the Bantu in order to get them jobs and therefore housing. We discharged him.

OFF-THE-JOB BEHAVIOR

The extent to which managers may or should exercise supervision over off-the-job behavior of subordinates is a delicate and much mooted question. The individual's right to freedom and privacy should be protected, but when a man substantially diminishes his worth to a company by irresponsible or socially reprehensible actions, it seems right that he be penalized. However, it is unfair to require a man to conform to arbitrary standards away from his place of work. The manager must therefore neither take on the role of "big brother" nor adopt the attitude that "his private life is none of my business." It would be helpful if some general guidelines about off-the-job behavior were established by agreement between management and elected employee representatives, and communicated to all employees.

That this problem is not imaginary is demonstrated by the one in every fourteen interviewees who told us about dismissing an employee for unethical behavior off the job. The usual reason was adultery or drunkenness—although many companies have praiseworthy programs for rehabilitating employees who are alcoholics. Typically, the fault was common knowledge and was causing, or about to cause, tension among employees. For example:

> I had heard from reliable sources that a man and a woman employee (both married) were going out together. It got to be general knowledge in the company. I brought both of them in and warned them to stop it, or else. I later heard that they had not stopped, so I fired the girl and gave him another chance because of his family.

Not surprisingly in the male-dominated world of work, the woman was dismissed and the man was given another chance. One wonders whether a complaint filed by the woman about the double standard used in this decision would be upheld according to Title VII of the Civil Rights Act of July 1964, which requires that all employees be treated without regard to sex in every phase of employment.

A dismissal that seems harsh is recounted by the president of a large company:

> In the case of a drunk, I gave him only one chance. If a man is drunk on or off the job, I fire him. Now I'm a teetotaler and I don't smoke; my religion tells me those things. If a man is drunk and walking on Main Street, he bespeaks the kind of business we are. I won't stand for that.

It is evident that one of the burdens of being a manager is the necessity, especially in dealing with subordinates, of acting as God's steward without "playing God." One of the tasks of stewardship, or leadership, is administering corrections. It is usually distasteful, but every manager is obliged to do it occasionally. Interviewees provided us with two examples of efficacious correction of unethical conduct. Because a reprimand is so rarely efficacious, we include these examples:

> Recently I corrected a younger man. He had been discussing the findings of some of our research with men who work for other companies. He also took advantage of an unusual opportunity to make money for himself and in doing so didn't consider the company's interest. My point was that he was wrong in failing to stop to ask himself what his obligations to the company and our clients were. I think he saw my point and agreed. It's hard to correct someone, but it's an exercise of responsibility, and I felt that this man would listen to me.

There was a salesman, 54 years old, who had been with the company for fifteen years. He had a below-average record of sales. He had been demoted from branch manager and wasn't selling enough to earn his keep, which was $12,000 a year. He had had a heart attack. There was some talk of getting rid of him, but I wanted to try to save him. I called him in and told him that I was moving him out of his private office—it was just a sop the boss had given him when demoting him—and that he would have to start producing. He hit the ceiling, started shouting at me. I was afraid he would have another heart attack right there and told him to go home for the rest of the day, but that he had to deliver or he was through. Just last month, I got the greatest kick since I've taken this job, when I was able to tell this guy that his work was so good he was being raised to $15,000. At 54, he reappraised himself and changed. That's something—and it made me look good too.

In summary, businessmen would like to put an end to unfair pricing, commercial bribery, and other unethical practices. But they feel most deeply about problems of employee relations. A 1964 study by the Opinion Research Company revealed that the American public is more sharply critical of business in this area than in any other.[1] Perhaps managers sense this critical attitude and this adds to their concern. But fundamentally the pressure they feel in situations involving dismissals, layoffs, or plant closings is probably related to the fact that the manager-employee relationship is personal and fiducial, while many other managerial relationships are competitive and less personal. The corporation is a social as well as an economic unit, and the person who excludes another person from this small society naturally feels concern.

[1] Harry W. O'Neill, "The Ethics of American Business," in *Business in a Changing Social Order*, ed. Daniel N. DeLucca (Philadelphia: Council on Business Ethics, St. Joseph's College, 1965), p. 162.

There are observers who insist that no ethical good can come from the business world. Others contend that none should be expected. One well-known professor of business administration claims that after observing managerial decision-making for many years and after many discussions with executives about their decisions, he has never known a business decision which could not be explained in terms either of profit or of personal gain for the decision-maker. The professor believes that when businessmen behave ethically, they are merely employing a useful means to the desired end, profit. He doubts that executives ever act for reasons that are primarily ethical, and he is not alone in holding this opinion.

I wanted to test this view, and since decisions which require personal sacrifice are more meaningful ethically than those which cost nothing, I asked the 100 interviewees:

Please try to recall a business decision which you made for ethical reasons despite your belief, at the time, that it would be less profitable for your company or for yourself than would an alternative decision. In other words, can you recall an occasion when you chose ethical behavior in preference to financial gain, or when you acted on moral principle even though you felt that your action would be criticized or might endanger your job?

Fifty-six men gave illustrations of decisions which they say were made on principle, and which seem to refute the notion that no ethical good can come from business. Twenty-eight others provided examples which may have been made on principle, as the men said they were, but which also lend themselves to the interpretation that they were made for the sake of long-run profits. Nine managers gave no answer to the query. Seven others preferred to speak in general, rather than specific, terms. Because I wanted instances of individual decisions, accompanied by details, these seven answers are not considered here.

Let us look first at two decisions which were made on principle, and also turned out to be profitable. A man from Madison Avenue detailed a decision, made for an ethical reason, which turned out to be profitable. At the time, there was a possibility that his advertising agency would lose a $5 million account as a result of the decision.

We handle a number of accounts for W Company, about $38 million in all. About $5 million of this has been advertising for the J-labeled items. However, W Company farms out some of the items that go under the J name to other ad agencies. Recently we looked at all the items sold under the J label and saw that some were not doing well. We agreed that W Company was missing a good bet by failing to coordinate all the J advertising; there were solid economic reasons for coordinating. At a group meeting of our executives we decided to recommend what we thought best for W Company, and that was to combine all the J advertising under a single theme. This, of course, meant that it would all be under a single agency, i.e., the $5 million we had and the $1¼ million that other agencies had.

As the largest agency, of course, we might well get the whole package. The items we have been advertising have been doing quite well, and some of those which other agencies have been pushing have not. However, there is up to this minute no certainty that we will get the whole package, and obviously we are risking an annual loss of $5 million, with the possible gain of $1¼ million. To round out the picture, I should point out that our agency does $38 million of business with W Company and that our decision undoubtedly will not fail to impress them with our integrity.

A general attorney for a large petroleum company provided an example of a personal decision made basically for a moral reason, but reinforced by other motives.

A lawyer is, in a sense, the conscience of a corporation. About a hundred times I have refused to invest in a stock which I was sure, because of inside information, would quickly appreciate. Recently our corporation acquired a small company whose stock went from 50, just before we bought it, to 77; I could have bought the stock under another name, but I refused. Why? Partly ethical, and partly fear of sanction if I were caught.

The two decisions cited involve mixed motivation. In each case it seemed to the decision-maker (and who would know better?)

that the main motive was ethical. Now let us look at several actions whose motivation is as unambiguous as human behavior can be. These decisions were made despite the probability that they would prove costly to a company or an individual. The first example came from a European administrator:

> There is no regulation against it, but I have never bought any shares of our company's stock. In my work, I become quite familiar with the bonus issues and other benefits, and if I wished, I could buy and sell at certain times and make a great deal of money from this knowledge.

The board chairman of a large utility cited similar personal behavior, adding some strong views about those who regard all businessmen as crooks.

> To say that businessmen never make ethical decisions unless they are also financially profitable is preposterous cynicism. I'm on the board of five other companies, and I never buy or sell stock in those companies on the basis of secret information which I obtain in board meetings. The same thing is true here. I own stock and buy some regularly, but I always buy in accordance with the employee purchase plan, twice a year. I never buy or sell on the basis of knowledge which I have as chairman.
>
> I also make some decisions that are ethical but unpopular. For instance, we filed suit against the electrical manufacturers after the federal government passed sentence. I've answered more than 600 letters as a result. Most of them were critical of us—we were the pot calling the kettle black. Didn't we realize what a terrible thing we were doing to our country by suing G.E., which is the number-two provider of defense goods? And some stockholders in G.E. were irate. My answer was that our position of trusteeship to our stockholders demanded that we sue in view of the action of the government in proving that there was price collusion.

Another board chairman was equally vehement in defending the integrity of businessmen:

> I can think of all sorts of decisions in answer to your question. When I was chairman of F Company, we were developing a major facility; it was a $25 million project and would benefit about 3,500,000 people. We needed the exercise of the right of eminent domain to make the facility possible. A prominent businessman came in to see me and tell me that unless I put a number of lawyers who worked for the state on our payroll, and paid some other expenses which I felt unnecessary, the project would never go through. I turned him down and said that if I couldn't get the legislation through without deals like that, I would drop the project. We got the legislation without any deal.

ETHICAL DECISIONS

Here are five illustrations which afford an idea of the variety of businessmen's temptations, as well as proof of the admirable character of some managers. From the president of a public relations firm:

Have you ever heard of Mr. A? Well, he sets up propaganda fronts. For example, he would set up a women's committee on behalf of B industry. That way the companies in the industry can release items favorable to themselves through the committee, which is not really active but just a propaganda front. Several times clients have suggested that we set up a front for them, but we have refused.

From a principal in a management consulting firm:

One of our clients makes a certain kind of machine. I did a thorough study for the client. Shortly thereafter, another company in the same industry asked me to make a similar study. I refused; it would have meant dealing in information which basically belonged to the first company, and so there was an obligation on me to keep those secrets.

I've got a tough job coming up. I've been working on a company for a while, and have decided that it's the president, who hired me, who is in the wrong. I'm going to tell him.

From an aerospace executive:

We were working on a middle-range intercontinental ballistic missile, along the lines of the Polaris project. We had a tough re-entry problem. When we sat down with the government representatives to negotiate this $2 million contract, I laid our cards right on the table and admitted how tough and insoluble the re-entry problem looked. We didn't get the contract, and our top management thought that I was the reason. They said, why tell the government everything you know even before you get the contract? But I did what I think was the right thing to do.

From the president of a transport company:

Last year I gave up a lease on a multimillion dollar facility. I sublet the facility to a group of workers for exactly what it was costing me. I was approached by an outfit I know is gangster-dominated, and they offered me a flat $50,000 more to give them the same deal I was giving the workers. I refused. Why? I won't have any truck with gangsters. I intend to keep my name free from blemish. I've long been associated with the area and I think that the workers' group will serve it better than that other outfit.

From the treasurer of a grain brokerage company:

Not so long ago I was selected the lone trustee of a profit-sharing trust to which our employees contribute; the trust owns stock in the company and the amount of stock is increasing. As the rules stated when I was appointed, I voted the stock in the trust. This gave me quite a bit of power, and with the amount of stock in the trust growing, could conceivably mean that I would eventually control the entire company. So the first thing I did when selected was to insist on an amendment to the rules to take this voting power away from me, the lone trustee, and give it to a five-man advisory committee. There was no financial gain to me; indeed, it could possibly cost me my seat on the board of directors of the company someday.

A personnel executive offers further proof of management's willingness to act ethically even when it hurts:

Years ago, my boss asked me to falsify an expense account by $100 and give him the money. He told me there was no chance that I could get caught, since he would approve the expense account. At the risk of my job, I refused because it wasn't honest. He didn't fire me nor rebuke me. I don't know why I did it; perhaps it was conscience, or cowardice.

GOOD RESULTS

Several experienced executives were convinced that the habit of making ethical decisions has two good effects. First, there is a chain reaction among subordinates; the good example of the boss is imitated by the employees. Second, and less obvious, word of ethical behavior gets around; the manager who refuses an offer or suggestion of unethical behavior will probably not be approached again on the same matter. In the words of our oldest interviewee: "One thing we have learned is that once you get a reputation for ethical behavior, there are fewer requests to act unethically." An executive in the communications industry said, "It's been interesting for me to note that when your position about ethical matters becomes known, you face fewer temptations. And your subordinates get the idea that you won't tolerate dishonesty or lying, so they make decisions in accord with your principles." These two comments contain a valuable insight.

Not every ethical action has salutary effects. In 1964, newsman Charles Nicodemus related the ordeal of Robert S. Snoyer, president of the Consad Corporation in Santa Monica, California.[1]

---

[1] Charles Nicodemus, "Robert S. Snoyer: His Ordeal and Triumph," *Chicago Daily News*, February 6, 1964, p. 41.

Snoyer informed the FBI, in June 1962, that Signal Corps officials had demanded a kickback of $48,000 before awarding a $2,400,000 contract to his company. In the ensuing twenty months until the conviction of three men for bribery, conspiracy, and conflict of interest, Snoyer was subjected to harassment and economic pressure, apparently because of the information he had given to the FBI. Time-consuming contract provisions not normally enforced were required of the Consad Corporation by the Signal Corps. Consad's bankers and creditors acted as though the company was no longer a good financial risk. Incoming contracts from industry and government slowed to a trickle; most businessmen felt that dealing with Snoyer would jeopardize their relations with the government. His willingness to undergo these hardships because of his principles was praiseworthy, especially since other businessmen severed relationships with him when he became controversial.

BEYOND JUSTICE

Among the examples managers gave of decisions of which they were proud, one frequent refrain was that in many business transactions today, what people think has happened is as important as what happened. Some decisions exceed the demands of justice in order that people will not misconstrue facts which may be hard to explain. For example, an interior decorator found himself in an awkward position despite excellent intentions:

Our airport recently added a new wing. I was hired by the city to write up specifications for the interior decorating. This I did, listing supplier firms with which our company has franchise accounts and from which our company gets maximum discount; I listed these men not because of the discounts but because I knew they would deliver the goods. I told the city officials that we were not interested in bidding on the interior decorating for the new wing because I had drawn up the specifications, and there would be cries of "unethical" if our bid was the lowest and received the contract. The man in charge agreed. However, some days later the city purchasing agent phoned me and said that as a citizen I owed it to the city to save it money if I could. So I submitted a bid, and it was the lowest. We got a $12,000 contract on which we profited about $100. I wish that we hadn't gotten it because I'm still afraid of criticism on the deal.

Even though the decorator's firm made little profit from the contract, the facts were such that, if they had become common knowledge, public confidence in the city government would have been shaken. The city official should have known that "where public confidence is at issue, what people think is true may be as important as what is true . . . public confidence is the single most important goal at stake in the field of governmental ethics."[2]

Examples of other decisions which exceed the demands of justice were offered by two stockbrokers, who told how they paid clients money which the latter did not deserve because they had omitted a minor, but necessary, requirement for a stock purchase. The brokers acted in this way because of the difficulty of convincing the clients that they did not deserve the money. This kind of behavior was described as "superethical" by one manager. Others might describe it as business prudence or good customer relations.

Another executive offered a similar illustration which seems to have been motivated by patriotism: "Our company has a number of on-going projects for the government right now on which we are losing money. We are continuing them because we think this is the right thing to do."

DOES CHARITY OBLIGE?

The three preceding examples point to a problem faced by the well-intentioned businessman who is unsure about what is required of him in certain situations. "How far must I go?" he asks himself; "must I turn the other cheek?" Usually the situations involve applications of the virtue of charity. A manager should keep in mind, however, that justice, giving to each person what is due him, is the businessman's virtue par excellence. Only after the requirements of justice have been met should the manager consider the possibility of a further obligation in charity.

In situations like these, some theologians make a distinction between a precept and a counsel.[3] A *precept* is a command, an obligation; a *counsel* is advice, an opportunity. As Thomas Aquinas put it:

[2] Association of the Bar of the City of New York, *Conflict of Interest and Federal Service* (Cambridge, Mass.: Harvard University Press, 1960), pp. 17–18.

[3] Lutheran theologians, and others, deny this distinction, which conflicts with their conception of a calling or vocation. Cf. Max Weber, *The Protestant Ethic and the Spirit of Capitalism* (New York: Charles Scribner's Sons, 1958), pp. 80–81.

This is the difference between a counsel and a precept . . . the latter implies necessity, whereas the former allows a choice . . . the precepts of the new law are to be understood as referring to those things which are necessary to reach the goal of eternal beatitude . . . whereas the counsels should be taken to mean the things by which a man can arrive at the aforesaid goal better and more easily.[4]

A common application of this distinction is made in theological interpretations of passages in the Bible: "Thou shalt not steal" is a precept; "If you want to be perfect, go and sell all your possessions and give the proceeds to the poor . . . then come back and be my follower"[5] is a counsel. That the latter is only a counsel is a conclusion suggested both by reason and by the actions of Jesus, who made the statement; He did not condemn the rich young man who did not follow His advice.

Knowledge of the distinction between precept and counsel is sometimes useful for managers, several of whom we have seen badly confused because they did not know it. When a man mistakenly regards the counsels of Jesus as precepts, he can have a serious problem of conscience.[6] Given his mistaken notion, the man reasons that he is being asked to do more than is humanly possible. Such a man might conclude that there is something wrong with a religion which puts intolerable burdens on men of goodwill. Then it is but a short step logically to conclude that business and religion are incompatible.

An illustration of a decision which went beyond the demands of justice was provided by a president faced with the need of firing a veteran engineer. The president gave the engineer severance pay equal to his salary for *five* years. Ethically the president had no obligation to make such a generous gesture. But he felt that it was the charitable thing to do in the circumstances.

In reply to my request for an example of a decision motivated by principle rather than self-interest, another president provided an example which was apparently motivated by charity, but which seems to have involved an injustice to stockholders:

Recently we purchased a division of another company. I acted in what I thought was good faith. We bought an entire product line: tool-

[4] Thomas Aquinas, *Summa Theologica*, I–II, 108, 4.

[5] *New Testament*, Matthew 19:21, from the translation by James A. Kleist, S.J. (Milwaukee: Bruce, 1956).

[6] In certain circumstances a counsel could be obligatory for an individual, but this is rare.

ing, catalogs, goodwill, etc. It was my first big purchase, and maybe I
was naïve. Anyway, I accepted the total dollar figure which the seller
proposed, rather than ask for an itemized listing. We didn't get what
we expected and we complained. We felt that the items which we got in
the purchase were only one-half of what we expected to get, so that
there was about $50,000 short. We didn't sue or anything. I talked
with the man who owned the division and I felt that he had been in
good faith, so I figured that I should keep my word about what we
would pay.

One wonders what would happen to the president if stockholders
ever discovered his reason for paying $100,000 for $50,000 of goods.
Presumably they would have something to say about charity beginning at home.

In this chapter I have described and categorized decisions made
by businessmen for ethical reasons. I think that they explode the
myth that profit is always the determining factor in business decisions. The illustrations in this chapter are as much a part of the
whole from which the public should form its image of business
ethics as are the facts about Billie Sol Estes and Anthony De-
Angelis. The businessman, who so often has his failures reported,
also deserves to have his virtuous acts catalogued.

Having described, analyzed, and categorized some business decisions, we will now consider which are the most constant factors leading to ethical decisions by businessmen. In Project Two, we asked the panelists about five influences which the pilot test had suggested were relevant to business decisions. A random half of the respondents (53.4 per cent actually) ranked these factors according to the influence they exert on a manager to make *ethical* decisions. The other half of the respondents ranked five similar factors according to the influence they exert for *unethical* decisions. Table 6.1 presents the results.

From these rankings, it appears that when a businessman acts *ethically* (Part A), he attributes it to his own ability to resist pressure and temptation, with some credit due to his superiors and company policy; when he acts *unethically* (Part B), he blames his superiors and the climate in his industry. These conclusions recall the playwright who attributed his failures to inept casts and stupid audiences, and accepted praise for successes as if they were one-man performances.

The human reluctance to blame oneself for ethical failings helps to explain why our respondents rank personal financial needs as *least* important of the five factors influencing unethical behavior. Another explanation for this ranking is that bad example and pressure from superiors or peers are felt intensely on a few occasions, while the need for money is a general condition. The findings here hardly justify the conclusion that money was unimportant to these businessmen, though 89 per cent of them had five-figure incomes. The possession of money and the things money can buy are certainly honored in the United States, but our respondents thought that this acquisitive spirit was a less important motive than the others given in Table 6.1.

Table 6.1
Influences on Business Behavior

A. What influences a businessman to make *ethical* decisions?

Possible Influence	Average Rank (N = 807)
A man's personal code of behavior	1.5
Formal company policy	2.8
The behavior of a man's superiors in the company	2.8
Ethical climate of the industry	3.8
The behavior of a man's equals in the company	4.0

B. What influences a businessman to make *unethical* decisions?

Possible Influence	Average Rank (N = 705)
The behavior of a man's superiors in the company	1.8
Ethical climate of the industry	2.6
The behavior of a man's equals in the company	3.2
Lack of company policy	3.3
Personal financial needs	4.1

Note: The rankings given are weighted averages of respondents' rankings of each item (1, 2, 3, 4, or 5), with most influential = 1, and least influential = 5.

A person's coworkers influence his behavior, but to what extent? Are businessmen "other-directed" rather than "inner-directed"; do managers look mainly to the company for their standards? Was the *Wall Street Journal* justified in its comment on the antitrust decisions in the electrical industry: "The simplest, if not the complete, answer [to why high-ranking executives had knowingly done wrong] goes back to the organization man"?[1]

Close examination of the data reveals a tendency in every age group, company milieu, and management level for a man to accept the values of his superiors. Questionnaire results encouraged deeper probing into the factors underlying ethical decisions, however, and

[1] John Bridge, "Antitrust and Organization Man," *Wall Street Journal*, January 10, 1961, p. 10.

for this purpose I designed eight interview questions. In this and subsequent chapters, I shall discuss the replies to these questions, i.e., businessmen's views about a variety of influences on decisions which contain an ethical component. For ease of analysis, I divide these influences into two groups: *inner* factors and *outer* factors. The former are personal to an individual, characteristics or possessions which are uniquely his or largely within his control; the latter are common to many men, largely beyond the individual's control and external to him. The arbitrary classification I shall follow is:

Inner factors: beliefs about business; conscience; age; income; education; religious affiliation and beliefs.

Outer factors: occupation; company; boss and coworkers; industry; national customs; government regulations.

GOOD ETHICS IS GOOD BUSINESS

First let us focus on a belief of businessmen about business, a belief related to the examples described in preceding chapters. It unquestionably affects decisions and appears in many speeches by executives: Good ethics is good business. What does it mean? How many businessmen support it? Why do businessmen like to repeat it?

In the first two projects, the respondents were asked for an opinion on the statement, "Sound ethics is good business in the long run." Agreement was nearly unanimous: 98 per cent agreed, 1 per cent were neutral, 1 per cent disagreed.

In the interviews, in order to begin the conversation with a question which respondents would find agreeable, they were asked: "Do you agree that good ethics is good business in the long run?" Only 1 per cent disagreed. A second query was then added: "Would you mind telling me why you think this is so?"

As might be expected, some first preferred to discuss the phrases "good ethics" and "good business." One president said: "If you define good business as maximization of profit, then I disagree." Another executive attached a pragmatic meaning to "good ethics": "I agree that good ethics is good business in the long run. You can catch more flies with honey than with vinegar. Besides, being nice to people doesn't cost anything." Throughout his interview, this man regarded ethical behavior as one among many means to business success. His view was atypical.

One reason for the unusually high percentage in agreement was that there were no qualifying adverbs like "always" or "frequently." Consequently, as long as a man thought that the statement was true more than half the time, he could agree with it. Logically, he could simultaneously agree that, in the long run, bad ethics is good business 49 per cent of the time. For instance, one president replied: "Yes, I'd say that more businessmen work on the basis of good ethics than on the basis of bad ethics."

With a few Pollyanna-like exceptions, the responses seemed realistic. One director of purchasing agreed despite a bitter personal experience: A subordinate had undermined the company president's confidence in him. The purchasing director had to leave, and his subordinate has since become a vice-president of the company. The victim of the undermining cited this as "obvious proof that bad ethics sometimes works."

Ten per cent of our interviewees added substantial qualifications to their basic agreement that good ethics is good business in the long run.

One manager said:

Perhaps it's so in the long run, but I've known a number of men who had to get out of business because of the unethical pressures. I know one contractor who refused to pay off the racketeers. He could have been a millionaire today, but instead he is a relatively poor man. I don't really believe that there is a necessary connection between good ethics and success.

A foreign businessman observed:

In general, it is so, except when there is a question of survival. In our country I often saw men of good will go out of business because they were too ethical. Some people said they were foolish. But they were not inefficient businessmen, they just tried to do business ethically. . . . One practice which I do not let my subordinates do is lie about product quality or performance in order to sell. Really, our customers appreciate that, and I don't think that I lose business in the long run.

A plant manager stated:

I agree, particularly with respect to dealings between management and employees. . . . However, it does happen that some of the most successful salesmen are the least ethical. It's not because they are unethical. But they have a hot item or a hot price. After all, we can't sell a salesman's good ethics; unless he has a good product, we don't buy from him. If he has a good product, we may buy from him despite his bad ethics.

REASONS FOR THE BELIEF

Professors Learned, Dooley, and Katz analyze the idea that good ethics is good business in the long run. They suggest that business-men's reasons for supporting this idea fit into three categories: (1) "a business that behaves ethically induces others to behave ethically toward it;" (2) ethical behavior is "a form of insurance against retaliatory acts;" (3) "a 'good man' who steadfastly tries to be ethical . . . somehow always overtakes his immoral or amoral coun-terpart."[2] This third category, virtue always triumphs, is a con-clusion that men can come to by two different routes: faith in "the operation of some divine force that ultimately assures a happy end-ing"; or a conviction that the unethical man naturally loses to the ethical man, whose "energies are freed for maximum productivity and creativity,"[3] while the unethical man is exhausted or cramped by the subterfuge in which he must engage. With one emendation, these categories serve well for classifying many answers I received; I would broaden the second category to include insurance against unforeseen harmful results which follow unethical actions.

About half the interviewees provided answers that fitted these categories, as amended. Eighty per cent of these replies were in categories 1 and 2, i.e., these businessmen explained their ethical behavior largely through reference to other businessmen, either as insurance against retaliation or as good example which prompts reciprocal treatment.

Professors Learned, Dooley, and Katz conclude that "the view that good ethics is good business is [not] a fully adequate or satisfy-ing guide for action."[4] Almost all of the businessmen I interviewed would agree. Rarely did I meet a manager who used "good ethics is good business in the long run" as a *major* reason or guide for his decisions. Though true, it is too simple and remote to be of sub-stantial help to a harried manager, most of whose decisions are complex and of short-run significance.

[2] Edmund Learned, Arch Dooley, and Robert Katz, "Personal Values and Business Decisions," *Harvard Business Review*, March–April, 1959, pp. 115–116.

[3] *Ibid.*, p. 116.

[4] *Ibid.*, p. 117.

BAD ETHICS IS BAD BUSINESS

The chairman of a large public utility thought that even a single unethical decision would turn out to be bad business: "After all, your employees and the other party with whom you work the unethical deal know about it." One manager recalled an unsuccessful attempt to influence a general to get an army contract by providing a call girl: "We did not get the contract, and the general raised a great deal of furor over this incident. We stopped that practice immediately." A vice-president in the aerospace industry resented subcontractors who were doing an inferior job, trying to put something over on him. "I caught it and we dropped those subcontractors. Bad ethics proved to be bad business for them."

As these examples prove, bad ethics can hurt income and profitability. When a manager has painful experience of this, he has a strong motive for acting ethically in the future. A president in a service industry was an eloquent spokesman for the dollars-and-cents value of moral behavior:

The ethical way is the only way to operate. When you do unethical things, it turns out to be expensive. For one thing, after you do something wrong, you worry; this is subjective, but it is important. It takes time and energy to worry, and that makes it expensive. Furthermore, you may have to take steps to cover your unethical move, and that will be expensive. Besides, many unethical activities are also illegal. . . . Also, with the improvement in communications, the penalties which a company must pay for unethical behavior have greatly increased. Word gets around.

This same president introduced a psychological reason that prompts businessmen to endorse the notion that good ethics is good business:

The most important motive for my acting ethically in business is, I'm afraid, the practical one: trying to be a masculine male, not doing right just in order to be right. . . . When I talk to our young men, I don't tell them to be ethical for the sake of ethics. I tell them that ethical behavior is the way to promotion and success.

This feeling that it is not virile to talk about ethics was also encountered by John B. Shallenberger, research director of the Comité International de l'Organisation Scientifique, in a globe-circling investigation. After interviewing 7,500 managers in 109 different countries, Mr. Shallenberger stated: "Managers are shy to speak openly of ethics, just as most people blush to mention God in daily conversation."[5] Similarly, editor Edward O. Bursk of the *Harvard Business Review* wonders: "Why do businessmen like to find practical reasons for doing unselfish acts?"[6] Part of the answer is found in the image of the successful businessman held by many managers. The image is that of an "economic man" whose ultimate norm in every decision is profit maximization. After describing in detail a decision he had made because he felt "a moral responsibility to our employees," one of our respondents added:

> Under ordinary circumstances, that is, if I were not talking to a priest, I might not admit this sense of responsibility for employees. We businessmen are embarrassed to say that we have any other motive for a business decision than profit. That's probably because of some image of the businessman that we all have.

As we have seen, our respondents believe that the successful businessman often acts for reasons other than those associated with his public image. They say that it is sometimes wrong for a manager to act like an "economic man," to make profit maximization the ultimate norm for decisions. On the other hand, after they make a decision, most of them prefer to present economic reasons for having made it. Presumably they fear that stockholders will be critical of a decision made for noneconomic reasons. In this era of social awareness, is this a reasonable fear?

Do businessmen realize the harm they are doing to their own reputation by insisting that they act solely for economic reasons? Executive-author James C. Worthy is sharply critical of the businessman's reluctance to admit the importance of noneconomic motives in his decisions:

> According to classical economic doctrine, business is assumed to be conducted primarily for pecuniary gain. . . . The businessman himself generally explains his actions in terms of self-interest. . . . Self-interest, whether narrow or enlightened, is an unstable basis on which to erect a system of economic institutions. . . . In terms of Christian ethics, the effort to explain and justify the workings of the business system on the basis of self-interest is to glorify greed. . . . Because of the insistence on a self-interest rationale, the business system is placed, by its own defenders and apologists, in moral conflict with the ethical foundations of its own society.[7]

[5] Raymond Baumhart, S.J., "How Ethical Are Businessmen?" *Harvard Business Review*, July–August 1961, p. 172.

[6] *Business and Religion* (New York: Harper & Row, 1959), p. viii.

[7] *Big Business and Free Men* (New York: Harper & Row, 1959), pp. 20–22 *passim*.

WHAT EXPERIENCE TEACHES

Finally, a majority of our interviewees were convinced that *experience* teaches that good ethics is good business, and some gave reasons for their conviction. The answers come down to four ideas pertaining to customer or employee relations, in the following order of importance:

1. Customers and repeat sales
2. Employees, union, and low turnover
3. Good reputation
4. Consistent behavior

A moment's reflection on the four ideas reveals how reasonable it is that a customer who is treated well may return to the same store or salesman; that employees like to work for a manager who respects them; that most men are pleased to do business with a company that has a good reputation; that consistent behavior is valued by manufacturers and retailers. In other words, experience teaches that ethical behavior and good business practice often coincide. Here are three illustrations, provided by our panelists, of how good ethics and good business dovetail.

A worker gave us two weeks' notice of his intention to leave our company. It was the beginning of summer, and he had summer vacation coming. So we gave him his full vacation with pay. This is not only good ethics, it's good business. If we hadn't given him his vacation pay, he would have been the last man to give us notice of his intention to quit.

Our advertising department wanted to use pictures of a scientific machine that we have in the lab in selling promotion for our tires. I refused to permit this because this machine did not really apply to problems encountered in normal tire wear. However, I was also thinking that the FTC [Federal Trade Commission] and our competitors would spot this and it would backfire on the company and me.

We have as a goal the making of a machine which will last for ten years without any major service changes. Quality is very important to us. All of this is desirable on a selfish basis, as well as on an ethical basis. For instance, it is not easy or inexpensive for the company to arrange for good service of its machines, so it will pay to make machines that don't need much service.

In the light of the data presented, how explain the dovetailing of good ethics and good business in the long run? Business decisions are made by people and affect other people. Those affected know who made the decision; at least, this is usually the case with employees and customers. Some business experiences are easily recalled. This seems generally true of unethical treatment. There is something about an injustice, about an affront to one's dignity, that calls forth instinctive disapproval. Remembering the past and moved by a proper self-love, a man will probably choose not to do business with a person who has mistreated him. But if a man is satisfied that he has been treated justly, he will probably choose to continue dealing with the same individual, other things being equal.

The business decisions of our country are made by several million men who do not like to be treated dishonestly or unfairly. They respond favorably to treatment that recognizes their human dignity. *Fundamentally*, that is why good ethics is usually good business in the long run. Usually, not always. Good ethics cannot meet a payroll, make a quality product, or be sold over a counter. Other factors, like lower prices, a better product, or fear of gangsters can outweigh for a time the natural tendency to favor the man who has treated a person fairly and to avoid the man who has not. But there seems to be operative in most human beings an instinctive desire for honesty and fairness, a desire whose cumulative result *in the long run*, in the areas of customer and employee relations, at least, is beneficial to ethical managers. Vis-à-vis competitors, good ethics and good business sometimes coincide, but the evidence provided by our panelists offers no basis for meaningful conclusions, or even optimism.

Why do men act ethically? There is disagreement over the answer. For many the only important thing is that man act ethically; his reason is unimportant. But surely there is a difference between a decision made for reasons of conscience, and one made solely because of the profits which will follow. Though the economic outcome may be identical in the two cases, the man who makes decisions according to his conscience gives us more hope that he will act ethically in the face of pressure and temptation. Sometimes a manager makes a decision for economic reasons, and it happens that satisfying noneconomic results follow. The man may like the psychic rewards of acting virtuously and so make future decisions for non-economic reasons. This is not to downgrade the decision motivated by a desire for reasonable profit. A motive, after all, is a reason that moves a man. Most men can be spurred by a variety of motives, some high, some low. Reasonable self-interest and a desire for profit can promote ethical behavior.

Through the Project Two questionnaire, as revealed in Table 6.1 we learned that 807 businessmen rank "personal code of behavior" as a most important reason for their ethical decisions. In Project Three, this idea was pursued by asking the 100 interviewees: "What, would you say, is the most important motive for your acting ethically in business?"

Conscience was the concept most frequently mentioned.[1] More

[1] This emphasis on conscience coincides with a finding of a Wayne State University survey of 84 men in middle management. Asked to identify the major source of solutions for their ethical problems in business, these mana-

than one-third spoke directly about conscience, many using the phrase, "I have to live with myself." Conscience is a practical judgment about the morality of performing or omitting an action; one or more principles or rules is applied to a concrete case. Popular usage identifies the human faculty which makes this judgment as the conscience. I will use conscience as most interviewees used it: the faculty which decides the morality of one's own actions, and urges one to do good and avoid evil.[2]

The principles utilized by man's conscience stem from nature, especially from his inclination toward reasonable behavior, and from education in its broadest sense. As a personnel manager said, "I try always to be honest with my conscience, but this is only a starting point; you have to develop your own conscience." This development can be inadequate, as the deliberate misbehavior of intelligent criminals attests. One's conscience can be poorly educated or become lax; when this happens, as a purchasing executive mentioned, "conscience can be an alibi," in the sense that unethical actions can be performed without remorse.

One manager stated, "After all, conscience is the only fixed standard you have, so you had better follow it." It is generally agreed that to follow one's conscience is to act reasonably, but is it accurate to speak of conscience as "fixed"? Conscience can be changed, in the sense that a man can learn or accept new norms for governing his behavior. The manager just quoted needs to have his conscience educated:

> I guess the main reason why I'm ethical is a weakness in personality: I don't have the guts to go ahead and take advantage of another fellow. For example, if I were in a strange store and a man gave me four dollars too much change, I would return it. But I certainly wouldn't feel bad if I had taken it.

More sensitive, the general manager of a chain of food stores offered his reason for acting ethically:

> I know that I'm more ethical now than when I was young. I'm more conscious of what's going on and more careful: that's my

---

gers named conscience most frequently. Company policy was ranked second. Cf. "Middle Managers' Views on Their Most Significant Professional Moral Problems," Program Extra No. 603, National Conference of Christian Employers and Managers, 1006 S. Michigan Avenue, Chicago, p. 26.

[2] Some philosophers regard conscience as a special moral faculty; others think it is the intellect judging the morality of a situation.

conscience . . . I feel uncomfortable if I gain an unethical advantage. Even if I'm only playing bridge and catch a glimpse of my opponent's hand, I feel uncomfortable and I don't enjoy winning as much: that's my conscience.

This manager has made a distinction between what moralists call antecedent and consequent conscience. Before a decision, one's conscience tells a man what to do or to avoid; afterward, conscience causes remorse or satisfaction. In the interviews I frequently heard about consequent conscience in terms like "peace of mind," "worry," "feel better," "sleep better," "at peace," "a clear conscience when you get home," "wouldn't be happy." Or as an investment manager expressed it: "Your mind is always with you; you can never escape a bad deed."

SANCTIONS

One way of classifying the foregoing replies is to consider them as sanctions, by which is meant either a reward for acting ethically or a punishment for acting unethically. The favorite way of saying that this sanction was a strong inducement for ethical behavior was: "I have to live with myself." In the words of a Negro who was conspicuous for courage in integrating an elementary school despite physical and verbal opposition: "I'd rather take a beating from a mob than from my own conscience."

The sanctions just mentioned are internal, originating within the individual whom they influence. Others are outside the individual influenced. One-quarter of our interviewees mentioned that such external sanctions promote ethical action. For example, several men agreed with the public relations counselor who said that "ethical behavior is the way to promotion and success. It is the easiest and the soundest way." Others, emphasizing the fear of retaliation for unethical behavior, simply announced, "You get back what you give."

The good opinion of other people, the desire to earn or keep a good reputation, is another external sanction which motivates businessmen. This desire is not only for the man's own sake, but also for his wife's and children's. Said one executive: "What a person thinks of me is important to me. I like it when somebody says, 'We like to deal with you and with your company because you are ethical.' " An executive who won Air Corps honors in World War II offered this explanation:

It wouldn't bother me substantially if I lost my job for doing what is right. . . . My wife tells me I'm proud. I guess she's right, but I'm proud of what we did in the war and I want to live up to that reputation for the rest of my life.

The president of a retail food company has a similar outlook for a different reason:

My father had a good reputation as a businessman. One of the stories they tell—it's good folklore—is about the time my father received a bag full of rolls of quarters instead of pennies for which he paid. He sent the quarters right back to the bank. So I felt that I had to live up to my father's good reputation.

Philosophers make a distinction between natural and supernatural sanctions. The latter term implies the idea of life after death, with the sanction being reward or punishment in that life. Supernatural sanction was given by one-fifth of our respondents as a major motive for their good behavior. As a company president put it: "I want to save my soul. If I do something wrong, I know that I must account for it to God," or, in the words of a young management consultant: "Reward or punishment for the way I use my talents. . . . I'm concerned about my score; all our actions go to make up this score." An advertising executive gave a similar reason: "I may jeopardize what is important to me, namely, heaven. I don't want to lose my seat up there." Supernatural sanction was mentioned by Catholic interviewees more than by those of other religious affiliations. There was no opportunity for in-depth questioning to determine why this was so.

Another frequently proffered reason for acting ethically is a sense of justice or obligation. For some men it is rooted in a conviction or instinct that the ethical way is "the right way." One who "sees" this truth feels little need to speak about the why of ethical behavior. Here are representative replies:

A Canadian: "Every day I have chances to cheat, but my response is automatic. I just wouldn't do those things, and reject them without thinking about them."

A small company president: "I don't know why. But I'm sure that ethics is right."

A banker: "Your response should be instinctive [in an ethical dilemma] and you shouldn't have to think. You should say, 'I just won't touch it.' "

A Japanese: "Ethics is not the sort of thing which requires reason. There is no reason why you love your mother."

"Love of God and neighbor" was seldom given as the answer to the query, "What is the most important motive for your acting ethically in business?" Natural sanctions, partly because they are immediate, seem to motivate more of our interviewees than do supernatural sanctions or a sense of justice, though these are also important. Even those who limited themselves to natural sanctions, however, usually conveyed a sense of the primacy of conscience.

THE PRIMACY OF SOLVENCY

Acting against one's own conscience was a central issue in another part of my Project Three research. Each interviewee was given a card containing a paraphrase of a statement by Marquis Childs and Douglass Cater:

The first responsibility of a businessman is to keep his business solvent, for if his business is bankrupt it will no longer provide a living for himself and jobs for others. Therefore, it is ethical for a businessman, in time of financial distress or severe competition, to make decisions directly opposed to those which his conscience dictates. Do you agree or disagree?[3]

In Project Two, five of every six questionnaire respondents thought it unethical "for corporation executives to act in the interest of shareholders alone, and not also in the interest of employees and consumers." It seemed doubtful therefore that many businessmen would agree with Childs and Cater. The Project Three result confirmed this thinking: Eleven managers agreed with them, 87 disagreed, and two declined to answer.

Before analyzing the elaborations of our interviewees, it is important to note that the statement is theoretical. Some men, apparently unaccustomed to abstract thinking, found it hard to disassociate theory from practice. Or perhaps these men were implying that learning the answer to this theoretical question is less important than finding out whether a manager, in time of competitive stress, will act against his conscience. No effort was made by the interviewers to direct respondents to one or other of the two debatable ideas contained in the assertion, namely, the primacy of solvency and acting against one's conscience. Most chose to speak about the latter. A dozen men addressed themselves to the problem

[3] *Cf. Ethics in a Business Society* (New York: Harper Mentor Book, 1954), p. 173, for the original version.

of solvency, and a few spoke about both ideas. The realism of the respondents is demonstrated by a distinction which many made: "That is what a businessman *should* do, I'm not trying to guess what he *would* do." They recognize the difference between an ideal, to which one aspires, and practice, which often falls short of the ideal. As a Chicago manager said: "Conduct like that is understandable, but it's unethical."

Among the majority who disagreed, one-quarter were strong in their conviction that acting against one's conscience is wrong:

> It's better to be financially bankrupt than to be ethically bankrupt.

> If this statement is so, we are a lost society.

Several interviewees asked for an example of conduct like that described on the card. Each was told a true story of a small company whose top management acted on the belief that staying in business justified, temporarily at least, lying to customers about merchandise and billing a supplier for advertising that was never done. Most reactions were unfavorable: "That's like taking the first pipeful of opium"; "Are they still in business?"

Opposition to solvency as the primary responsibility of the businessman was emphatic on the part of several:

> I disagree. His first responsibility is to himself, to keep his principles unblemished. That's a hell of a lot more important than staying solvent.

> If you agree with that statement, you make solvency the norm of conduct and I see no sense in that.

Eight men rejected, for economic reasons, the view of Childs and Cater that it is sometimes ethical to act contrary to one's conscience:

> If this man cannot make money by operating a legitimate business, then there is either no market for his product or he is a poor manager. If this is true, regardless of his short-run decisions, he will go broke sooner or later.

> A company that reaches a crisis like this probably should not be in business. By making solvency the norm, inefficient companies would go on and on, and that's no good.

Once again, from a different quarter, we hear the theme: Economics and ethics dovetail in the long run.

The statistics are clear: Our respondents think it unethical for a businessman to act contrary to his conscience, even to avoid

bankruptcy. What of the minority viewpoint? Here are their sentiments:

> In a small degree, decisions such as these are necessary to keep the
> business going. This necessity to compromise whittles away at your
> ideals.

> I would feel that I must keep the business going and this would
> perhaps justify some of my unethical actions.

> You have got to keep your business solvent. This is your first re-
> sponsibility. If you are soft and a patsy, you deserve to go broke.

A few executives were stymied by the insolvent-or-unethical
dilemma. Under pressure from the interviewer, one finally concluded, "Maybe it's sometimes ethical to be unethical."

Although the thinking of 100 businessmen is hardly going to
settle the problem of the "technical must versus the ethical ought,"
our respondents' views help to reveal the ramifications of the problem.[4] Let us consider some of them in greater depth.

To do good and avoid evil is the basic principle of moral order,
known intuitively by every human being. The conscience applies
the first principle, and others that are secondary, to specific human
actions in concrete situations, and judges that a proposed action
would be good or evil.[5] If the action would be evil, the conscience
urges that it be avoided. To perform such an action would be to act
against one's conscience, which—assuming that the conscience is
properly formed—causes moral disorder and harms society, at least
indirectly.

Why would anyone act against his conscience? Because he felt
that it would be to his advantage. The statement of Childs and
Cater implies that there is something about a free enterprise economy or the role of the businessman that occasionally persuades him
it would be advantageous to act against his conscience. There is
support for this view from the eleven interviewees who agreed with
the statement, and from the 70 per cent of questionnaire respondents who acknowledged the presence in their industry of generally
accepted business practices which are unethical. Does our economic
system cause businessmen occasionally to act against their con-

---

[4] The phrase is Benjamin Selekman's. A full discussion can be found in
Sylvia and Benjamin Selekman, *Morality in a Business Society* (New York:
McGraw-Hill, 1956), Chap. V.

[5] The secondary principles are not known intuitively, but are rational de-
ductions from the first principle.

sciences? If so, does it happen to all, many, or just a few? If a few, are they men who manage inefficient, undercapitalized, marginal operations whose demise would not harm the economy seriously? Or are they key men in nationally known companies like the executive who said: "Let's get down to brass tacks. Sometimes in business you have to be unethical. We do it. Just tell us what our penance is. We'll pay it. Then we'll get on with what we are doing." This sounds very much like "business is business," which most observers contend is passé. While the businessman quoted may not be representative, he is an officer in a large corporation in an important industry. If his company acts that way, can other companies compete effectively without descending to the same kind of behavior?

MAKING MONEY COMES FIRST

Today's businessmen are said to be aware of their responsibilities, to be socially conscious. Perhaps they are. But there are prominent businessmen who contradict this common view. For example, *Forbes* magazine described United States Industries' president, I. John Billera, as a man who "wants to change the company's image from one that is preoccupied with 'corporate social responsibility' to one that 'makes a buck.' "[6] Billera describes his self-image quite simply: "I'm employed to make money. I have no other aspirations."[7] This country has no monopoly on businessmen with mercenary ambition. Roy Thomson, an English publisher, declared: "I buy newspapers to make money to buy more newspapers to make more money. As for editorial content, that's the stuff you separate the ads with."[8]

There are academicians who defend the businessman's single-minded pursuit of money and profits. Professor Paul Donham regrets that the businessman feels that he

must utter pious platitudes about his social enlightenment and lack of self-interest, while at the same time he knows that the law of the jungle still holds in his competitive environment. . . . The sooner all business administrators stop trying to play God and concentrate on their *raison d'être*—the maximization of profits—the sooner will our

6 "New Broom," *Forbes,* October 1, 1965, p. 43.

7 *Loc. cit.*

8 *Time,* November 26, 1965, p. 53.

society benefit . . . their primary devotion is to the dollar, and . . . *this is as it should be.*"9

Professor Robert Freedman apparently agrees with Childs and Cater; he writes: "There is often no escape from compromising what is right and what is necessary. In the end the business role demands that the businessman protect his business . . . it is society's job to ensure social justice, not his."10 The president of Maremont Corporation feels much the same way: "It's a game. . . . We in business are playing to win and make profits, and to the extent that people are affected, they will sooner or later be protected by Government."11

More typical of the opinions of businessmen participating in our survey, however, is the view of American business expressed by the president of Jamieson Incorporated: "Its first objective must be to properly serve the material needs of others. It must, in effect, serve the common good."12 In his view, profits are the result of serving others. Bernard Erf, publisher of the *Brewers Digest*, pushes this concept a bit further: "The enabling of men to achieve the fullness of human being becomes the core function . . . of the economic institution."13

There is disagreement about the primary responsibility and basic purpose of a business corporation. But there is a consensus that the businessman has broader horizons than making profits. In Project Two there was presented the following abbreviated version of the thinking of Professor Theodore Levitt:

The businessman exists for only one purpose: to create and deliver value satisfactions at a profit to himself. If what is offered can be sold at a profit, then it is legitimate. The spiritual and moral consequences of the businessman's actions are none of his concern.14

9 "Is Management a Profession?" *Harvard Business Review*, September–October 1962, pp. 67–68.

10 "The Challenge of Business Ethics," *Atlanta Economic Review*, May 1962, p. 12.

11 Letter written by Arnold Maremont to the editor of the *Harvard Business Review* on November 4, 1965.

12 Edward Jamieson, "The Businessman's Vocation," *New City*, September 1, 1964, p. 6.

13 "Beyond Self-Regulation," *Brewers Digest*, April 1966, p. 7.

14 "Are Advertising and Marketing Corrupting Society? It's Not Your Worry, Levitt Tells Business," *Advertising Age*, October 6, 1958, p. 89. The author's exact words are: ". . . the businessman exists for only one purpose, to create and deliver value satisfactions at a profit to himself. . . . If what

From top to bottom of the corporate ladder, 94 per cent of the respondents said, "We disagree!" As one personnel man put it, "This man lives in a vacuum, ignoring the society that gave him his opportunity, his responsibility to make it better rather than worse as a result of his existence." Our respondents also revealed that they regard untempered profit maximization as unethical, agreeing with the thesis advanced by Professor Robert N. Anthony.[15] Five of every six managers reacted affirmatively to this paraphrase of his judgment: "For corporation executives to act in the interest of shareholders alone, and not also in the interest of employees and consumers, is unethical." A production manager from Texas voiced a viewpoint to which many subscribe: "The aim of the corporation should not be profit maximization but rather a performance of excellence."

UNETHICAL OR BANKRUPT?

Convincing though this consensus may be, it does not help a man confronted with the crucial dilemma proposed by Childs and Cater. To put that dilemma in its most extreme form: Is it always wrong for a man to do something unethical in order to avoid bankruptcy? Most moralists hold that a good end never justifies a bad means. But there are differences of opinion over what constitutes a bad means. To help man make reasonable decisions in a world that is often ethically gray, rather than black or white, moralists have developed principles like the double effect and have made distinctions between formal and material cooperation in evil.[16] In effect, they have reduced the number of situations in which a means is absolutely bad. Businessmen find these insights helpful, but feel that problems like that of the firm faced by bank-

---

is offered can be sold at a profit (not even necessarily a long-term profit), then it is legitimate. . . . The cultural, spiritual, social, moral, etc., consequences of his actions are none of his occupational concern." *Advertising Age* later published eleven letters from businessmen about Levitt's view. Ten were unfavorable.

[15] "The Trouble with Profit Maximization," *Harvard Business Review,* November–December 1960, pp. 126–134.

[16] For a discussion of double effect and cooperation in evil, see Herbert Johnston, *Business Ethics,* 2nd ed. rev. (New York: Pitman, 1961), pp. 86–93.

ruptcy due to unethical competition have been neglected. One
executive expressed his feelings in these words:

> Here's the way some businessmen feel about the unethical practices
> into which their company is forced by competitors: Better a company
> with a few unethical practices than no company. Besides, how is the
> industry ever going to get cleaned up if all the ethical men have to leave
> it, or are never permitted to enter it?

There are industries in which solvency requires performing an
occasional unethical action. Must every person desiring to enter or
remain in such an industry be told that to do so is wrong?

A Japanese businessman added another dimension to this consideration. In defense of one's life, most moralists permit physical
resistance, including the use of weapons if necessary, on condition
that the person has not initiated the attack and uses a defense that
is proportioned to the attack of the aggressor. Hence, in defending
against armed assault, it can be ethical to kill another human being.
Moralists add that if a man attempts to steal a person's lifetime
savings, the latter may defend his material possessions, even to the
death of the aggressor, if this is necessary.[17] Why is similar reasoning not applicable to business competition? Is unethical business
competition essentially different from armed robbery? Is the economic life of a company so much less important than physical life
or a family's lifetime savings that there should be a substantial
difference in the defenses available when corporate economic life
is threatened?

These businessmen have a point worthy of the moralists' attention. There can be excusing causes for cooperating in unethical
behavior (for example, coercion). It seems that there can also be
business situations in which a manager is justified in fighting fire
with fire. The Reverend Thomas Garrett, S.J., thinks that

> . . . there may be cases where extreme measures could be justified in
> order to protect clear rights. These cases would be rare, since they would
> occur only when a businessman had good reason to suspect that a com-
> petitor was planning to use illegal or unethical means against him. To
> put it another way, there would have to be a situation of almost un-

---

[17] *Theologia Moralis*, Alphonsus Liguori, 4 vols., Vatican, Rome, 1907,
number 383: ". . . licet defendere bona fortuna magni momenti cum oc-
cisione furis, si aliter . . . retineri non possint, probabilius," which I translate
loosely as: "It is the more probable theological opinion that a man is permitted to defend his possessions of great worth even to the extent of killing
a thief, if he cannot otherwise retain these possessions."

limited war rather than normal competition. This is to say that unjust and unethical attacks can so change the nature of competition that an honest businessman may have a proportionate reason for using extreme measures that would be unethical in ordinary, fair competition. It should be noted, however, that the ethics of self-defense or warfare demand that the attack be unjust and that all normal means of defense, such as the courts, should have been tried before extreme measures are taken.[18]

Clearly, the burden of proof must be on the businessman who thinks that he has an adequate reason for an action that would be unethical under ordinary conditions. The danger is that inefficient managers, and managers of companies that are marginal to an industry or are inadequately capitalized, will convince themselves that any kind of behavior is permitted to avoid bankruptcy. Good ethics is usually good business, but even when good ethics is bad business—in the sense that it is uneconomical or costly—the businessman ordinarily must follow the ethical path, though it be narrow. To be ethical must be more important than to be profitable. The challenge facing our businessmen is to prove to the world that the free enterprise system can produce an abundance of material goods for humans while nourishing and enhancing the human values of our Judaeo-Christian culture. The data from our survey, as well as the injustice and inequities present in our industrial society, indicate that the challenge is not being met with a vigor or imagination sufficient to achieve the desired result.

[18] *Business Ethics* (New York: Appleton-Century-Crofts, 1966), p. 98.

Conscience is man's inner guide. But men's consciences differ from one another. Why? Because men grow up in different cultures and environments, because their education is different. Although we know little about the acquisition of moral knowledge and attitudes, it is clear that they depend in large measure on the advice and example of the adults with whom a person spends his childhood. These include parents, teachers, and clergymen. The acquiring of moral knowledge continues throughout life, for example, through one's wife, boss, or peers. Wondering which persons have the most influence on the conduct of businessmen, we asked our interviewees: "Who, would you say, has been the most important single influence on your acting ethically in business?" When necessary for clarity, the interviewer added that the influences encountered throughout the person's entire life were to be considered. The answers are shown in Table 8.1, including secondary influences volunteered by some men. It is evident from these replies that the persons with the most beneficent influence on the decisions of these businessmen are those who dealt with them when they were young. This suggests that, for ethical business decisions, attitude may be more important than knowledge. By attitude I mean a conviction that it is important to act ethically and a desire to do so.

PARENTS MOST INFLUENTIAL

One or both parents were named as the main influence by the majority of respondents. In light of the phrasing, "most important

Table 8.1
Personal Influences on Ethical Actions (N = 100)

Influence	Number Ranking It First	Number Ranking It Second
Father	26	1
Both parents	18	7
Boss	11	5
Mother	9	1
Teacher(s)	8	6
Clergy	8	5
Wife	8	2
Business associate	2	4
Other	6	4
No answer	4	0

single influence," it is worth noting that many saw their father and mother as a single influence.

Father is the number-one influence, which is not surprising, since almost all the respondents were men. Also, in nine cases, the father had a superior-subordinate relationship in business with his son; this opportunity for double influence was present in the case of only one mother. Here are the statements of three men who named their fathers as the main influence on their acting ethically in business:

My father taught me how to handle men. I use his system: treat people honestly, don't hoodwink anyone.

Every Saturday night when I was a kid, my father used to get us kids together and teach us the Baltimore Catechism. After we had memorized the answers, he would tell us: "Don't ever do anything that would make your mother ashamed of you."

My father not only educated me when I was young, but he has regularly discussed with me the ethical implications of all his business problems.

Not every father succeeded in passing on his ideals to his son, as is evident from the comment of a 29-year-old: "My father is silly about ethics. He practices professional ethics even to his own detriment."

Mothers also play a prominent role in educating managers to the importance of ethical actions. Three men provided detailed examples of the way their mothers taught them the importance of honesty. In each case, the mother used a small incident to teach a lesson that proved to be unforgettable.

Some managers were unable to pinpoint one most important ethical influence on their lives because several influences were simultaneously operative in their youth, and reinforced each other. Parents, school teachers, clergymen, friends—all said the same thing about the importance and the content of ethics. These managers used broad statements to answer our question: "my entire background"; "my Christian heritage"; "a group of people and my environment." A Japanese manager put it this way: "Ethics is an accumulation; it comes from parents, teachers, friends, and others. It is as they say, 'Rome cannot be built in one night.'"

TEACHERS AND CLERGYMEN

One in every seven interviewees named one or more teachers as a leading influence on his ethical conduct in business. There were references to "early training and examples given at school"; "the headmaster at prep school"; "an instructor I had in college"; "aviation cadet training impressed me at an important time in my life."

Ranking roughly equal with teachers in the replies to our question about ethical influences were clergymen. Several managers preferred to speak not of a single clergyman, but of a complex of people and institutions whose basic orientation was religious. So an investment analyst stated: "The church was the main influence, in the sense that my parents, school, priests, and others all were insisting on the same ideas, and these ideas came from the teaching of the church." A purchasing agent named "church influences, supported by environment."

Two managers described the influence of religion on their business actions in the following terms:

My religion is most important. When I go to Confession, and I want to do that regularly, I must have a purpose of amendment; otherwise, the Confession is no good. So I can't keep on doing something that's unethical.

With respect to any aspect of my life, it would be fair to say that the principal influence has come from a combination of clergymen and philosophical writings. One man has spent a lot of time coaching me; he directs my reading and for a long time we met two days a week for two hours to discuss spiritual matters.

These two comments are meaningful because, in the remainder of the interviews, these managers gave evidence that their religious beliefs were operative in their industrial decisions.

The individual teacher and the individual clergyman are key figures in forming the conscience of the student or believer. But this research was not designed to learn much about the influence of these individuals. Rather, I investigated businessmen's reactions to educational institutions and churches. These will be treated at length in Chapters 17 and 18.

WHAT WIVES CONTRIBUTE

Eight per cent of our interviewees named their wives as the most important single influence on their acting ethically in business. Most of these men pointed out that there was good communication in their marriages: Husband and wife talked about what he did at work. This gave her an opportunity to be constructively critical about his business actions. Seldom did the husband praise his wife for her knowledge of his field, but he lauded her sensitivity to personnel problems, "her appreciation of human factors."

A director of research said: "If I ever did anything wrong and were caught, I would catch hell at home." The young president of a midwestern company, grateful that his wife placed ethical concerns before success, said he didn't know "how men who have wives who are always thinking and talking about money can stay in a tough, competitive business and take risks." "A couple of times," he continued, "I had a chance to make money by doing something unethical. We talked it over and she said, 'What's the problem? There's only one thing to do, whatever is right. We'll always manage somehow.' So I have never had to worry about her opinion of me if the company went bankrupt."

The same point is made by contrast by an interviewee who had to deal with a foreman who stole $3,200 from his company. Investigation revealed that the foreman's wife nagged him for more money so that she could take vacation trips which were beyond his regular income.

SAME STANDARDS AT HOME AND AT WORK?

Having described the influence of parents and wife on the businessman's ethical decisions, we turn to a comparison of his values at home with his values at work. The businessman is frequently criticized for having two sets of ethical standards; that he has one measuring stick for his actions on the job, and another for his actions off the job. The usual implication is that the businessman's standards of conduct at work are lower than they are at home. To probe the meaning of this popular criticism and to get the businessman's reaction to it, the respondents were asked: "What do you think of the common opinion that the typical businessman has two sets of ethical standards, one of which he applies to his business activities, the other he applies to his private life?" Only 30 per cent of our interviewees agreed with this opinion about "the typical businessman." Their thinking was pushed further by inquiring: "Thinking for a moment of the three most ethical businessmen you know, do you think that there is a difference between their private morality and their business morality?" Only one in three of the 30 per cent agreed that this difference exists.

Underlying the second question was a desire to secure information about the notion that the environment of American business is so permeated by unethical practices that even the best men cannot act honorably. Some critics view business as an irresistible seducer. From the answers given by the 100 men, I conclude that, though environment and generally accepted practices are frequently not conducive to ethical behavior, the manager with a well-defined personal code and good motivation can still act ethically.

Seven of every ten respondents said that the typical businessman does *not* have two sets of ethical standards. "The leopard doesn't change spots," one said. "An s.o.b. is an s.o.b." Another manager suggested, "In my experience, the fellow who cheats on his wife is also financially pretty shaky."

Among those who believed that the businessman has a double standard, two-thirds said that he is less ethical in business than in his private life. Several added that the gap between the two standards is closing through improvement of business ethics. A management consultant guessed that "ethics are about 50 per cent lower at the office." A young sales manager commented: "I know only one man who has not split himself. The others in my company are in the same boat as myself."

These managers do not approve of the double standard whose presence they acknowledge, but they think it understandable. As an Oregonian put it: "After all, if you don't *have* to be unethical, why be unethical?"

A big reason for an ethical differential between private life and business life is the dissimilarity between the purposes of the home and of the office. These purposes, according to a hotel executive, "are so different that the decisions a man must make in the two areas are almost impossible to compare." Decisions at the office are "objective," "rational," "impersonal." At home, "decisions are emotional," "personal." It is permissible to be inefficient at home, but not at the office. Not only members of the family, but also workers around the house, may be forgiven for inefficiency, according to the president of a merchandising organization: "We have a fellow who cleans up around the house, a handy man. He is not too dependable, but I keep him. If he was in my plant, I would fire him right away." One man summed up the difference between home and office in terms of attitudes toward money. "I'm here at a desk to make all the damn money I can; work is a necessity. I spend money at home; it's like a vacation." An import manager suggested that "love for his family may lead a man to be unethical in business."

The comparison between home and office elicited other useful observations:

A man can give individual attention to his family. But there are so many people involved in business—stockholders, workers, suppliers, competitors—that it would be impossible to give individual attention.

Success in private life means success as a community member and trying to give happiness to others. Success in business means acceptance based on performance, based on who you know.

In a company there is usually a buffer of some kind between the man who makes the decision and the people affected. Also, you don't have to live with the people to whom you are unethical in business.

The presence of competition in the business world was cited by ten men as the major reason for lower standards at work than at home. As one manager admitted, "Within the company, advancement is necessary; a man doesn't worry about advancement in his own family—he starts out in the top seat."

An unexpected answer was provided by nine of the interviewees. They opined that there is a double standard, that the typical businessman is *more* ethical in business than at home. One company officer referred to "a very passive accountant who is a real 'hell-raiser' at home." Another manager reported employees with low personal standards who justified themselves by saying that their personal life is their own business. The main reason given for men being more ethical at work is simply, "They can get away with more in their private lives." One junior executive admitted, "It is easier to ride a white horse on the corporation's money than on your own; it's easier to be good when you have the resources of a large corporation supporting you."

Note that 68 per cent of our respondents stated that they have the same ethical standards at home and at work, and that 61 per cent ranked their parents or wives as the most important influence on their ethical business decisions. It seems reasonable to conclude that businessmen who operate on a single standard of ethics bring that standard from home to work, and not vice versa.

In many social science surveys, one uncovers differences in outlook among men of different age groups. Without descending to
a multitude of statistical details, let us consider three age-related
differences which emerged from Projects One and Two.

From replies to queries about padding an expense account
(question 4 in Appendix A), conflict of interest (question 8a), call
girls (question 8b), and exchange of price information (question
8c), it is evident that older businessmen are more inclined than
the young to call some practices "always unethical." The fact that
the younger men are apt to be more situational or relativistic in
their approach to ethics is not necessarily blameworthy. For example, in regard to the questions about conflict of interest and exchange of price information, I think that "always unethical" is an
unrealistic guide for business conduct (my answers to these questions are in Appendix D). There are surely some exchanges of price
information which are innocent, and some possible conflicts of interest which do not constitute an occasion of misconduct. In other
words, exchanging prices and owning stock are ethically neutral
acts in themselves; whether they are right or wrong will depend on
the circumstances in each case.

A second difference between the replies of the young and the
old is that the young tend to be more pessimistic—they would say,
realistic. This is seen in several ways:

1. More of the young admit the existence in their industry of
unethical practices, and agree that "the American business executive tends to ignore the great ethical laws as they apply immediately
to his work."

2. Fewer of the young feel that a written code would raise the ethical level of their industry, or that a code would be easy to enforce.

3. A larger percentage of the young agree with the idea, "Let the buyer beware."

4. A smaller percentage of the young think that executives are unethical if they ignore the interests of the employee and consumer in favor of the shareholder.

Another way of interpreting this difference between the younger men and the older is that the older identify more closely with "the businessman," and so are somewhat defensive in their answers.

BETTER WHEN AGED

The third, and most significant, difference among age groups showed up in both Projects One and Two: The older the businessman, the more ethical is his attitude, as indicated by his answers. This conclusion is documented in Table 9.1, where the replies to six Project Two questions are grouped by age. To come to this conclusion, I had to evaluate the respondents' answers to these questions as being more ethical or less ethical; my reasoning is con-

Table 9.1
Age Makes a Difference (N = 1,512 for 1e and 8b, 807 for the rest)

	Under 40	40–49	50 and Over
1e. Agree that "For corporation executives to act in the interest of shareholders alone . . . is unethical."	80%	83%	85%
2. Would use confidential corporate information for private financial gain.	48	41	39
3. Would probably hire personnel from a competitor to acquire scientific discovery.	56	48	43
4. Regard padding of expense account by $500 as unacceptable regardless of the circumstances.	81	87	88
5. See no ethical dimension in status-symbol advertising.	43	33	27
8b. Think that providing a call girl for a customer is always unethical.	84	88	93

tained in Appendix D. The data in Table 9.1 are convincing because the differences in replies to all six questions are in the same direction. Items 2, 3, and 4 had earlier been investigated in Project One. After dividing the 100 businessmen in that survey into two groups with the fortieth birthday the dividing line, it was found that the answers of the older group were more ethical for these three items, just as they were in Project Two.

AFFLUENCE NOT THE REASON

Why this age-related difference? Perhaps the young were more honest in their replies, though there was no evidence in their essay-type answers for thinking so. If the older men really are more ethical, perhaps this is because they can afford to be more ethical. This suggests that the answers in Project Two are more closely related to size of income than to age, an inference which statistical investigation did not sustain. In fact, the answers of men over fifty whose income is relatively low were more ethical than the replies of men of similar age with a higher income. Of course, a manager's annual income ordinarily increases with his age, so the statistical variances are small.

In order to investigate further this age-related difference, Project Three interviewees were asked:

In a survey in which 1,600 businessmen were asked what they would do in certain situations, or what they thought about certain statements, the responses of the older executives were more ethical than those of the younger executives. Does this surprise you? Why?

Three of every four were not surprised. It is noteworthy that the interviewee's age made no difference in his opinion; young managers were as convinced of the accuracy of our finding as were older managers.

The reason most often given in support of the opinion that older businessmen are more ethical was that "experience teaches." Apparently experience teaches a variety of things, depending on the learner; here is what it taught three managers:

Experience counts; when you are older, you have proved to yourself that good ethics works out for the best. As you get older, your values shift from the material, partly because you have material goods, partly because you appreciate the importance of spiritual values more.

In our industrial society, you get more secure as you get older. You lay your ambitions behind you, and pick up wisdom along the way. The young must start with a proper value system, but ought to improve with age.

Older men have learned that good ethics is good business in the long run; some of them have learned the hard way, through a suit brought by the government.

An engineering manager spoke of the resentment of the younger executives in his company after the electrical manufacturing industry scandal:

The young seem to feel that they were misled; following the example of their elders, they had put aside their own ethical convictions and adopted industry practices, apparently thinking that if such reputable men as they assumed their bosses to be would do things, the things were all right. Having been disabused of this notion by the indictments, the young men are faced with a much tougher selling job than they ever had before. These young fellows seem to resent having been hired into an industry under one set of conditions, and then—after committing themselves for some years—finding out that a new and more difficult set of conditions has been put into effect. I knew one young fellow who often carried around a ledger with all the prices of all the bids on certain equipment in the industry; he knew just when we were due to get a certain kind of contract. He was told one day, "All that sort of thing is out from now on."

Cynicism about business was present in several replies, including this one from an experienced marketing executive: "Ethics comes with age. Men get tired of fighting. You get a younger man to do the dirty work. Of course, you get more clever as you get older. People will always do the same things; the trouble is that some are more clumsy than others." A young consultant felt that "men try to be more ethical as they get older in order to salve their consciences," and pointed to the philanthropy of the robber barons.

IS IT YOUTH, OR THESE YOUTHS?

About a dozen interviewees felt a need to reconcile two apparently contradictory opinions they held. On the one hand, they felt that the trend of business ethics was upward; on the other hand, they thought that the young were less ethical than their elders. To reconcile these views, one man noted that the decisions which significantly influence business conduct are made by those who

hold the reins of top management, usually older men; consequently, the lack of ethics on the part of the young is not as harmful
as it might be. Other managers who attempted to reconcile an upward curve in business morality with a relative lack of ethics among
young businessmen, distinguished the *period* of youth from the
persons passing through the period. Youth is to blame, not these
youths; the present ranks of older managers were similarly lacking
in high standards twenty years ago. Here is a typical expression of
this view: "The young are tempted more, have many more pressures, especially economic; and they are less sure of themselves, and
so will do some unethical things to prove that they have the stuff
necessary to succeed in business."

Several interviewees felt that there is an inverse relation between
ambition and ethics. Thus a European manager stated: "All men
want to achieve. The young are very ambitious to achieve, while
the old are less so." The president of a small western company
agreed: "The older man has settled for some definite, not-so-
ambitious goals, and ambition is related to ethics. Maybe ethical
behavior is proportional to a lack of ambition." A slogan I heard
more than once, which acknowledges the ambition of the young
as well as the higher ethics of the old, was: *Get on, get honest, get
honors!*

A marketing executive paraphrased this as, "Make money first,
then become respectable." Money pressures are at the root of some
transgressions by the young, although—as Table 6.1 revealed—not
as important as some other pressures. Perhaps it will be helpful to
picture in detail the difference in financial pressure on men of
different ages. Consider two men having similar abilities and education, working in the same company. Each has a wife and three
children. Mr. Older is fifty, a department manager whose annual
salary is $15,000. Mr. Younger is twenty-eight, a junior executive
earning $7,500. The difference in income is related partly to age
and to the experience accompanying it. Accentuating the income
gap is the difference in expenditures faced by the two men. Mr.
Younger has a large mortgage on a home, owes money on his furni-
ture and car, and is wondering how he will finance the education of
his children. He has never owned a home before, nor successfully
raised a family. Contrast his outlook with that of Mr. Older, who
owns a home and a car, and has almost completed financing his
children's education. Now place the two men in identical situations, with money the bait for performing an unethical business

transaction. Other things being equal, is not Mr. Younger more likely to succumb to the temptation?

"O TEMPORA, O MORES"

One final reason for the ethical superiority of the older business-man was endorsed by one in ten interviewees: The young are children of their time, and their time is less ethical than times past.

I'm not happy about the downward trend of the ethics of our cul-ture in the past 15 or 20 years. The old virtues are less potent than they used to be. There is too much dependency on government; there is too much emphasis on group philosophy instead of on the importance of the individual. I feel that things like these undermine our moral stamina. We are a prosperous nation today, and are softer than we were.

I went to a military academy and we had an honor system which we all followed. We tossed out a cheating football team by living up to what was demanded of our honor system. Many people thought that we were wrong in throwing out the football players, and even protested that "everyone does this." But there were no excuses under our system. The old breed of managers was more stable and careful. The new breed is not as stable and do not come from the same solid backgrounds. They have made their money and power too quickly and easily.

A board chairman who is a world traveler revealed a similar concern about modern youth:

I'm afraid that the United States, in favoring our economy, has been pushing into the background some of our social concepts. One of the things that disturbs me is the way that the position of the family in our society is giving way. The family doesn't stick together any more. The corporation sends families here and there so that the corporation will benefit. But who watches to see if the family benefits?

In primitive societies, the elders are respected as the wisest. Here everything traditional is thrown out; the younger even complain that the older people are holding them back. They no longer look to the family for approval of their actions; they look to their peers.

Eloquent indeed were the minority of interviewees who regis-tered surprise that the answers of the young were less ethical. The reason most frequently given for their surprise was personal experi-ence: "The young businessmen I know are more ethical than their elders." Or, as an experienced personnel officer who recruits col-legians put it:

I'm really impressed by young men today. Many are men who went through World War II; they are better educated, think more seriously and deeply than their predecessors. Why, in the thirties there was all sorts of playing around by businessmen; the young men of today don't do that. I deal with thousands of these young men; they are better than their predecessors. Perhaps the trend of the mass of young people is down, and I am working with a privileged group.

A corporation secretary said:

I feel sure that the mentality of young businessmen today is more responsible than that of their forerunners. The entire community depends on my father's factory, and our family has a responsibility to the workers and to the whole community. In the old days, all the bosses looked to was the profit and loss statement.

This chapter has raised the question: Is business behavior more ethical than it used to be? The writer answers it affirmatively. Although the improvement of business behavior over a period of time is impossible to document empirically, history testifies to advances that are striking: Wages, hours, working conditions, and employment opportunities have improved dramatically.[1] So has the quality of manufactured products, food and drugs. Without attempting to divide the credit for these advances—legislation, government regulation, and labor unions have played prominent roles —it is beyond dispute that business behavior has become more ethical in this country in this century. The motivation for the improvements undoubtedly has been mixed, but the advances have been remarkable.

The key question raised in this chapter is: Do businessmen typically become more ethical as they grow older? Our respondents answer affirmatively, saying that success in business, with its accompanying sense of financial security, satisfies the personal ambitions of most men and reduces the likelihood that they will do wrong. In addition, experience demonstrates the heavy psychological, and sometimes legal, costs of unethical behavior, and also teaches that good ethics is usually profitable. At the present time, however, the desire of young businessmen to act ethically may be lessened by the myth that to be successful, the businessman must be unethical, and by an overemphasis on the acquisition of material goods to the detriment of higher values.

[1] For a sketch of working conditions, wages, and hours at the turn of this century, see Frederick Lewis Allen, *The Big Change* (New York: Bantam Books, 1961), Chap. 3.

Earlier we noted the opinion of questionnaire respondents that the boss is a major influence on employees' behavior. By *boss*, respondents meant not only the chief executive of a company but any one who directs workers. Table 8.1 revealed that some men feel that the influence of the boss on their business behavior is more important than the influence of their wife, clergyman, or former teachers. Interviewees added that a man's *first* boss is more influential than his successors. A Dutch executive spoke of his "first boss with whom I worked for nine years. Some thought he was cranky and hard to get along with, but I felt he was always fair and just." A New York consultant named "two business leaders whom I met early in my career; the way to learn is to watch a man handle ethical problems."

Table 6.1 showed that the boss is often blamed for subordinates' unethical behavior, but gets little credit from them for their praiseworthy actions. One author, who believes that it is difficult to be promoted in business without using unfair tactics, and that undermining one's associates is the usual practice, concludes: "The blame rests squarely on the highest levels of company management."[1]

PRESSURE

When Project Two respondents told about their interactions with superiors, they frequently used the word *pressure*. They meant

[1] Harrison R. Johnson, "How To Get The Boss's Job," *Modern Office Procedures*, May 1961, p. 18.

that some demands of superiors distressed and troubled them. Since the interviewer heard only one side of the story, of course, it is not clear that their resentment was always well-founded. The pressures described were of two kinds: those resulting from performance expectations which the employee felt were unreasonable or too demanding of his time and energy, and those which the employee regarded as pressure to get results, regardless of the means used.

A young supervisor exemplified the first kind when he complained of "pressure to get too much work out of too few people in too short a time." Such a process can wear a man down physically and psychologically, leaving him overtired at the end of every day and old at forty-five.

There were also demands to reach an economic goal, which were implicitly an encouragement to do wrong:

The sales manager of a very large corporation castigated "the constant everyday pressure from top management to obtain profitable business; unwritten, but well understood, is the phrase 'at any cost.' To do this requires every conceivable dirty trick."

An assistant manager was worried because "my management has, in effect, required that I go along with certain antitrust violations involving restraint of trade."

Another executive said: "As controller, I prepared a profit and loss statement which showed a loss. An executive vice president tried to force me to falsify the statement to show a profit in order to present it to a bank for a line of credit. I refused, and was fired on the spot."

A young engineer testified that he was "asked to present 'edited' results of a reliability study; I refused to defraud the customer, so they had others do it."

Of course, the task of management is to get results. To do so, every manager must motivate subordinates. At times, in order to obtain excellent work, some pressure may be necessary. As one manager put it, a good boss ought to have the ability to "stretch" his men. But it is important that he not "overstretch" them, physically, psychologically, or ethically.

How can a manager guard against pushing his men too far? When asked this question, an executive replied, "By knowing them. By taking the time to understand them. By reflecting on the kinds and amount of pressure he is applying to them." To gain such knowledge requires excellent two-way communication between the superior and his subordinates. Such clear communication is especially important in large, decentralized corporations.

Without thorough knowledge of what is going on, a superior can unwittingly make impossible demands, for example, insisting on a certain share of the market, or setting an impossible sales or profit goal for the period. Such a superior is as unjust as a father who insists that his son, whose I.Q. is 100, get a straight-A report card.

Impossible demands, say our respondents, especially if accompanied by an implied "produce or get out" attitude, can quickly result in unethical behavior. The lonely subordinate, faced with demands like these, occasionally dreams about a union for middle management, complete with seniority and grievance procedures.

A common defense by top management is that it is only fair that pressure be kept on subordinates since stockholders and competitors keep the pressure on top management all the time. This may be true, but few executives in our survey mentioned stockholder pressures. It is doubtful that widely disparate and anonymous stockholders exercise pressure on top management comparable to the pressure that executives bring to bear on their subordinates.

Many managers told us about an unethical request or suggestion made by a boss. Most of these examples were of a type identified by moralists as cooperating with another person's fault. It is a thorny problem, but some guidance can be obtained for solving it from a traditional distinction: *formal* cooperation (taking part in and consenting to the unethical deed of another) is always wrong; *material* cooperation (unwillingly taking part in an unethical deed) is often wrong, but permissible in certain circumstances.[2] Some interviewees quit jobs rather than cooperate formally with the misdeeds of their superiors:

I sold new and used cars for Mr. M and did what he wanted me to do: lie, cheat, etc. I couldn't take it, and quit after six months. M doesn't sully his hands; his salesmen have to carry out his dirty policies.

I quit a construction firm. They told me to build a certain building for which they had contracted and to bring in a profit, which was impossible. They wanted me to use defective material and to reduce the number of coats of paint on which there had been agreement. A couple of old women would be victimized.

[2] For a thorough treatment of this complex topic, see Henry Wirtenberger, S.J., *Morality and Business* (Chicago: Loyola University Press, 1962), pp. 109–119.

As a student I worked for three months for a small firm selling securities. It was a profitable business but I left when I discovered that they were making false claims for the securities they sold.

Nineteen per cent of our interviewees said that they had quit a company for ethical reasons. In addition to those subjected to unreasonable pressure for performance, or asked to cooperate with wrongdoing, several managers left companies because of personal mistreatment by superiors:

I left the mail-advertising company because the boss wouldn't show me the company records of income. I had an agreement entitling me to five per cent of sales. He would never let me see the record on repeat orders. I'm still not sure that he was cheating me, but . . .

I had an agreement with my associates to merchandise their product to a segment of the trade. After a few months they told me not to contact a large user in Chicago; they said they did not want to do business with this firm. I found out that they kept the contact and supplied the firm, but did not pay me the commission.

As our examples show, when an employee dislikes the standards or behavior of his boss, one recourse is to find another job.[3] When the roles are reversed, the boss has a number of ways of punishing the misbehavior of his subordinate, including dismissal. In situations involving reward or punishment, ethics and authority are often intertwined. Reward and punishment are at the end of a one-way street that runs from superior to subordinate. This arrangement assumes ethical superiority on the part of the boss, and underlines his importance in creating the ethical climate for a department, division, or plant. One of our questions, mentioned in Chapter 4, provided the interviewees a choice of speaking about either rewarding or punishing:

Please try to recall an occasion when you rewarded some person in your company for ethical behavior (for instance, by promotion, pay raise, or congratulations), or when you penalized someone for unethical behavior (for instance, by dismissal, demotion, or reprimand). Would you mind describing the occasion?

[3] Our evidence casts doubt on the opinion of Elizabeth and Francis Jennings: "Here is a curious article in the industrial code of behavior. . . . It is unrealistic or stupid to resign because of involvement with ethical principles" ("Making Human Relations Work," *Harvard Business Review*, January–February 1951, p. 35).

THEY DON'T REWARD ETHICAL BEHAVIOR

Of the men who described such an occasion, 82 per cent recalled a punishment. Why did so many more recall penalties than rewards? Probably part of the explanation lies in the general expectation of ethical behavior. Eleven men made this point before describing a time when they penalized a subordinate. As one of them said, "If I praised my men for doing things ethically, that would imply that I thought it unusual." Another pointed out, "You don't compensate an individual for being ethical. Rather, a man accumulates a reputation by a series of ethical actions, and eventually his promotion depends on it."

What about this attitude that ethical behavior ought not be rewarded? A man is paid a salary for doing a job; it is assumed that he will do it ethically. When he does what he is paid to do, why praise him? The reasoning is logical, but is it psychologically sound? Few men work solely to make money, as has been shown in recent motivational studies.[4] Human beings regularly need satisfaction and assurance that their work is appreciated. Dostoevsky wrote, "If it were desired to reduce a man to nothing . . . it would be necessary only to give his work a character of uselessness."[5] Employers might ask themselves how long it has been since they praised employees whose trustworthiness they value. A salary increase offers an appropriate occasion for mentioning that ethical behavior is partly responsible for the raise—if, in truth, it is.[6]

THE MAN AT THE TOP

Members of top management in a corporation are in positions of power. They make the crucial decisions. In the public mind, they stand for the corporation. When employees at lower levels are irked at a decision, they blame "the administration." This phrase always includes the chief executive officer of a company. Our research in-

[4] For example, Alexander Heron, *Why Men Work* (Stanford, Calif.: Stanford University Press, 1949).

[5] Fyodor Dostoevsky, *The House of the Dead*, quoted in "Human Relations," *Time*, April 14, 1952, p. 96.

[6] The 18 per cent of our interviewees who rewarded employees for ethical behavior typically used words of praise, though there was one promotion and three cash awards (all for returning goods to customers who had lost them).

cluded one question aimed at gathering opinions about the extent of the influence of the chief executive:

> Let's talk for a moment about the person who makes the most important decisions in your company. Obviously, his words and actions imply certain views about the place of ethics in business, and about what constitutes unethical behavior. Would you say his views have had a significant influence on yours?

A minority felt that the top decision-maker was "too far removed" or "impersonal" to have influence on them, although in some cases, he "reaffirmed my ideas." Most respondents, however, felt that the chief executive had a significant influence on their outlook, and he got credit for enforcing company policies: "We have a strong influence from the top; policies don't mean a damn thing unless they come from the beliefs of a chief exec." There were many variations of Ralph Waldo Emerson's statement, "An institution is the lengthened shadow of one man."[7] A transportation executive said: "The president's conduct and the manner in which he does things are very good. I try to copy him." Other managers added:

> It's especially important that the ethics of the top man or top men be good. I was very impressed by one man who gave unique good examples. He limited his own perquisites. He was a man of principle, and his principles permeated the company. He strictly defined the lines of authority among management. Also he won the goodwill of the community.

> My boss has been of tremendous importance in showing me the value of ethics in business. Really, I think that this attribute of high ethical standards accounts for his success as top executive. He lacks some other very important qualities which a top man in the retail business usually has.

Subordinates are not alone in thinking that they mirror the superior's ethics. Superiors agree, as is shown by the following comments of presidents:

> An unethical action depresses everyone connected with it. The employees lose respect for the boss who acts unethically; I have lots of employees who would leave our company if I started to act unethically. This is related, of course, to the fact that in our industry at the present time it is no trouble to get another job.

[7] *Emerson's Complete Writings* (New York: William Wise, 1926), Vol. 2, p. 61.

This may sound egotistic, but I'll say it anyway: My partner and I set a pretty good example, both in hiring and day-to-day behavior. The top people in any organization set the tone for the behavior of the other people.

One chief executive unwittingly motivated good behavior by his bad example:

I saw the damage he had done to his company and to his own reputation by unethical behavior. After all, many of the employees, the sources of supply, and customers whom the president had mistreated were still around when I became plant manager. They told me of some of his ridiculous promises and sharp practices, and I know that I would never act that way or make those mistakes.

The long shadow of the ethical standards and actions of the boss falls across all his subordinates. The longest shadow in a company is that cast by the chief executive. As Charles G. Mortimer recently said:

A corporation's ethical attitude is the result of its *chief executive's beliefs*. It reflects the decisions he makes about the kind of company he wants to have. Equally important, the corporation's ethical attitude is a measurement of how effectively the chief executive has communicated his desire for unimpeachable dealings—both by the company and the individuals managing it. It is not enough merely to enunciate a set of high principles. The chief executive must follow through—consistently and forcefully—by establishing procedures which say loud and clear that he will brook no shenanigans, whether in the area of price fixing, conflict of interest, "insiders' information," or whatever.[8]

One result of subordinates' tendency to follow superiors' ethical standards is unhealthy. It is the practice of blaming unethical decisions on the boss or, more frequently, on "the administration." Weak subordinates justify themselves by saying, "I just carry out orders." The anonymity of a large corporation prompts some employees to carry out orders which they would be ashamed to give or approve as private persons. It is part of the boss's responsibility when making policy or decisions to bear in mind the likelihood that he will not hear criticism, especially about ethical matters, from his subordinates. Most men are sufficiently insecure in their jobs to want positive signs that the boss welcomes criticism before they will offer it.

In summary, our data reveal the tendency of men to accept

[8] "The Purposeful Pursuit of Profits and Growth in Business," quoted in *Personnel*, November–December 1965, p. 2.

the values of superiors. This tendency, stemming from a respect for the talents of the superior as well as for his authoritative position, should be acknowledged by every administrator as a part of his power for good or evil. The larger the number of his subordinates, the greater is his power in this matter. And it is natural for the community to expect responsible action from someone with much power, and to blame him when anything goes wrong.

Judge J. Cullen Ganey, in his statement on the electrical industry antitrust cases, despite the absence of proof, castigated the top management of the involved companies. He said, "The real blame is to be laid at the doorstep of the corporate defendants and those who guide and direct their policy."[9] And the public was reluctant to accept the idea that the electrical equipment companies' chief executives were blameless; even if these men were unaware of the collusion, their position seemed like that of parents of a 21-year-old who has done serious wrong. Though the parents are liked and respected, they must endure the common opinion that they should somehow have prevented the son's mistake. Our data indicate that this public reaction is based on a fact of business behavior: Men do look to their superiors for guidance. What the public may not adequately comprehend is the difficulty, even for a chief executive, of controlling the administrative complexities of a large, decentralized, multinational corporation. However, if this difficulty is advanced as an excuse for chief executives' failure to be aware of corporate misconduct, it is appropriate to ask: When it is practically impossible for the man who has ultimate responsibility for an important decision to know its principal details, is this a sign that the company is too large?

In conclusion, our respondents agreed that managers, through their policies and decisions, have tremendous opportunities and responsibilities for influencing the actions of subordinates. Obviously, then, it is important for the welfare of the business community that every manager possess a well-defined code of behavior and a way of approaching the ethical aspects of business problems. Without these, a manager can hardly be worthy of the imitation he so often receives. With them, he will attract young men with high standards. Like does attract like. And high-principled young men embarking on business careers will follow the advice of several of our respondents: If you want to be ethical in business, find a good boss.

9 *New York Times*, February 7, 1961, p. 26.

11 Managerial Level and Occupation

Many concepts and terms used in business have been adopted from older organizations like the military. Such seems to be the case with *staff* and *line*. In the military, a line officer is in the line of command; a staff officer is not. Typically the staff officer advises, informs, and helps line officers. In industry, a similar relationship exists between line and staff. Line management has full and final responsibility for directing a firm to its goals; staff managers assist. Staff men are specialists; for example, in law, purchasing, or personnel. Line men are generalists. As drawn here, the distinction seems sharp. In reality, it rarely is.

As part of Project One, in order to find out whether men in staff positions have different views about business ethics than do men in line positions, replies were scrutinized according to the line-or-staff variable. None of this analysis was productive of differences. It had been conjectured that staff managers, usually being away from the center of productive action, would hold opinions on action-oriented questions somewhat different from the views of line managers. Not so. Replies were so consistently similar that the line-or-staff variable was dropped after Project One.

Why the similarity? Perhaps because many men now in staff posts were earlier in line positions, and vice versa; consequently, their views are almost identical. Or, perhaps the similarity indicates that the significant differences between line and staff are related to the use of authority, a topic on which the questions did not focus.

MANAGERIAL LEVEL

Decision-makers in business are usually divided into three managerial levels: top, middle, and lower. Wondering whether the level of management at which a man works strongly influences his opinions about ethics, I examined the replies of Project Two respondents to nine questions.[1] Analysis revealed that the answers and opinions of top management were not significantly different from those of middle and lower management.

Why the lack of correlation between managerial level and ethical responses, despite the correlation between age and ethical responses which were described in Chapter 9? Because, in our sample, the relationship between age and managerial level was not as close as it usually is in business; in fact, the coefficient of correlation was but .19. Apparently it included many young men who received promotions relatively rapidly.

As a man successfully ascends the corporate ladder, expectations of his ability to handle ethical dilemmas rise. His co-workers expect middle managers to be more knowledgeable and capable of solving conflicts of interest and similar problems than are junior executives. There are great expectations, especially on the part of the community, of top management's ability in this respect. Consequently, it is disappointing that the higher levels of management seem to possess ethical views no different than their subordinates'. Perhaps executive development programs should devote time to remedying this situation. I will say more about the education of managers in Chapter 17.

While opinions about ethics may not vary much from one managerial level to another, the problems themselves do. For example, a unique feature of the chief executive's post is that his decisions, at least the more complex ones, are not regularly reviewed by others. This means that he may occasionally be tempted to benefit personally by his corporate decisions. This can mean a temptation like the one described by the owner-manager of a food chain: "We frequently have salesmen come in who try to 'buy' our business. If I accepted the money, I would benefit directly; I

---

[1] Job titles and positions included in each of these levels can be found in Table 1.2; they follow guidelines used by the editors of the *Harvard Business Review*. The questions are the ones used in Chapter 9; more information about them can be found in Appendix D.

could put the $100 right into my pocket; it would never get into the company's books or into an income tax statement."

Because of the secrecy with which a president's decisions are sometimes cloaked, he can be involved in conflicts of interest like those described by a young executive:

A president's actions are examined by no one; they say that the board examines them, but they can't really know the details. There is no full disclosure of the relevant facts unless the president wants to reveal them. I've often wondered, especially in mergers, how much presidential self-interest is involved. Even the vice-presidents don't get to know much about mergers. The president usually does all right in the new company, and you wonder how much he gains in stock and other benefits because he agrees to the merger.

STOCKHOLDERS SUFFER

Several interviewees made the point that presidents are in a spot to be unethical: "They can get contract kickbacks with nobody in the company being the wiser. The president of one of the companies I worked for had a barn built for him by company suppliers, and also had cement walks put in on the farm."

When the president owns a large block of company stock, the rights of the minority stockholders can be violated. This may have been the case when a chief executive acquired real estate from his company appraised at a half-million dollars, for which he paid the price listed on the company's books, less than half that amount.

The president of a small company, admitting the possibility of fraud by men like himself, suggested that top management members have their decisions recorded and available for examination. "Secrecy promotes unethical behavior. It would be helpful if top managements' decisions were made public—not right away, because that would benefit competitors; but at a later date."

MIDDLE MANAGEMENT

Top management has some unique ethical problems and temptations, as well as a few built-in pressures for ethical behavior. The same is true of middle managers, who translate general plans and policies into workable programs, who interpret top management to their subordinates, and who communicate employee attitudes and needs to top management.[2] A Wayne State University study of 84 middle managers revealed that the three "most important moral problems they encounter in their jobs" are:

1. Complying with superior's requirements when they conflict with your code of ethics
2. Job demands infringing upon home obligations
3. Methods employed in competition for advancement.[3]

The same study also showed that the middle manager's most important moral problems relate to his superiors. A handful of middle managers told me of opposing unethical proposals by their bosses. When this handful—none of whom felt the disagreement serious enough to prompt them to leave the company—is added to the 19 per cent who left a company because of an ethical disagreement (see Chapter 10), it is evident that the self-serving schemes of some executives are vigorously opposed. Three interviewees, who would themselves have benefited, told how they had challenged presidential plans aimed at providing management with increased shares of profits. They believed that stockholders or nonmanagement personnel would be deprived of a just share in the profits. For instance, a chief engineer said: "We are now having a problem dealing with employee relations. We pass out a liberal bonus every year but it is only split among the supervisory group. I am pushing against top management to split this money among all the workers."

A purchasing executive related how his action reduced the under-the-table income of the company president:

The president, for reasons that were not clear to me, had a policy that all purchases were to be made through a middleman. The middleman got ten per cent for his services. Well, after I had thought the whole thing through, I went to the president and suggested that we cut out the middleman. I could tell from his reactions that he was irked, but I pushed my arguments and he couldn't get away from the logic of the presentations. So we got rid of the middleman, but I was a *persona non grata* around there from then on.

[2] See, for example, Thomas F. McMahon, C.S.V., "Moral Problems of Middle Management," *Proceedings of the Catholic Theological Society of America*, Vol. 20, 1965; he analyzed my data with middle management in mind and verified the similarity of their replies to those of other respondents.

[3] "Middle Managers' Views on Their Most Significant Professional Moral Problems," Program Extra No. 603, National Conference of Christian Employers and Managers, 1006 S. Michigan Avenue, Chicago, 1966, p. 26.

It wasn't until I was with another company that I got the complete story, namely, that the president had been getting a good chunk of the middleman's commission, and that I had eliminated this lucrative source of income—maybe worth $25,000 a year to the president.

Another executive told of opposing the chairman of the board:

A competitor had planted a man in one of our plants for a full year before the competitor moved into that city. We found out about it when the man walked out, taking with him a lot of information about customers in the area, and also taking three of our personnel; the man was put in charge of the new plant of our competitor in that city. I have never seen our chairman so angry; he wanted to fight fire with fire. I got together with a couple of vice-presidents and we decided on a tough but honest way of competing with that company. We had openings for salesmen, and could probably take some of the competitors' top men away from them.

When we got into the meeting which the boss called, he outlined his plan: we would send one of our execs who was unknown to the competitor, a young fellow who would pose as representative of a company which bought the competitor's products. That way we would get all kinds of information about the competitor from their employees. Not one person in the meeting said nay to the boss's idea, though some of them had said before the meeting that they would probably oppose unethical activities. I spoke up and said that we ought not stoop to the level of unethical competitors by getting information through a lie. With no support, my dissent failed, and the company went through with the boss's idea.

A few days later, he was in my office and remarked that he wasn't getting a great deal of support from me. I knew he meant my comment at the meeting. I told him that it's one thing when a decision has been made, and it's another thing when a matter is still in the discussion stage. I won't oppose a decision that has been made, but if I can't speak up my opposition before a decision has been made, then I don't belong in the company any longer. He was silent for a while . . . I wondered whether I had lost my job . . . and then he walked out.

While this executive's rule of thumb not to oppose an unethical decision after it has been made is debatable, his action in the situation described was obviously praiseworthy.

The extent of a personal obligation to oppose the misuse of power or authority by superiors has been the subject of countless playwrights and novelists, as in *The Caine Mutiny*. It can require heroic courage for a manager to be the first, and perhaps the only, person to question the morality of a course of action handed down by top management. Even when a number of middle managers band together to oppose a boss, they may be risking their jobs. One interviewee told me how several men blocked a chief executive's attempt to make himself a dishonest million dollars. Over the next five years, the thwarted executive eased these men out of the company.

Intracompany differences of opinion about ethics were mentioned by numerous interviewees. In most of these cases the manager did not leave the company, probably because the disagreement was not about principles but about applications of principle. Several men who were asked to act against their own conscience resigned. However, some who did not have to participate or cooperate in their company's unethical actions did not take the usually costly step of quitting.

COMPETING FOR ADVANCEMENT

The organization chart of a firm always resembles a pyramid; there are more persons at the lower levels than at the middle, and more at the middle than at the top. Inevitably there is intracompany competition, and just as inevitably many men do not advance. In the competition for the boss's job, unethical behavior is apparently common. A farcical presentation of this pattern can be seen in the Broadway success, *How to Succeed in Business Without Really Trying*. In this play, the hero advances rapidly from window-washer to chairman of the board by discrediting and eliminating incumbents as well as competitors for promotion. He skillfully steals ideas, verbally knifes an absent coworker, withholds important information, and tells big lies. That these practices are not limited to the stage was evidenced by a survey reported by Harrison R. Johnson, editor of *Modern Office Procedures*. He tells the reader: "You probably hold down your present position because you jerked the rug out from under someone in the past."[4] When he asked more than 100 businessmen, "Is it possible for a man to move up through the ranks of management solely by honest, decent measures?", the majority answered, "No."

Although our interviewees thought that dishonesty and unfairness while competing for advancement are less prevalent than do the men quizzed by *Modern Office Procedures*, they acknowledged

[4] "How to Get the Boss's Job," *Modern Office Procedures*, May 1961, p. 15.

that such competition is the occasion of unethical conduct. For example:

> I think that I've seen enough men go to the top in business, so that now when I see a man on top, I look around to see the crushed and bruised bodies he's stepped on in order to get there.

> I resent repeatedly having to act contrary to my sense of justice in order to please. In upper middle management, apparently, one's own ethical will must be subordinated to that of interests at the top—not only to advance, but even to be retained.

Competition among peers can spawn improper behavior. This explains why, in Table 6.1, we saw that businessmen regard their peers as having less influence on their *ethical* decisions than on their *unethical* decisions. When total sales volume or profit percentage is valued more highly than honesty by top management, competition among middle managers can quickly result in a level of behavior which is the lowest common denominator of the group.

Reactions to competing for promotion extended from repugnance ("I am convinced that it is not the work load that kills people in a large company, but the politicking and back-knifing that goes on.") to a kind of primitive zest ("I have two men's feet tracks all over my back, but the day will come when I can get them.")

Competition for advancement by middle managers includes attempts to replace the boss. There were several cases of subordinates who went directly to the president and put the actions of their superiors in a bad light. Of course, not all of the unsavory actions are performed by subordinates. One executive noted: "I've seen a number of men take credit for the ideas of their subordinates."

Remarks by and about the lower levels of management were similar to those by and about middle managers. There is pressure for performance and conformity from above, and competition for advancement from peers. Here are typical comments from men at the bottom of the managerial ladder:

> Everyone is moral at the top; upper management is very good and they preach to the younger men. But the temptations are at the lower levels.

> Sometimes the men on the lower echelons are not intentionally unethical, but the pressure on them to produce profits makes them so.

In summary, each level of the corporate hierarchy has its own prevailing winds of temptation. At the very top, men are tempted to fashion a private windfall under the cover of a mass of figures and complex considerations. Lower on the corporate ladder there are high-pressure areas, usually caused by superiors' demands for sales or profits. At the middle and lower levels is also found the temptation to backstabbing in order to gain a promotion.

OCCUPATIONAL DIFFERENCES

Rarely does a person advance in industry or commerce without first devoting years to one functional area. Exceptions are management consultants and sons of the president of a family-controlled corporation. Usually men are educated and trained in an area like finance, personnel management, accounting, economics, or production management. Typically they spend at least ten years in this specialized area, dealing with the problems pertinent to their occupation.

The kind of work to which a man devotes his early years in business reveals and shapes his personality; it may also reflect the values he prizes. There are behavior-influencing forces peculiar to each occupation, and these forces operate on everyone engaged in that kind of work. In Projects One and Two, indications were found of relationships between some occupations and ethical behavior. So in Project Three, the interviewees were asked: "Do you think that executives in certain occupations or doing certain kinds of work act more ethically than executives doing other kinds of work?" Affirmative answers came from 87 per cent of the men, who were then asked two more questions: "Would you please name one kind of work that you think is very ethical, or one that you think is unethical? Why is that kind of work so ethical (unethical)?"

The phrase, "act more ethically," can mean either the quantity or the quality of ethical actions. For example, a bank teller who resists the opportunity to shortchange careless customers many times a day may act ethically more often than the bank president. But one decision made by the bank president can affect thousands of employees and depositors; if the decision is ethical, it will be more influential—in terms of people and dollars involved—than a year's activities of the teller.

Many respondents reworded the first question to something like: In which kind of work is there the least, or most, exposure to temptation? Salesmen were regularly said to have "the opportunity" to be unethical, while purchasing agents were identified with "gifts" and "bribes." The answers to the second question are given in Table 11.1.

Table 11.1
Occupational Influence on Behavior (N = 75)

OCCUPATION	NUMBER WHO SAY IT IS	
	Ethical	Unethical
Accounting	11	2
Engineering and research	6	0
Purchasing	2	16
Selling	0	28
Others	9	1

It is clear that our panelists think it easier for accountants and engineers to be ethical than for salesmen and purchasing agents. With this in mind, it is revealing to look again at Table 4.3, which names unethical practices that Project Two respondents wanted to see eliminated. The practices named there are frequently associated with the activities of selling and buying, seldom with accounting, engineering, or research.

Ethical behavior is related in part to the frequency and intensity of temptation. As a board chairman phrased it: "There is such a thing as evil, such a thing as temptation. Men who take money from the till more frequently than others are the men in a position to put their hands in the till." Another chief executive reinforced this view:

In the restaurants which we took over, there were several hundred waitresses. When we put in cash registers, the average day's income increased tremendously over what it had been when every waitress was handling money. Many people are dishonest whenever they feel they can get away with it, when they have the opportunity. This is especially true when they work with money instead of, for instance, machinery.

Management consultant Norman Jaspan, in *The Thief in the White Collar*, thoroughly documents the propensity of ordinary, trusted employees to yield to temptation. Every year, white-collar employees in the United States steal more than $1½ billion from their employers. This is, incidentally, at least eight times as much as is stolen from companies by burglars. There are two obvious reasons for employee theft from large companies: the company's affluence ("they will never miss it"), and the employee's inability to identify with the company. Evidence of this inability is the frequent reference to "they," "the administration," and "company policy."

FAILURE TO USE INTERNAL CONTROLS

Despite the large losses to thieving employees, many managers continue to have a marvelous trust in the behavior of company personnel. So naively trusting are many managers that they neglect to take ordinary precautions, for instance, in internal financial control. One interviewee told of a purchasing manager who tried to get a kickback from him. Though the purchasing manager bought more than $50 million of goods annually, his superiors made no check on his activities. Eventually top management stumbled onto his salary supplementing and fired him. As one management consultant stated:

> One thing that strikes me is the lack of adequate controls in many companies, so that they don't know and can't tell when somebody is cheating them or stealing from them. These companies don't have adequate measures of performance, and there is no policing. A company is more ethical if there is less exposure, less temptation.

THE PURCHASING AGENT

The carelessness of top management increases the temptations of purchasing agents, but it should also be kept in mind that if an agent feels that he is underpaid he is more willing to consider kickbacks. The president of a very small company explained his unhappy experience with purchasing agents on this basis:

> This purchasing agent phoned me one day and suggested that I start bidding on some of their needs. I did, and before the year was out, he had given me two orders totaling $87,000, which was about 60 per cent of our total annual sales. The next year I wanted to rebid on the same orders; so we had lunch. During lunch he put the pressure on me; he told me how underpaid he was, how his worth to the company wasn't appreciated. Then he asked if I wouldn't be able to make some kind of financial arrangement to his advantage, if my company got the orders.

A top executive who spent many years in purchasing thought there was less cheating now because the men were better paid and the purchasing agents' association had established patterns of conduct. The comments of another experienced purchasing agent showed an interesting combination of human concern and tough-mindedness:

> I'm willing to work with a supplier if he's in trouble. One man who had been a good supplier to a number of companies became an alcoholic. A number of us who bought from him worked as a group to get him back on his feet. He recovered. But I can be a hard guy. I recall working with one supplier whose prices gradually got out of line because he wasn't pushing his work force. I went to him and said, "Look, your prices are almost 10 per cent out of line for this coming contract. We are not going to give you the business unless you give such-and-such a price." He was stunned and asked how he could cut his costs that much. I told him to fire 10 per cent of his men. He left, thought it over and fired 10 per cent. When he next saw me, he said, "Do you know what happened? Our production is higher now than it was before I fired those men." That didn't surprise me. His men had been dogging it, and I saw that.

THE ACCOUNTANT

In all three stages of our survey, respondents regarded account-ants as more ethical than men in other areas of business. The principle reasons given for this view were: (1) the historical func-tion of the accountant as recorder and steward; (2) the absence of pressure on him to make profits; (3) the likelihood that his written records will be checked by auditors; (4) habitual adherence to accounting regulations, which makes adherence to all guidelines, including the ethical, easier; (5) professional status—certified pub-lic accountants are professionals, having their own admission stand-ards, a written code, and penalties for misbehavior. The majority agreed with the interviewee who said, "The more your books are required to balance, the more ethical you are. Accountants have little leeway."

One man, however, complained of "the shenanigans I've seen accountants pull with inventory records." Another resented the fact that accountants didn't seem to make any decisions. A sales-man was irked that the accountants "don't put anything on their records about the number of calls and contacts I make without any-thing happening; they just sit at their desks and when I click on a deal that brings me $1,000 commission they try to reduce the com-mission."

Engineers too have occupational aids to acting ethically. Their work goes onto charts, into written reports or formulas, and is subsequently tested in the laboratory, on the production line, and in use. As a result, an engineer's work is identifiable, can be checked at any time, and is proved by the results. For much of an engineer's work, sheer professional self-preservation dictates ethical conduct.[5] Another help to engineers is that they usually work with men in the same company as themselves. It is psychologically harder to wrong an acquaintance or coworker than someone you do not know. Also, unlike salesmen and purchasing agents, engineers are seldom in situations in which ethical conduct will produce results that are so economically satisfying that their boss will overlook the means by which they were obtained.

THE SALESMAN

The salesman is in a unique position in our economic system: He is the man on the firing line. In our competitive economy, it is the salesman who—more than anyone else—competes. The salesman is tempted both when there is too little competition, a sellers' market, and too much competition, a buyers' market. In a sellers' market, the salesman is apt to be offered money under the counter for scarce items. In a buyers' market, the salesman is pressured from top management and may offer payola to purchasing agents. Pressure for performance can be accompanied by a refusal of the boss to share the blame for unethical actions, an inconsistency that was mentioned by an interviewee:

In yesterday's paper there was a story about the X Company. One of their salesmen was thrown out of the state for bribing an official. A payoff of $150,000 was made by the salesman. Company officials denied that they had approved this in any way, but I talked to some of them several years ago, and they told me that the only way they could get state contracts in a couple of instances was by making a payoff.

Why do interviewees name selling as the kind of work in which it is most difficult to act ethically? They offered a variety of reasons:

A sales manager: "Salesmen have to deal with more people who

[5] Cf. Raymond Baumhart, S.J., "It's Easy to Be Ethical—Sometimes," *Chemical Engineering Progress*, February 1965, pp. 16–20.

have their hands out. They face more temptations, but they also yield often."

An engineer: "There is a psychological something about the role of the salesman in a company. Only a salesman brings money into the company, every other department just spends it. That leads to a different, more lenient attitude on the part of top management with salesmen."

Several interviewees subscribed to the view that many salesmen fit a stereotype: an extrovert who is talkative and confident, wants to make money fast, is highly motivated by commissions but not by delayed rewards or long-run goals.[6] As a personnel executive put it: "Salesmen are a different breed. A good salesman has to be attractively egotistic: He has to impose his will on the customer." If this is so, there remains the question whether men with these traits become salesmen, or whether salesmen acquire these traits as a result of their job. But it is agreed that the worth of many salesmen decreases with age at a pace unmatched in other occupations, and this is a reason for the salesman's desire to make money quickly.

A president provided an illustration of common attitudes toward salesmen and accountants:

Salesmen have to lie, exaggerate, and make claims about their product. But an accountant who did the same thing would be fired. Let me give you an example. The other day I went to Washington on a business deal. My accountants had to work overtime the night before to prepare some figures. In Washington, someone spotted an error which my accountants had made, and I had to phone to get the correct figures. But I could have told half a dozen lies about our product to the same men in Washington and they would never have discovered it.

Summing up the evidence about occupational differences, it appears that there are more temptations in jobs involving competitive relationships, like the salesman's or purchasing agent's, than in those involving fiduciary relationships, like the accountant's or engineer's. In a limited sense, then, it is easier to be ethical in some occupations than in others.

[6] From Plato to Arthur Miller, the intellectual's stereotype of the salesman has been unkind to those who earn a living by selling; see *The Republic*, Book II, 371B–373B.

As an old saw has it, a man is known by the company he keeps. This prompts the question: Can a man be known by the company which keeps him? If you are familiar with a company's ethical posture, will this tell you much about individual executives in the company? In other words, does a manager's ethics depend on the corporation which employs him? Using the data, I shall investigate these questions, then offer some ideas about whether a company with a good reputation attracts young men with high ideals, and then look at the relationship of company size to ethics.

From Chapter 10, with its evidence of top management's prominence in determining the standards of subordinates, it follows logically that ethical views and practices differ from company to company because one top management team differs from another. Having said that a corporation is the lengthened shadow of its president, respondents have implicitly affirmed that many employees think as their president thinks about ethical matters. This is to aver the existence of a "company response." Some executives, like public relations man David Finn, are convinced that such a response exists: "Each company has its own threshold of what it is comfortable in doing from an ethical standpoint."[1] Presumably new employees gradually discover where the threshold of comfortable behavior ends, probably in the same variety of ways that children learn that stoves are hot. One interviewee related how he discovered the height of his company's threshold:

[1] "Struggle for Ethics in Public Relations," *Harvard Business Review*, January–February 1959, p. 51.

About six years ago I first ran into evidence of strange dealings in our pricing. I saw invoices from three customers of approximately the same size in the same area: A was paying book price, B was getting a 15 per cent discount, C was getting a 20 per cent discount. I brought up the matter in an informal chat with three other men. Two of them walked away and the third, a senior salesman, said, "That's a question for another day. We don't ask questions like that around here." Some time later, I took a bid into my boss's office and asked why $5,000 had been added to the price which I had calculated. He said, "Don't ask questions. Just leave the $5,000 in." So I did, and we got the contract. It was our turn to get it; so he added $5,000.

At the time of the electrical industry antitrust cases, there was a split in public opinion concerning culpability for the price collusion. A large segment of Americans regarded the conspirators' action as proof of the moral weakness of *individuals*. The management of the General Electric Company, by dismissing executives who had been convicted by the government, espoused this view. Oversimplified, this viewpoint may be stated: Bad men make bad companies.

Many observers, however, felt that individual weakness was an inadequate explanation for the wholesale failure of men whose conduct was, in most respects, admirable. This school of thought hypothesized the existence of a company attitude so strong that it was very difficult—morally impossible, some theologians would say—for the individual to take an opposing stand. Professor William Kennedy argued that William H. Whyte's insight about the existence of a social ethic in U.S. corporations was verified:

His [Whyte's] point is well illustrated in the history of Policy Directive 20.5 of the General Electric Company. Over the years hundreds of executives faced the dilemma of either standing by their affidavit to comply with the directive and obey antitrust laws or going along with the predominant "ethic" of meeting with competitors. The Kefauver Report gives only one instance of an executive who stood by his affidavit. In doing so, he had to sacrifice his position with the company. The man was Walter F. Rauber. . . . That 99 out of 100 men, who constituted a fair sample of the population of corporation executives, failed this test of personal morality demonstrates the overwhelming power of the "social ethic" of the organization. . . .[2]

An oversimplified version of this viewpoint is: Bad companies make bad men. Contrary to the action of General Electric, the

[2] "The Ethics of Conspiracy," *Atlantic Economic Review*, August 1962, p. 17.

Westinghouse Company did not dismiss its convicted executives. Presumably, Westinghouse top management not only admits that there is an organizational social ethic, or company response, but also thinks that it was partly responsible for the price collusion decisions.

What do our data reveal about the existence of a company response? No questions were asked that elicited replies providing direct evidence, but by comparing answers given to the same questions by several men employed by a company, evidence was secured about several firms which suggests the presence of a company response. The evidence includes marked similarities among the managers in: defining the term *ethical*; degree of sensitivity to ethical issues; quality of their ideas and reasoning about ethics; rating of their own company's practice of ethics; and their attitude toward the utility of codes of ethics.

Ten of the interviewees volunteered the view that a company response explains many similarities in managers' views about ethics. One executive affirmed that "it's easy for us to take a noble position because of the top men. All we have to do is follow the party line. . . . There is an ethical attitude which is prevalent here." Other managers, however, felt that the company response often had a negative influence on employees' decisions.

Company policy, if it is genuine and not mere window dressing, is the official equivalent of a company response. As Table 6.1 indicated, company policy is regarded by businessmen as a helpful influence for ethical decisions. The Wayne State University study of middle managers showed that they had a similar high opinion of the value of a "company's policies or regulations" in solving moral problems.[3]

As a detailed illustration of a company response or posture toward ethical problems, the company history provided by a merchant is enlightening:

Let me tell you a bit about this company, because its history has some relevance for a study of ethics. Its president in the early 1900s had no real need for money, and decided to make the store something of a monument to his name. He wanted the store to have the finest type of reputation for quality merchandise, careful treatment of customers, the highest type of business ethics. He could afford to make these his objectives, while competitors were taking a different tack, emphasizing low prices, sales, and the like. When he retired, he found a man who

---

[3] "Middle Managers' Views on Their Most Significant Professional Moral Problems," Program Extra No. 603, National Conference of Christian Employers and Managers, 1006 S. Michigan Avenue, Chicago, 1966, p. 27.

had no special need for money either. So this was the image that the
two men decided to create, and they succeeded. Even during the depression they never traded down nor fired people. All merchandising
has been and is aimed at preserving the same, single reputation.

Especially in a retail operation like this one, the personality of the
chief executive carries down through everything the store does. For
instance, the president still walks through the store greeting everyone
and chatting about their personal problems. He also picks up pieces of
paper which he sees on the floor; so everybody else in the store picks
up paper when they see some on the floor. The top executive has created
the kind of environment he wants; it is calculated, but it is good and
promotes good ethics. Furthermore, our customers—who are mostly
women—like the courteous and kind treatment given by our sales
people. Now we get these sales ladies from the same pool of personnel
that other retail stores in the area get their help, but our help is more
courteous because of the reputation which the president has established.
New sales ladies catch on; their better side shows through in their
work. And we don't pay any more than other stores around here either
—probably we pay a little less.

Another fact about our stores, we don't take advantage of discount
situations. In this business, let's say you get a bill payable on the first of
the month at 2/10, net/30. If we don't pay the bill within the ten
days, we don't take the discount. Just about every other store does take
the discount whenever they pay, even if they are not entitled to it. The
manufacturer doesn't object; he can't because he wants to sell the same
customers again. In the same way, some stores—if they have made a
deal to buy some item and the item has cooled off before it arrives—
will cancel the deal if the item is one day late. We never do a thing
like that. Our actions pay off because the resource, that is, the manufacturer or manufacturer's agent from whom we buy the garments in
New York, will give us breaks on hot items, help us when we run
short, and so forth. We try to cultivate this buyer-resource relationship.

We are also square with contractors. For example, the painters
underestimated how much a job would cost them here. We heard about
it and, instead of holding them to the original price, agreed to split the
difference with them.

A final piece of evidence that a company response to ethical
problems really exists comes from the instances in Chapter 10 of
men who left companies with whose standards they were dissatisfied. Presumably these men moved to companies where they
found the ethical threshold and moral standards more to their
liking.

We conclude that respondents think that a company's response
to ethical problems is a significant influence on employees' actions.
If this is so, a corporation (i.e., top management) has a responsibility toward its employees to provide them with a policy and a

climate conducive to ethical decisions. The right policy and climate bring out the best in employees and enable them to be human, to act ethically, as in the department store situation just cited.

COMPANY REPUTATION AND RECRUITING

Since the kind of young men hired by a company will determine the company's future, in matters of ethics as well as of economics, the interviewees were asked: "If a company has a reputation for ethical behavior, do you think that this is a significant factor in attracting young men who possess high ethical standards? Why?"

Seventy per cent replied affirmatively. Included in this majority viewpoint was some disagreement over the degree of influence; in other words, over what "significant" means. The range of affirmation extended from "probably significant" to "most emphatically important." The views were not all of equal value, as some interviewees had no experience in hiring and only one experience of being hired. Others, like personnel officers and managers who regularly engage in recruiting collegians, had pondered the question at length; the views of these men offer enlightenment.

Almost all of the respondents agreed that salary, title, and economic security are the most important factors in a young man's choice of a job. As one president saw it:

> I'm cynical about these young fellows looking for a job. They want to know all about how much money they will get, what sort of guarantees we will make, and what kind of security they will get. They wouldn't know much about ethics in business.

An interviewee who reflected on his own attitude years earlier while job-seeking admitted: "My question was: Can I grow in that company? I did not think of the ethical practices."

What of the 70 per cent who affirm that a company reputation for ethical decisions is a significant factor in attracting young men who possess high standards? It is noteworthy that Morris Rosenberg, in a study of occupations and values involving 10,000 collegians, found 70 per cent in disagreement with the statement, "In order to get ahead these days . . . you can't afford to be squeamish about the means you use."[4] Rosenberg interprets this disagreement

[4] *Occupations and Values* (New York: Free Press of Glencoe, 1957), pp. 96–97.

as revealing faith in people. This same faith is undoubtedly operative in many of our respondents.

Some interviewees felt that it is less likely that a reputation for good ethics attracts young men than that a bad reputation keeps them away. One trainmaster lamented that it is no easy thing to outlive a reputation for unethical behavior: "We still have people who remember the old robber barons such as the Goulds. These men were very unethical at the time and the result of their operation still hurts us today." A manager in the electrical manufacturing industry made the same point: "The students really quiz us since the indictments. They want to know whether collusion has stopped and what company policy is."

Most respondents feel that a reputation for ethical actions does attract high-minded young men. Some companies attempt to give the impression that ethics is important to them. This is well brought out by an executive in a midwestern company:

One factor which makes for ethical conduct in business is the ability to recruit each year, for management ranks, a large pool of idealistic, informed young persons. For several years, I was in charge of recruiting here. One of my selling points was our leadership in fair employment practices. I felt that if a man was attracted by this kind of a sales pitch, we wanted him.

A vice-president of an advertising agency recalled that the industry had a bad reputation in his mind:

I was quite apprehensive about entering the industry because of the amount of drinking, the amount of money spent—which I thought would tend to unbalance a man's views of what is important—and the way some advertising men acted like "big dealers." But it also occurred to me that there were probably some very ethical agencies, so I looked for them. Fortunately I ended up with five job offers and could pick on the basis of ethics. I think that I made a good choice.

This man admits, however, that he made his choice on scant information; he thinks it unlikely that a job-seeker can know much about a company's ethical practices. A dozen other men echoed this thought, suggesting that a man must work for a company for a year or two before he can know what is really happening. The consensus is that the typical student's impression of a company is garnered from newspapers, television, and radio, plus a smattering of secondhand information from friends.

A management consultant feels that the image presented by the public relations departments of big corporations often misleads the young. There is, of course, no defense for falsehood, misrepresentation, or artificial image making. But it does seem that the popular image of the businessman has been distorted by the predilection of news editors for scandal, and by the occasionally irresponsible words of a politician more eager to get votes than to get at the truth. Responsible public relations releases admittedly focus on the virtues of business, but these are just as real as its vices and far less likely to be reported by communications media. Furthermore, students are not completely naïve about what is happening in industry, as is shown by the words of one interviewee: "When I graduated from the university, a certain company had the reputation of hiring two men for one job, and then firing one of the two. We all agreed to stay away from this company, and no one in the class went to work for them."

Alert and sophisticated job aspirants utilize sources of information which are closer to the company than communications media, especially the candid opinions of men who have worked in the lower echelons of the company, or faculty members who have acted as management consultants for the company. And students exchange information about the interviews conducted by company placement officers; such exchanges quickly reveal insincerity on the part of the interviewer. An interested job applicant will be able to get some information about what I called a "company response" if he takes the time to try the various approaches mentioned above, including that of securing interviews with men from different managerial levels and departments. Nevertheless, he will have to make his choice without knowing all of the facts—but, after all, business decisions are made under the same condition.

Since the value of experience cannot be exaggerated in regard to the question we are considering, the reply of a personnel officer who, over the last twenty-five years, has hired 6,000 young men for one company, deserves special attention:

I agree that a good reputation attracts young men with high standards. Our company has a wonderful reputation in this city; for example, we might treat some sick person very generously, as we did a man with tuberculosis, whom we kept on the payroll for more than a year while he was ill even though he had only been with us for three years. And we help the widows of our workers. Word of this gets around; it's talked about at home and over the dinner table. Also, many promising young men investigated our company because of a public service advertising series which we sponsored; they said that any company which believed in ideas like the ones which appeared in our ads interested them.

COMPANY SIZE

Now we turn to another question: Does company size influence ethical behavior? Some critics believe that *bigness* is practically synonymous with evil: "The jungle ethos of big business is peculiarly its own, and has very little relation to small or family owned business."[5]

David Riesman, however, holds that *smallness* is conducive to unethical behavior:

Today, only small businessmen (car dealers or furnace repairmen, for instance) have many opportunities for . . . sharply manipulative property-pyramiding.[6]

In a similar vein, Richard J. Nelson, a vice-president of the Inland Steel Company, said:

Instances of personal corruption are more widespread in the area of small business then they are in large corporations. In small business the managers are frequently the owners and are accountable only to themselves. I would guess that there are more abuses of expense accounts and misuse of company cars and planes in relatively small companies than there are in large corporations. The reason is fairly simple. The owner-manager is trying to avoid, if not evade, taxes. The more personal expenses he can charge to his business the less out-of-pocket he is. If this expense money came to him later as a profit he would have to pay a substantial percentage of it in personal income tax.[7]

What did our investigation reveal? In Project One the respondents were asked to agree or disagree with the statement, "The executives of large corporations are typically more honest than the executives of small business enterprises." The replies were inconclusive: 28 per cent agreed, 30 per cent were neutral, 42 per cent disagreed. However, cross tabulation revealed that the answers were related to the size of the company for which the men worked. Managers of large corporations tended to agree with the statement; small-company managers tended to disagree.

Project Two differences were interesting. On eight of the nine questions which I used to learn about the influence of variables like

[5] Jerem O'Sullivan-Barra, "Dear Sir and Brother," *Integrity*, Vol. I, No. 10, pp. 5–6.

[6] *The Lonely Crowd* (New Haven: Yale Press, 1954), pp. 265–266.

[7] Richard J. Nelson, "The Ethical and Moral Standards of Labor and Business," speech delivered March 1, 1960, to the Chicago chapter of Industrial Relations Research Association, p. 2.

age, education, and religious affiliation, the managers from companies with fewer than fifty employees answered less ethically than did managers from companies with more than 10,000 employees. However, the replies of the managers from the smallest companies were as ethical as those from men working for companies employing 1,000 to 9,999 persons. The answers from managers whose companies were neither very small nor very large fit no pattern. About all that can be said, as Table 12.1 indicates, is that managers from smaller companies seem less ethical than those from larger companies, but the differences are neither consistent nor statistically significant.

Table 12.1
Size of Company Related to Responses

	NUMBER OF EMPLOYEES IN COMPANY				
	1–49 (N = 195)	50–249 (N = 234)	500–999 (N = 128)	1,000– 9,999 (N = 330)	10,000 and over (N = 297)
1e. Agree that "For corporation executives to act in the interest of shareholders alone . . . is unethical."	80%	79%	83%	85%	85%
1h. Agree that ". . . the spiritual and moral consequences of the businessman's actions are none of his concern."	4	4	5	5	2
2. Would use confidential corporate information for private financial gain.	51	45	47	44	34
3. Would probably hire personnel from a competitor to acquire scientific discovery.	42	56	43	48	50
4. Regard padding of expense account as unacceptable regardless of the circumstances.	85	82	88	85	89

	NUMBER OF EMPLOYEES IN COMPANY (cont.)				
	1–49	50–249	500–999	1,000–9,999	10,000 and over
	(N = 195)	(N = 234)	(N = 128)	(N = 330)	(N = 297)
5. See no ethical dimension in status-symbol advertising.	32	35	33	36	28
8a. Think it always ethical for executive to own stock in company with which his company regularly does business.	2	3	2	3	1
8b. Think that providing a call girl for a customer is always unethical.	83	86	93	88	89
8c. Think it always ethical for executive to exchange price information with other companies.	7	4	1	6	3

(For questions 2, 3, 4, and 5, there were approximately half as many respondents as for the other questions.)

In the 100 interviews of Project Three, company size was brought into the conversation only when comments about industry differences made size a likely topic. On this basis, one man in five related company ethics to size. Again the interviewers heard men defending companies of the same size as the one they work for, and voicing doubts about companies of other sizes. Listen, for example, to the president of a Fifth Avenue manufacturer's agency:

Every year, no matter who the income tax adjuster is, we get a visit. Because we are a small company with two owners, the adjuster automatically cuts our expenses heavily. He assumes we are guilty of cheating on our expense claims. That puts an unnecessary burden on us little guys. Nobody bothers the big fellows on this point.

Compare that reply with the words of a lawyer for a large corporation: "The tax returns of large companies will certainly be audited. So large companies are very careful of tax returns. . . . I don't want to generalize, but small companies are under more pressure [to act unethically] because money means more to them."

When these data are sifted and weighed, what can be said of company size and ethics? Although there was no consistent relationship discernible, the data suggest that respondents from large companies were more ethical than those from small companies. Going beyond the quantitative evidence, I offer my own impression that small companies are both the most ethical and the least ethical in our economy. How can this be? Leadership is the answer. In a small company, the actions and attitude of the chief executive are often known by all the employees and used as benchmarks for their own behavior. If the chief executive's actions and attitude are marked by integrity and high principles, the corporate acts will habitually be ethical. If his actions and attitudes are selfish, dishonest, or greedy, employees who value ethics will rarely remain with the company for long, and corporate acts will often be unethical.

Apart from leadership, there are three factors which seem to provide an ethical advantage for the small company over the large:

1. Accuracy of communication. When the boss of a small company wants all his employees to act in a certain way, he can communicate his wishes quickly and correctly. In a large company, because of the many levels of authority, messages downward sometimes are garbled, and complete information does not always find its way up to the decision-maker.

2. Ease in demonstrating managerial interest in employees. The large corporation tends to be impersonal; the efficiency it seeks fosters anonymity. The failure to recognize individuality results in employee reluctance to show personal responsibility. Anonymity can lead to anomie.

3. External checks on managerial actions. These checks, principally from stockholders but also from the community, are closer in small companies than in large, assuming they are publicly owned. Because of the complexity of the problems faced by giant corporations, it is difficult for even an intelligent and interested stockholder to secure information if top management prefers to conceal it. However, the company that is privately owned—usually a small one—can, without external checks, degenerate into a front for cheating both employees and the government.

On the other hand, large companies usually have two assets which can give them an ethical advantage over smaller companies:

1. Adequate capital. The large company is rarely caught in a financial crisis. Many small companies are undercapitalized from birth. Pressure for sales and profits is present in companies of every size, but the pressure of imminent bankruptcy seldom hits a large company. One division of a large corporation can lose money for several consecutive years but, because it is part of an economically integrated operation, never be in financial difficulty. The choice of going out of business or acting unethically is the small business-man's dilemma par excellence.

2. Career executives. These men, well educated and highly skilled, take a professional attitude toward their work. They are more often employees in large companies than manager-owners of small companies, and their future depends in part on a reputation for integrity. Success in their career does not require that they stay with any one company; it may require a reputation for ethical decisions. So the temptation to cut corners in order to help the company is strongly restrained by the desire to maintain a good reputation in the industry.

13   Industry Climate and Competition

Early in Project One, businessmen told us that some industries are more ethical than others. This seemed deserving of study, in part because of the stated preference of many promising young men for an industry with a good reputation.

Over the years an industry develops its own way of doing things. These generally accepted practices significantly determine the climate of the industry which, as we saw in Chapter 6, businessmen regard as a strong influence on their decisions. To find out how prevalent unethical actions are among everyday practices, the interviewees were asked: "In every industry there are some generally accepted business practices. In your industry are there any such practices which you regard as unethical?" As reported in Table 4.2, 70 per cent of the 1,459 respondents acknowledged the existence of practices which are accepted although they are unethical.

This candid admission is a call for corrective action. Generally accepted practices are the sun and rain of an industry climate. When a goodly number of these practices are unethical, how can the climate be otherwise? It is hardly possible to justify the continued existence of industrywide practices which are unethical, unless one argues that certain economic goods are more valuable than ethical behavior.

There are differences in the number of unethical everyday practices in various industries, as is evident from Table 13.1.

The industries listed in Table 13.1 are those shown by members' replies to be well above or below the average. Clearly, men in transportation and public utilities companies have a relatively high regard for the generally accepted practices in their industries. Not so the men who work in construction, consumer services, advertising, and other communications industries; one-quarter of these men said that they face *many* unethical practices in their industries. One in every three men from construction and consumer services companies stated also that he "occasionally" or "very frequently" (as opposed to "never" or "rarely") finds himself in a situation where he "has to make a decision so quickly that there is no time to consider its ethical implications." Only one in every five of the other respondents made a similar admission.

Table 13.1
Industry Differences Regarding Unethical Practices (N = 1,279)

	HOW INDUSTRY MEMBERS REPLIED TO QUESTION, "ANY GENERALLY ACCEPTED UNETHICAL PRACTICES?"		
	No	Yes, a Few	Yes, Many
Transportation, public utilities	50%	42%	8%
Banking, investment, insurance	26	65	9
All others	20	70	10
Advertising, media, publishing	12	65	23
Consumer services	10	63	27
Construction	9	65	26

Managers from advertising, media, and publications differed notably from all other respondents in two respects: a higher percentage (54 per cent compared to 42 per cent) said that they "find it more difficult to know what is right than to do it"; and 47 per cent acknowledged an ethical component in status-symbol advertising, compared to 66 per cent of the other respondents. Also, compared to other businessmen, construction and advertising managers gave distinctly less favorable opinions of the amount of guidance provided them by clergymen. This could be because men in construction and advertising face more, or more difficult, ethical problems than other businessmen. In the light of this evidence, it is no surprise to find that men from the construction, consumer services, and advertising industries were more favorably disposed toward industry codes than were other respondents.

Having these and other indications of industry differences from Project Two, I inserted into Project Three interviews the query: "Do you think that some industries are more ethical in their decisions and actions than other industries?" Eighty-two per cent of the replies were affirmative. Because the answer required a comparison among industries, the views of management consultants and public relations counselors, who usually deal with many industries over a period of years, are especially meaningful. The fourteen consultants and public relations men were more affirmative than the average respondent, with only one seeing no difference among industries.

Two more questions were asked of the yea-sayers: (1) "Would you please name one industry that you think is very ethical, or one that you think is unethical?" (2) "Why is that industry so ethical (unethical)?" The answers to question 1 are given in Table 13.2.

Table 13.2
Naming One Ethical (Unethical) Industry (N = 72)

	NUMBER WHO SAY IT IS	
	Ethical	Unethical
Banking, investment, insurance	8	2
Transportation, public utilities	1	1
General manufacturing	8	10
General marketing	2	3
Advertising, media, publishing	0	4
Construction	0	5
Garment	0	10
All others	8	10

These businessmen saw certain industries as more conducive than others to responsible behavior. Note again the preference for singling out unethical rather than ethical behavior. In addition to the one industry named by interviewees for the tabulation in Table 13.2, many commented at length on several industries. Banking, investment, and insurance received a favorable rating; a closer look revealed that all of the favorable votes were cast by men employed by these industries. Only a handful of other interviewees were similarly proud of their own industry. The bankers and insurance executives took no personal credit, insisting that ethical behavior was built into their industries.

Advertising, media, and publishing received none but unfavorable votes. One president attributed the lack of ethics in advertising to the fact that "the men are trying to impress one another" with striking results. Another executive stated that "you can make out quite well in the newspaper business with low standards because newspapers are looking for scandal in order to sell papers." A top-ranking executive in communications was opposed to:

. . . the lurid magazines you can buy at any magazine stand. It's not just the factor of competition; for instance, there is stiff competition in the shoe business but it seems to stay ethical. But with magazines or movies or other fields of entertainment and information, the design of the product is crucial. Editors and publishers know that if they appeal to the lower instincts of men, they will sell some readers or listeners.

THE CONSTRUCTION INDUSTRY

The construction industry, including residential and nonresidential sectors as well as home improvements, fared poorly in the interviews. Several managers gave examples of vicious behavior in construction, including one threat of murder. Construction and repair jobs on homes are so seldom repeat business that some builders take chances on inferior materials, thinking that it will be a long while before the misdeed comes to light. One executive offered this comment: "There is graft and corruption in the building of offices, schools, and houses. They all get together and fix prices. They take turns accepting contracts, and then the low bidder pays off the companies who knowingly bid high."

Another executive, who deals with companies which make aluminum sidings for home insulation, warned: "They're like TV repairmen; you have to watch them." A marketing consultant refused to take part in an ingenious plan for selling fallout shelters at the time of the Cuban missile crisis:

This fellow had manufactured swimming pools, but they leaked. His big idea was to invert the pools, which were like shells, and sell them as fallout shelters. I knew that the basic material was ⅜-inch corrugated steel, which would rust in two years, and that the whole idea was a fraud. The man's reaction was, "Well, if they don't work, who will be around to complain? And if they wear out in two years, the people will be so glad that there's been no war that they won't complain." I won't help to market that kind of product.

A young executive, who was appalled at the behavior of companies which do roofing, ended his analysis of factors which prompt roofers to act unethically with a nice insight: "What I'm saying is that it is important how measurable an industry's product is, that it will be ethical in proportion to its measurability."

One businessman nominated the highway construction industry as the worst:

This is because of its dealings with politicians. The customer is always a state government, and there is only one in a state. A small clique in the state government has a lot of power, for example, on just exactly where a new highway will run. Consider how many chances for easy money there are when a decision is to be made on where to extend a highway for fifty miles, that is, through whose property it will run, which town will benefit, and so forth. It would be very hard to change the unethical way they do business because it's been done that way for so long.

The actions of some union leaders and management members in the construction industry have had a bad influence on college students, who are hired in considerable numbers during the summer. Collegians like the heavy, high-paying work, but many are troubled by what they see and hear on the job: cheating on quality and quantity of material, stealing building material for personal use, featherbedding.

A series of discussions by building contractors in the Detroit area revealed their concern about an industry situation "in which deception, breaking faith, and mutual suspicion come to be the accepted mode of operation; one must indulge in these things oneself in order to survive."[1] From their conversations, it appears that cutthroat competition results in bidding practices which regularly require corner-cutting when fulfilling the contract, if any profit is to be made. The individual contractor may be powerless to correct an unfortunate situation like this.

THE GARMENT INDUSTRY

The most striking statistic pertains to the garment industry, which garnered more unfavorable votes than any other pair of industries. Why? A veteran observer of the garment industry, who has worked in the New York garment-making district for twenty-five years, analyzed the situation this way:

I suppose that in big companies like IBM there is a serene atmosphere, but the garment-makers have to claw their way to a living. The garment manufacturers are just little guys, many of whom go in and out of business yearly. The way to start in business is to get a confirmed

[1] Robert C. Batchelder, "Building Contractors and Associates," *On-the-Job Ethics*, ed. Cameron P. Hall (New York: National Council of Churches of Christ, 1963), p. 32.

order, for example, from Woolworth. On the basis of the order, you can get a loan from the bank, rent machinery and a loft, get felt and other material on consignment. Then you get some women to do the work. When it is done, you close unless you have another order.

Even the union doesn't buck the mobsters. There are still "protected shops," that is, shops that are protected against being unionized. This protection is bought from the mobs and the union can't fight it. I know a fellow who was run out of town when he tried to organize a protected shop; several gunmen gave him the message personally. He phoned a union leader who apologized for not having informed him in advance that the shop couldn't be unionized.

At the delivery end, the industry is dominated by the truckers. Unless you send clothes in by their trucks, you can't get in or out of the market. The mobsters have a stranglehold on what enters the market; they are the "muscle" by which the industry is kept under control. Their power extends across the nation to Los Angeles.

Between manufacturing and delivery is a key group of middlemen, who know the buyers of all the big stores across the country. The buyers want assurance of quality, so they deal only with men whom they know, which keeps the number of middlemen small.

The severest competition is at the manufacturing end. It used to be worse, but the union helped matters by removing wages from competition, and by refusing labor to shops which made bids lower than their costs. The manufacturers can compete in technical efficiency and other areas, but not in wages. But it's still a tough industry.

A look at the history of the garment industry verifies this analysis. In the twenties, some members of management invited thugs to help keep unions out of the industry. Most of the activity took place in New York City, where about two-thirds of the clothing worn in the United States is made. After some sluggings, the union organizers also invited thugs to join their side. In time, Louis Buchalter Lepke, called "the most dangerous criminal in the United States" by J. Edgar Hoover in 1939, organized the industry by forcibly controlling the garment cutters union and the truckers. The labor-management battle was a savage one. *Murder, Inc.*, written in 1951 by an assistant district attorney of New York, contains two dozen references to the garment industry.[2] The book gives details of bombings, sluggings, and murders of union officials and management men. Although conditions have obviously improved in the last thirty years, the garment industry is no exemplar of business ethics. Here are observations from interviewees:

[2] Burton B. Turkus and Sid Feder, *Murder, Inc.* (New York: Farrar, Straus & Cudahy, 1951).

Those who buy and sell are under pressure to be unethical, for example, in department stores. There is excessive entertainment provided to buyers for department stores. The buyers are all-powerful in their selections.

The garment workers on Seventh Avenue in New York are a lot different from the companies on Park Avenue. We find it harder to negotiate with the garment makers. The differences have something to do with customary actions in the industry. But I don't think it is so much different ethical standards as the fact that the men are making decisions about different things.

To speak of the ethics of an entire industry is to lapse necessarily into overgeneralizations. In every industry there are admirable companies, known for honesty and square-dealing. Also, an industry may be praiseworthy in all its activities except one, like pricing, while another industry has an impeccable pricing practice but consistently cheats customers on quality of goods sold.

INDUSTRY CHARACTERISTICS

Why are some industries more ethical than others? Among the reasons are these industry characteristics:

1. Heavy dependence on repeat sales to customers
2. Relatively stable demand for the industry's major product
3. Large sum of money is required for a new firm to enter the industry
4. Quality of the product can be determined with comparative ease by the buyer
5. Industry is old enough to have developed customs
6. Product quality is watched by a government agency.

The history of an industry, including the kinds of leadership provided by its pioneers, also helps to explain its standards and behavior. For example, the use of strike-breaking mobsters by management in the garment industry in the 1920s had unfortunate long-run effects. A similar instance was provided by the president of a company selling materials to building contractors:

Our own industry is so unethical because, in our area, it has been dominated for years by a single company with a domineering boss. He was very unethical, and he got into the business first. Everybody who followed felt that to compete against him—he was the biggest—they had to do business the way he did. But lately, competitors have cut into his position by being better businessmen, so things are improving.

New inventions and industries often lead to ethical crisis. A new industry, like that born through U.S. efforts to master space, attracts many entrepreneurs because no one has much of a start over anyone else in technical knowledge. Many men try to make their fortune in a new industry. Most inevitably fail, and some resort to unfair tactics in the scramble for success. To be a loser is no easier in business than in any other competitive activity, and is usually more expensive.

Great variations in the demand for a product, such as the seasonal variation in the toy and garment industries, cause pressures for unethical actions. Opposed to these variations is stability of demand, as in large parts of the food industry. Stability of management and ownership also helps business behavior. According to one president: "The reason that the retail bakery business in our area is ethical is the stability of ownership. There is a large percentage of second- or third-generation owners. There has not been a great deal of growth, and this has helped the ethics."

COMPETITION

The most important influence on an industry's ethical practices is competition, both the amount and the kind. Competition is related to factors like elasticity of demand, homogeneity of product, ease of entry into the industry, and the rate of growth of demand for the product. One-half of the interviewees spoke at length about the relationship between competition and industry ethics. Their main theme was: Beyond a certain point (call it the ethical optimum of competition), as competition increases, so do unethical practices. This theme can be graphed as in Exhibit 13.1.

In other words, the entire or partial absence of competition is harmful to good ethics, as is illustrated by some construction contracts. Erring on the left side of the ethical optimum, however, is relatively rare. Severe or cutthroat competition is more frequent. Business ethics is injured by both too little and too much competition, with the latter more prevalent.

"The invisible hand" of competition cannot, by itself, achieve desirable ethical results. It may even be that the absence of competition which theoretically prevails in a totalitarian country results

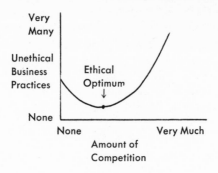

Exhibit   13.1

in fewer unethical practices than occur in a democracy during periods of severe competition. If this is so, it reveals the confidence that a democracy reposes in its business leaders; the people depend on responsible managers to keep competition within reasonable bounds. In a democracy, the people so highly treasure individual liberty and the human results it brings that they are willing to accept occasional inhuman competitive tactics as part of the price of liberty and a high standard of living.

Of course, there are other kinds of competition found in business besides that between companies in the same industry. In Chapter 11 we discussed competition between managers trying to advance in the same company. There is also interindustry competition as new uses are found for raw materials or as machinery is adapted to new purposes. There is international competition. But our interviewees thought that intra-industry competition puts the most strain on their standards. Content analysis of their comments shows that most were about "competition from other *companies.*" The next most popular expression was "competition for *sales.*" Listen to these managers:

> Ethics is not an easy thing to decide. We have some coal mines, and we could easily have the safest mines in the state. But could we afford it? That's quite a dilemma: Do you blow people up or do you starve them—devices are so expensive that your mines are no longer competitive.

> When a competitor in any industry uses unethical means, this makes for difficulty because the unethical action quickly becomes an economic pressure, and you feel that you have to compete economically.

> I have strong personal feelings against Germans. I hate them for

what they have done, and I cannot forgive them. But they make good machines, better and cheaper than others make. I don't want to buy their machines, but I have to because competition does.

INDUSTRY-WIDE SOLUTION NEEDED

There are business problems which seem soluble only if the competitive advantage resulting from an unethical action can be eliminated. Presumably this requires joint action by all the companies in an industry. Theodore Thau, former secretary of the Business Ethics Advisory Council, reports that businessmen told the council, "We would like to [take the lead in being ethical] very much, but our industry is highly competitive. If we take the lead we're liable to find that our competitors will cut us to ribbons. If there is to be any raising of the standard or of the performance of ethics in our industry, it will have to be done not on a company by company basis, but an industry by industry basis."[3] To illustrate this type of industry problem, an example taken from game theory is useful; it is called "The Prisoner's Dilemma." Here is one version:

Two suspects are taken into custody and separated. The district attorney is certain that they are guilty of a specific crime, but he does not have adequate evidence to convict them at a trial. He points out to each prisoner that each has two alternatives: to confess to the crime the police are sure they have done, or not to confess. If they both do not confess, then the district attorney states he will book them on some very minor trumped-up charge such as petty larceny and illegal possession of a weapon, and they will both receive minor punishment; if they both confess, they will be prosecuted, but he will recommend less than the most severe sentence; but if one confesses and the other does not, then the confessor will get lenient treatment for turning state's evidence whereas the latter will get "the book" slapped at him.[4]

An over-all view of the dilemma, in terms of years in prison, is presented in Exhibit 13.2.

It is evident that both prisoners would benefit most if neither confesses; but unless there is complete trust between them, both

[3] "The Business of Government and the Government of Business," *The Concept of Business Ethics*, ed. Daniel N. DeLucca (Philadelphia: Council on Business Ethics, St. Joseph's College, 1964), pp. 113–114.

[4] R. Duncan Luce and Howard Raiffa, *Games and Decisions* (New York: John Wiley and Sons, 1957), p. 95.

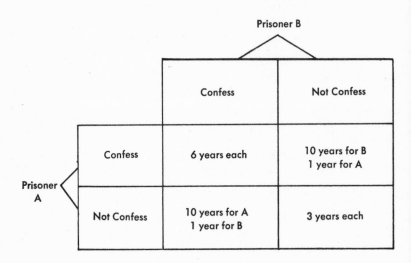

Exhibit   13.2

will confess. There is nothing perverse about their choice; it is rational self-love in operation.

In Chapter 3 we noted a prevailing attitude of mistrust among businessmen: "I'm more ethical than he." Given this attitude, situations analogous to the prisoner's dilemma regularly arise. Here is a hypothetical example:

There are five hotels in a city whose hotel guests are accustomed to racial segregation. The managers of hotels A and B want to correct the existing practice of refusing admittance to Negroes. They think that the practice is wrong and probably uneconomical. These two managers acknowledge that, unless they get cooperation from the managers of the other three hotels, hotels A and B will probably lose more business than they will gain by the change. Exhibit 13.3 shows how the economic situation looks to the managers of hotels A and B.

Desiring to do what they think is right and at the same time to avoid financial loss, for they have obligations to stockholders, the managers of hotels A and B will probably try to convince the other

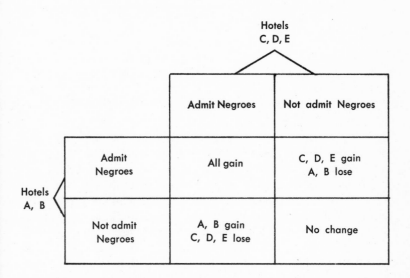

Exhibit 13.3

three managers to cooperate in changing the practice of refusing admittance to Negroes. If the trio refuses, the segregation will probably continue. In industry or geographic situations like this one, which is far from unique, there is an opportunity and a need for creative leadership. The communications media and consumer organizations can provide invaluable assistance to the businessmen so that the unethical practice is stopped without any one company suffering undue economic hardship.

If business leaders in a democracy fail to cooperate in efforts aimed at correcting generally accepted practices in their industry which are unethical, they should not be surprised if the government or some other group representing the common good takes action to force them to act responsibly. Corporation executives who give speeches about improving the business climate can prove their sincerity by working to eliminate unethical practices existing in their own industry.

Throughout this chapter, it has been apparent that the individual executive's personal attitude toward competition is of major importance. Consider the strong and unique views of one president:

> This problem of ethics worries me a little. I'm a competitive person. I try for 90 per cent of any market that I'm in. My objective is to put my competitors out of business. I don't happen to think that's unethical. Like I tell them, they needn't have any fears that I'll ever put a knife in their back, but if I can, I'm going to slit their throat.

Such a man is likely to have an outlook on many aspects of business that is different from the personnel executive who said: "Competition is too extreme in some cases. It needs moderation, to be kept within bounds. Competition can get vicious and inhuman."

It is worth noting that 40 per cent of our Project Two respondents agreed that "competition today is stiffer than ever. As a result, many businessmen find themselves forced to resort to practices which are considered shady, but which appear necessary to survive." Those who agreed with that statement were more cynical than others about the behavior of businessmen. For example, 63 per cent of them thought that "the American business executive is preoccupied chiefly with gain," compared to 39 per cent of the disagreers. Are the agreers reacting in an aggressive manner in the belief that "you have to fight fire with fire"? Are they rationalizing business decisions which would otherwise disturb their consciences? Or are they more realistic than others in acknowledging the difficulty of squaring economic competition with upright behavior?

MORE COOPERATION, LESS COMPETITION

Reflecting on the opinions and analysis in this chapter, it is appropriate to ask whether we Americans have not had an inordinate, almost blind, faith in competition. It seems evident that business ethics would improve if competition were moderated. Earlier we noted that a group of Detroit building contractors had met regularly to discuss the problems of their industry. They "were painfully aware that excessive competition can be destructive and can lower rather than raise the quality of goods offered to the consumer. They ended by searching for structures and arrangements that would preserve the values of competition while avoiding its excesses."[5]

Economic competition as we know it is an American phenomenon; it is a major cause of our high standard of living. Competition is unquestionably necessary, an accepted principle of activity in our economy. But can we, should we, rely on competition as the sole organizing principle of our economy when there is no assurance that it will be effective? Indeed, history has demonstrated that competition can be socially ineffective at times. Of course, we have laws against too much and against too little competition, but the admission of widespread unethical practices by businessmen in our survey suggests that the legal solution is inadequate.

Competition is a means, a secondary principle. What is the primary principle by which competition should be limited? As a nation we have never decided the answer to this question, and therefore, we find it very hard to identify unfair or unethical competition.

The problem is that competition has its roots in self-interest, and experience has shown that unlimited self-interest and competition produce, in addition to a rising standard of living, some results that are socially undesirable.[6] It is worth noting that in other areas of behavior few Americans have faith that competition fostered by self-interest will singlehandedly produce desirable results. Usually the competition is moderated by capable, well-informed people who are less involved than the competitors. For example, no one would think of permitting two professional football teams to play without several referees. Why not? Because in the heat of competition and the desire to win, despite the many rules and good intentions, players will be tempted to take unfair advantage of opponents. The competition between business firms is at times no less vigorous than that between professional football teams. How can it be moderated, and by whom?

Looking at other areas of modern life, we see that the churches have concluded that it is essential that competition among them must give way to cooperation. Also, our nation as a whole insists that opposition between racial groups must yield to cooperation. Perhaps the time has come for us to emphasize the cooperative aspects of American economic activity, rather than the competitive.

[5] Batchelder, *op. cit.*, p. 38.

[6] Economist Frank H. Knight wrote, "There is truth in the allegation that unregulated competition places a premium on deceit and corruption" [*The Ethics of Competition* (New York: Harper & Row, 1935), p. 50].

14 Culture, Customs, and Business

A very significant trend in United States commerce and industry today is overseas expansion. Never before have there been so many American managers working abroad, nor so many others flying regularly to and from foreign branches. Angel's *Directory of American Firms Operating in Foreign Countries* listed 4,200 United States corporations having more than 14,000 overseas operations in 1966. Most of the largest American companies are multinational corporate systems. The tremendous interest in international business is reflected in the curriculums of business schools and the research of their faculties.

When men of different nations do business with each other, their transactions are complicated by differences in language, laws, monetary systems, and managerial styles. These differences often stem from customs, which have grown out of the national culture. These customs influence businessmen's views of what constitutes ethical behavior. In Project Three, data were gathered about customs and ethics in international business by interviewing thirty businessmen: eleven were from eight foreign countries, two were United States citizens working abroad, and the rest were Americans experienced in overseas business. Then the findings were discussed with persons who have done research in international business. This chapter is the result.

"Business in my country is more ethical than it is elsewhere," was a comparison I heard from many of these men, as I mentioned in Chapter 3. That sounds like the age-old distrust of foreigners. However, a number of interviewees gave details of a business transaction in which they or their business associates were treated in a way they felt was unjust. They were not presenting themselves as paragons of virtue, though one executive from abroad complained: "Most American businessmen I've met act as though they have halos."

ABOUT U.S. BUSINESSMEN ABROAD

The managers we interviewed made both general and specific criticisms about American business behavior overseas. These criticisms ranged from "innocents abroad" to "ugly Americans." Here are some representative remarks:

U.S. businessmen are more ruthless; they compete harder. They figure all the angles. I'm amazed that even in this executive development program all the Americans are figuring how they can impress people, or wondering why somebody asked a particular question.

Our working agreement with the companies in country A is 50–50. Since they are somewhat suspect of us, we strive to carry out our part of the bargain, but are under pressure from our owners in the United States. For example, one of our American owners who buys from us in large quantities forced us to sell them at twenty per cent below our stated price agreement with the nationals of country A.

I know of many contracts which the big oil companies have made with poor people in country B. There's always plenty of small print, and when oil is discovered, then the companies rely on the small print and the poor people get nothing.

One of the reasons why businessmen in other countries have a poor impression of American managers is that some of our least reputable citizens have gone abroad. But the question naturally arises: Do U.S. businessmen act differently abroad than they do at home? It does not permit a simple answer. Some businessmen do not act responsibly. A professor told us, for instance:

My proposal for a research project about the benefits of U.S. enterprise for a Latin American country was turned down because the U.S. executives were fearful that the harm their companies had done would outweigh the benefits.

Another university researcher felt that some United States companies abroad act hypocritically. Though executives do not ask employees to take part in dishonest behavior, they close their eyes to the behavior of nationals who act as agents. To these nationals the executives give the instruction, "Do what is necessary to get the contract." Unless qualifications are added to instruction, the nationals may understand that the only limit on their actions is financial.

Increasing the temptation to be less honest when dealing with a customer who lives abroad is the distance between buyer and seller. The president of a small company said:

> One thing is obvious to me from my dealings with people in country C. If the customer or other party is geographically distant, ethics is of slight importance. Once the item is on the ship and you have your money, it doesn't much matter what happens to the item. Country C is a long way off.

Not all interviewees were critical of the business behavior of Americans. Here were the observations of a Japanese who, as his comments show, has had a special interest in cross-cultural comparisons since he began to work in the United States four years ago.

> Last week I talked to the president of an engineering company from Stamford. He was like most American businessmen in saying that he would quit rather than be forced to deal unethically as a regular thing. This is probably realistic in the U.S., and I think they would quit. But if they were living in place of Japanese in Japan, they would not. This is big difference between the two countries. In Japan there is no allowance, no cushion, no money in the bank, nothing to fall back on. Japanese have no savings; many business decisions are matters of financial life or death. Unlike U.S., many people in Japan are critically poor, absolutely poor. Business decisions often mean food in the baby's mouth. Always in Japan, and sometimes in U.S., the businessman is walking on the edge of ethics because of too much competition.

An American consultant, experienced in dealing with multinational companies in Latin America, affirmed: "United States companies and accounting firms have been instruments for raising ethical standards in quality of product, accurate sales messages, and many other aspects of business."

While managers from outside our borders were critical of the actions of United States businessmen, the reverse was also true. Here, for example, is the experience of the president of an import-export firm:

> We've had some dealings with companies in country D. They're very unethical; their word is worthless. I took part in two deals in country D: in one we grossed $400,000 on a two million dollar deal, and on the other we made $150,000 on a million dollar deal. In both cases the

businessmen there were urging me to make more profit. One retail merchant in appliances told me he wouldn't put something on his counter unless he made 150 per cent on it.

The "haves" really take advantage of the "have-nots." Why, just outside the capital city, there is a country club which costs $15,000 for an annual membership. I heard club members sitting there talking about business ethics; those same men pay their workers $15 a week.

An incident related by Professor J. George Robinson indicates that American companies buying goods from abroad sometimes feel that they have been cheated.

At a meeting of industrial purchasing agents, one of the participants . . . related an experience with a foreign business firm in which his company had procured foreign-made goods at prices considerably lower than those offered by domestic manufacturers. According to this statement the company had found that the quality of the imported goods was lower than had been represented by the seller and, in addition, the delivery of the goods was slow, resulting in costly delays. It was not surprising to see that this participant's comments received spontaneous applause from other purchasing agents in attendance.[1]

More striking than the unethical behavior in this story is the spontaneous applause, which suggests that behavior of this kind is not rare.

As is evident from previous chapters, there are many business situations in which men act unjustly toward their countrymen. In such situations the unjust behavior is rarely associated with the nationality of the wrongdoer. But when a businessman suffers an injustice from someone from another country, he tends to blame the injustice on the national difference. Let us consider whether this tendency is a manifestation of prejudice, or whether there are reasons for this reaction. We will proceed by looking at some ethical problems facing United States businessmen overseas, problems which do not confront them at home.

DILEMMAS OF U.S. BUSINESSMEN ABROAD

A large American company (call it USACO) with a history of involvement in underdeveloped nations has encountered several typical difficulties. USACO employs thousands of workers, for whom it provides good vocational schools and hospitals. USACO

[1] "Ethical Standards of Foreign Business," *Ethics and Standards in American Business,* ed. Joseph W. Towle (Boston: Houghton Mifflin, 1964), p. 222.

tries both to respect local practices and to exercise responsible leadership. The company has been criticized on three counts.

Although USACO pays wages equal to the highest going rates in the host nation, the general level of wages is still low. When criticized for not breaking the upper limits of the local wage scale, management replies that it has so many employees it dares not do so. If it did, local businesses would lose some of their best employees, and consequently would persuade government officials to harass USACO until the changes were rescinded.

The company is also castigated in one country for firing employees with nine years' seniority if there is grounded suspicion that they might cause trouble. Dismissals like this are relatively common in the country because of a law which makes it practically impossible to fire an employee after he has been on a company payroll for ten years. USACO justifies its dismissal of a small number of workers on the grounds that it must motivate and maintain control over the work force.

Finally USACO is blamed for paying different salaries for the same jobs; U.S. citizens receive more than do nationals. Management defends the practice because of its need for competent managers, and the high salary demands of competent Americans who work abroad. Critics maintain that if USACO paid nationals as well as it pays United States citizens, it would soon have ample local talent. Management replies that it would then be accused of pirating talent from the ranks of local government and industry.

The dilemmas faced by USACO call attention to a crucial question in many ethical problems in international business. When in Rome, do you do as the Romans do? Or do you use the same standards and practices that you employ at home? This difficulty deserves our special attention. The comments of two investment brokers, the first from abroad, the second from the United States, illustrate this difficulty.

I personally have found the standards on Wall Street very high despite a great many temptations. I am afraid many of these temptations would be exploited in my country. There, in the operation of the stock market there has always been an accepted practice of trading among partners of a firm. They can often make a good deal of money trading on someone else's funds.

After I make a careful study of a company and recommend that our clients be advised to buy some of the company's stock, sometimes our management decides not to advise our clients about the company. I don't buy any of the stock because I wouldn't feel right about making money when our clients didn't have the opportunity. Of course, our company insists that all its employees report all the securities in which we invest that are handled in any way by the company.

If the second broker were to go to the homeland of the first, would he be justified in following the accepted practice there? Or should he apply the same standards of behavior he uses in the United States?

Corporations with branches in many countries—like banks, hotels, and auto manufacturers—run into trouble if they try to administer all the branches by the same ethical standards. An American who spent many years in country E made this comment:

No contract is observed there unless the party for whom the work is being done has power to force the workers to do it. There are frequent work-stops, accompanied by demands for more pay or different working conditions. In general, the only thing that is respected is power. Men do something as long as it is to their advantage; when it is no longer to their advantage, they stop.

The phrase, "we must operate according to our ethics, not theirs," points up the dilemma facing some United States managers overseas. The hotel industry has a peculiar problem because its customers can be the same people in different countries, as another hotel executive pointed out:

We try to interject our own ethical ideas into the nationals who work for us. I don't know that U.S. standards are more objectively right than theirs. But we are an international organization and we want the same standards in our properties all over the world. If the hotel were only for the people of country G, I think that we might run it by their ethical standards. But we have people from all over the world staying at our hotels, and we want them to know what they can expect. As a result, I think we have upgraded standards in some lands.

This view leaves the basic dilemma unsolved. Which nation's custom is to be followed when there is a difference, for example, in interpreting collusion, bribery, or fulfillment of contract?

One merchant related how an associate of his handled such a problem. In effect, the associate was following the saying, "When in Rome, do as the Romans do."

Recently I was chatting with a leading broker of our town. He had for many years owned a sugar plantation in country H. Our conversation started with how hard it was to get something done in our town without paying off some politician. We agreed that this wasn't ethical and that we wouldn't do it. But then he told me that in country H he habitually bought off the politicians. That was different, he said, because everybody did it. He is ethical here because of the kind of business he's in; he has two different standards depending on where he is. He said that he couldn't bring himself to lose the plantations just because some payoffs were required.

Actually the owner of the sugar plantation, when he follows the local custom in country H, may not be acting unethically, even though a similar payoff in the United States would be unethical. But he should realize that the custom of buying off politicians is harmful to the common good and to social order, and that he has an obligation to work for the abolition of the custom. To let the custom go on as though it were beyond reproach would be socially irresponsible.

Differences in custom are the source of much anguish in international business. Here is an example provided by a U.S. administrator:

It is very difficult to tell what the role of custom is in determining what is ethical. For example, it is necessary to give five per cent of any deal to the chairman of the board in any company in country I; this is the custom and you can't do business unless you give the five per cent. Well, everybody understands it.

What is an administrator to do if the only way his company can get the required approval to enter another country is to give money or expensive gifts to the officials there? One of the top-ranking executives in our survey said, "Stay out." So did Clarence B. Randall, retired president of Inland Steel Company and special adviser to President Eisenhower on foreign economic policy:

I know whereof I speak, and I say that there are many otherwise respectable companies which still buy their way in when it comes to securing a mineral concession or establishing an operation in a remote part of the world. . . . I reject the argument that other nations are doing it, and therefore we must if we are to compete. Better to lose the business than to deny our heritage. . . . In the host countries, someone always knows the facts. . . . What will be our position when some demagogue from the desert calls his people to arms with the cry, "Drive the filthy Americans into the sea. We have been robbed of our ancient heritage"?[2]

One might ask whether Randall's view is broad enough. Conformity to a common practice is rarely the fault for which United

[2] Clarence B. Randall, "For a New Code of Business Ethics," *New York Times*, April 8, 1962, p. 127.

States firms are driven out of a country. Before deciding whether or not to make a payoff in order to open a plant in an overseas location, should not consideration be given to the beneficial economic influence that entry of the United States company would mean for the country?

In situations like the ones Randall is talking about, large sums of money can change hands. I heard of an approval that came from a foreign government only after the payment of $400,000. But I also heard of another payoff which differed not only in amount, but also in kind, from those that Randall was talking about. This payoff involved a local custom. The American businessman had been unable to secure a permission in a large foreign city, and asked a native what was the reason. He was told to enclose a $5 bill with his request. This he did, successfully, with each of three clerks whose approval was required. When the businessman finally arrived at the desk of the clerks' boss, he also enclosed $5. But the boss returned the money, explaining that it was unnecessary since he was independently wealthy. The payoffs were necessary for his subordinates, he said, because their income from the job was inadequate to support their families. If this is true, the payoff becomes like a tip in the United States; it is customary and is generally regarded as part of the recipient's salary. Ethically, however, the payoff is not identical to a tip. A person who cannot afford a tip in a restaurant can eat at home, but a government permit is not available from any other source.

THE INFLUENCE OF CUSTOM

In this example, and many of those quoted in this chapter, the customs of a nation influence the ethical evaluation of a business practice. Since variations in custom cause businessmen abroad some of their most puzzling problems, let us consider the interrelationship of custom, ethics, and culture.

Etymologically *ethical* and *moral* are related to *customary*, although they are not synonymous.[3] Since customs proceed from the

[3] Originally the Greek word *nomos*, which is usually translated as "law," meant a sacred custom. Pindar, a Greek poet about 500 B.C., wrote that "custom is the king of all men," which suggests the importance of custom, especially in a nation whose laws are not fully developed. In preliterate societies, custom, which generally indicates the consent of a majority, helps to regularize expectations and thus leads to that minimal order necessary for communal living. The

practices of men sharing the same human nature, customary behavior is usually an excellent indication of what constitutes ethical
behavior. Exceptions occur, however, when through malice or bad
education or misguided leadership, a custom develops in opposition
to the nature and rights of man.

Anthropologists have demonstrated that every person is, in large
part, the creature of his culture, that body of learned behavior which
is handed on from parents to children. Culture includes the customs
of a people, the unwritten laws which grow naturally out of the soil
of every society. The less civilized the society, the more important
are customs. In a primitive society, "morality is the fulfillment of
custom . . . the customary is both the right and the permitted."[4]
In the more advanced societies, ethical judgments are less likely to
be simple extensions of custom. Even in an advanced nation, custom
determines the meaning of certain actions and so can lead to a moral
obligation. One example is the finger motions in the trading pits at
an American grain exchange.

The customs, common ideas, and values of its people constitute
the cultural treasury of a nation, its uniting force, its spirit. Customs
embody the ethical values of a nation. These values influence the
cultural institutions of a nation, and vice versa. The role of custom
in helping to determine ethical standards is illustrated in the matter
of women's clothing. History reveals wide variations in the amount
and kind of clothing worn by women at different times and places.
A designer of women's clothing wondering how much of the female
body must be covered in order to avoid ethical condemnation will
find that the guideline offered by moralists is: In women's clothing,
what is customary does not affect man, and so is ethical. Marked
exposure of portions of the body usually covered in a given society
is morally reprehensible. With such a norm, the customary dress of
an inhabitant of the tropics might be regarded as immoral if worn
in Boston.

As our data reveal, the business customs of different countries
vary. What kind of guidelines can we offer to businessmen who want
to know whether it is ethical to follow the custom of the country

---

Greek word *athos*, from which *ethical* is derived, means custom. Similarly
moral is derived from the Latin word *mos, moris*, which means custom. These
derivations do not say that *customary* is synonymous with *ethical* or *moral*, but
they do indicate a close connection among the three words.

[4] R. M. MacIver, *The Modern State* (London: Oxford University Press
paperback, 1964), p. 38.

in which a business transaction occurs? If we say that whatever is customary is ethical, this is tantamount to endorsing the notion of ethical relativism. If we espouse the idea of fixed absolute values, we imply that there are some transcultural criteria by which we can evaluate customs regardless of culture.

Experience indicates that the culture in which ethical judgments are made influences those judgments. This is as true in business as in other areas. Experience and cross-cultural studies show that there is no one culture which has ethical criteria so enlightened that all cultures may be evaluated by them. However, ethical norms are not the result solely of cultural patterns. There are ethical universals, standards of behavior found in most of the hundreds of cultures studied by anthropologists. After reviewing anthropological research, Clyde Kluckhohn concludes:

> Contrary to the statements of . . . extreme cultural relativity, standards and values are not completely relative to the cultures from which they derive. Some values are as much given in human life as the fact that bodies of certain densities fall under specified conditions. . . . No culture fails to put a negative valuation upon killing, indiscriminate lying, and stealing within the in-group. There are important variations, to be sure, in the conception of the extent of the in-group and in limits of toleration of lying and stealing under certain conditions. But the core notion of the desirable and non-desirable is constant across all cultures."[5]

Richard Beis adds:

> The ethical *content* in all cultures is in a large degree the same but relativity enters in at that point in different cultures where it has to be decided which aspects or parts of the ethical content are more important and should, therefore, receive the greater emphasis.[6]

Ethical principles and varying cultural values are compatible theoretically and practically. Behavioral ideals need not mean fixed ways of decision-making without regard for cultural content and customs. The good businessman must evaluate the specific problem in the light of the principles; this is an art, though it depends on the knowledge of what constitutes ethical practice. This knowledge

[5] "Values and Value Orientations," *Toward a General Theory of Action*, ed. Talcott Parsons and Edward Shils (Cambridge, Mass.: Harvard University Press, 1951), p. 418.

[6] "Some Contributions of Anthropology to Ethics," *Thomist*, April 1964, p. 208.

grows with the systematic analysis and classification of business practice in different countries.

Customary behavior in business or affecting business must be scrutinized to determine its origin, its historical purpose, and whether the purpose perdures. The ethical congruity of a custom depends largely on whether the common good benefits from the custom, which can hardly be the case if the custom originated because of the selfish purpose of business interests.

Rather than debate the merits of ethical relativism or fixed ethical absolutes, it seems more beneficial to acknowledge that the fact of differing business standards in different nations is best explained by the concept of the progressive knowing of moral values by mankind.

Our knowledge of moral laws is progressive in nature. The sense of duty and obligation was always present, but the explicit knowledge of the various norms of natural law grows with time . . . the knowledge of the particular precepts of natural law in all of their precise aspects and requirements will continue to grow until the end of human history.[7]

We are still left with the question of whether it is right for the businessman from a more advanced culture doing business in a less advanced culture to follow the practices of the latter. There is no general answer. What is right will depend on the facts in the individual case. But one thing is clear: When a decision-maker faces an ethical problem in a foreign country, he should first learn the facts and their entire setting. This means that he should have sufficient knowledge of the social and economic organizations of the culture so that he knows what the situation means to the members of the culture. Only then can he determine what he should do, how to apply his principles in this case.

INTERNATIONAL COMPETITION

One problem that is receiving increasing attention in international business is that of different ethical standards among competitors from different nations. It has proved difficult to persuade all the companies in a single industry in *one* country to agree to certain ethical practices. How much more difficult will it be to convince all the companies in an industry throughout the world. Yet how else

[7] Jacques Maritain, *On the Philosophy of History* (New York: Charles Scribner's Sons, 1957), p. 105.

can a problem like the following be satisfactorily solved? In a number of countries, I was told, ship captains get a payoff from the company to which they bring the ship for repairs. This is an under-the-table payment, which the ship-repairing company typically recovers by falsifying the report of hours of labor spent on the ship. The captain tacitly approves the falsification. If this practice is widespread, as my informant says it is, what chance has a single ship-repair company to halt it? Except for emergency repairs, ship captains will delay repairs until they find a congenial conspirer.

Another industry in which ethical standards differ from country to country is public accounting. Some large U.S. public accounting firms have discovered themselves at a competitive disadvantage abroad, when local accountants made it a practice of approving understated income on corporate statements. The reason for this practice is usually to enable underpayment of taxes.

There exist bilateral tax treaties which reconcile conflicting requirements on taxpayers who are subject to two national tax systems. Perhaps these treaties can be used as a precedent for agreements concerning international competition. But if they are so used, it is obvious that the respective governments will be deeply involved in their construction. Perhaps this is inevitable. It is noteworthy that the American Iron & Steel Institute asked the U.S. government to strive for "an equalization of the rules under which all world steel producers would compete for the available markets. . . . Our nation's commitment to the leadership and economic support of the free world and to free trade places a great burden on us as an industry to find acceptable procedures to achieve rules of fair competition in international trade."[8]

LAWS AND POLITICS

That international business is subject to laws and government officials of more than one nation differentiates it markedly from domestic business. The laws dictate some decisions, and government officials are regularly involved in transactions.

None of our interviewees who lived abroad complained about United States government personnel. However, there were a goodly number of complaints by Americans about corrupt government

[8] John P. Roche (president of the American Iron and Steel Institute), "A Third Force," a speech given at White Sulphur Springs, West Virginia, May 1, 1964, pp. 12 and 15.

officials in other countries, especially in those which are developing economically.

The national attitude toward law and government is worthy of investigation by any American firm beginning a commercial relationship in a foreign country. The obvious approach is to speak to representatives of American companies already doing business there in order to learn whether the foreign government makes demands which are extreme by U.S. standards.

Management should also investigate the possibility that the foreign government is acting unethically—for example, by limiting personal freedom through coercion and violence. For a company to support or encourage a government which is essentially racist or militarist is socially irresponsible.

It is, however, impossible to decide whether a government is unethical unless one has all the important facts, and even then it is difficult. This is illustrated by the difference of opinion about investment in South Africa by U.S. firms. This difference was strikingly illustrated by an incident which took place in New Jersey in February 1966. Charles W. Engelhard, president of Engelhard Industries, was scheduled to receive a brotherhood award from the National Conference of Christians and Jews for his humanitarian efforts in New Jersey. His approach to the site of the award was temporarily halted by pickets from the National Association for the Advancement of Colored People. The pickets charged that Engelhard was not making a reasonable effort to improve human rights in South Africa. Engelhard, who "directly controls nearly 15 percent of South African gold production and almost 20 percent of uranium production,"[9] and who is a director of more than a dozen South African companies, retorted, "As a businessman, you have certain obligations as a guest in the country in which you do business. One of these obligations consists of not criticizing what they do at home, since you don't want them to criticize what we do at home."[10] This is hardly an adequate answer to the charges.

The Coca-Cola Export Corporation was also recently involved in a political-ethical problem of broad dimensions. In March 1966, allegations were made that Coca-Cola was opposed to giving a bottling franchise to any company in Israel. These allegations were denied by the chairman of the board of Coca-Cola, James A. Farley, who related his company's unhappy experience in dealing with an Israeli beverage company. Several months later, Coca-Cola

---

[9] "Citizen Engelhard," *Africa Today*, January 1966, p. 29.
[10] *Newark Evening News*, February 18, 1966, p. 13.

granted a bottling franchise to an Israeli concern. This action resulted in a warning from the Arab nations, whose attitude was explained by King Faisal in a visit to New York in 1966: "We consider those who provide assistance to our enemies as our own enemies."[11] In November 1966, the Boycott-Israel Office in Kuwait notified the Coca-Cola Export Company that its products were banned in thirteen Arab states and sheikdoms.

Under present political conditions, it is well-nigh impossible for a company to do business with both Arab and Israeli firms. But a company which refuses to deal with any firms in one of the two nations is liable to be charged with discrimination. It is not hard to sympathize with managers confronted by this dilemma. They must consider the rights of their shareholders, as well as the rights of the people in Israel and Arab states who wish to manufacture or distribute the product. The crucial ethical issue is whether the Arab attempt to boycott is just, a judgment which seems to require a prior judgment about the guilt or innocence of the nations in their warlike opposition. In any event, it is certainly difficult to understand how Coca-Cola can be described as "assistance to our enemies."

Perhaps the ethical-political problem most common to United States multinational companies is that of dealing with companies in Communist countries. One midwestern company president told us: "Our management committee turned down a $30 million order from the Polish government for patriotic reasons, even though we were looking for work." Two Seattle firms refused a Russian offer for $600,000 worth of machinery. Would it have been unethical for these three companies to sign the contracts? That would depend on the equipment which the order covered, and the purpose for which the equipment would be used. It would also depend on the judgment of informed United States government officials about the impact of such decisions on the Cold War. It is relatively easy to evaluate the morality of decisions on either end of the spectrum, e.g., it would be unethical to sell guns to Red China if that nation is supplying guns to the Vietcong, and ethical to sell grain to Cuba if people are starving there. But the majority of cases fall between these easily identified extremes. A company incorporated under the laws of a nation, and employing the people of that nation, has certain minimal obligations of patriotism. The limits of these obligations are debatable, but surely within the limits is the responsibility of management to discuss with government representatives the likely political impact of a contract with a company or government behind the Iron Curtain. Unless United States government officials, presumably well informed about the situation, indicate disapproval of a commercial transaction, it would ordinarily be ethical for an American firm to sign such contracts.

CONCLUSION

It seems likely that United States companies will continue to be the leaders in generating multinational enterprises.[12] They will have many opportunities (not to say obligations) to make socially responsible decisions. Besides the questions they usually ask themselves before making a decision in the United States, top management must ask other questions. Perhaps the most important of these is: What are the social and political implications of this economic decision *in this culture?* Since a culture is an economic-political-social system, a change in one part of the system affects the rest of it.

Another important question is: Does this decision reflect the fact that in this situation our company represents the United States in the minds of many observers?

In those situations where a businessman has the opportunity to impose his own standards on business operations in another country, he should proceed carefully. Changes in behavior patterns rarely occur by fiat; usually they evolve. This point was made by the chairman of a food distribution company. Active in the international Boy Scout movement, he has been struck by the inapplicability of some aspects of the Scout movement in certain countries, for example, how little appeal Scouting activities have for a boy in an underdeveloped country who regularly sleeps outdoors and cooks over an open fire. He concluded that if Scouting is to be a guiding force in the development of a boy's character, it must preserve the virtues and culture of his own people, and that the same can be said of actions directed to improving the business ethics of a nation. The actions should be evolutionary rather than revolutionary, based on the noblest ideals of the nation and utilizing education to achieve the upgrading.

Though the possible pitfalls in raising international business standards are many, the opportunities for leadership by American businessmen are great.

[12] Cf. the opinion of Raymond Vernon in "Multinational Enterprise and National Sovereignty," *Harvard Business Review*, March–April 1967, pp. 156ff.

15 Does the Government Help?

In the colonial era of our country, reflecting our English ancestry, there was a relatively close relationship between business and government, as has been true in most nation-states since the decline of feudalism. Although the American Revolution was, in part, a protest against economic regulation, the heritage of its leaders was mercantilism, an economic policy whose aims included national unification, protectionism, a favorable balance of trade, and monetary advantage over other countries through governmental regulation of the national economy. There was ambivalence, therefore, about the ideal relationship between business and government at the time of the Declaration of Independence. Since then the needs of the growing nation and of American industry have evoked governmental intervention in a variety of forms. This intervention, which has changed over the past 190 years, can be described in four categories, which are here arranged in a roughly chronological order: (1) efforts to promote certain kinds of free enterprise, e.g., protective tariffs, aid for the railroads; (2) attempts to eliminate practices harmful to workers, e.g., working conditions and child labor; (3) laws to prevent the concentration of private economic power from seriously harming democratic government, e.g., the Sherman Antitrust Act of 1890, which was designed to restrict business practices that were in restraint of trade; (4) interventions which contribute directly to general welfare, e.g., old age pensions and the minimum wage law.

Individual states carried on most of these activities in the eighteenth and nineteenth centuries, with the federal government gradually increasing its part. The role of the federal government as a service agency with few regulatory functions ended with the advent of the New Deal in 1932. Since then the federal government has grown in size, complexity, and power.

From a free enterprise economy with a minimum of direct governmental activity, the United States has moved to a mixed economy, much of it guided by government. Some observers have suggested that the power of big business called forth the countervailing power of big government. This growth in government intervention has complicated the life of the businessman. He must now make his decisions within boundaries laid out by the government.

Whatever the reason for the increased involvement of government in business, businessmen generally oppose it. The scholarly authors of *The American Business Creed* summarize this opposition in these terms:

. . . [consider] the nature of government, the proper functions of government, the inherent evils of government activity, the nature and dangers of the democratic process, and the threat of socialism which government action creates. On all these matters, the dominant tone of the creed is negative. . . . The creed classifies government servants into three groups: the politician, the routine bureaucrat, and the impractical academic bureaucrat. . . . Their heads are neither clear, hard, nor level . . .

The creed contains a generalized distrust and scorn of politicians and bureaucrats, whatever their party and whatever the policies they advocate and execute.[1]

In a sophisticated analysis, these same authors provide some reasons for the antipathy of American businessmen to government. The government is

. . . a convenient personification of the obscure forces which cause the outcomes of business decisions to differ from expectations . . .

The government's actions . . . provide the major ideological explanation of business instability. The mechanisms by which the government produces depressions and inflations may vary, but the fact that the government is responsible is an invariable article of business faith.[2]

It is well to note a paradoxical gap between businessmen's behavior and their rhetoric about government activity. They regularly praise the free market and competition. But when a government

[1] Francis X. Sutton *et al.*, *The American Business Creed* (Cambridge, Mass.: Harvard University Press, 1956), pp. 185, 192, 193, 369.

[2] *Ibid.*, pp. 369, 372.

agency acts to promote intra-industry competition or to halt abuses which unduly limit the consumer's freedom of choice, the businessmen directly affected often complain. For example, the proposal to deregulate the transportation industry in 1962 was not endorsed by some railroad men who had earlier spoken in favor of deregulation. Government assistance to business in the form of subsidies or tax concessions is seldom praised in the abstract, but is often accepted in the concrete.

One sensitive observer has written: "Government's role in economic life is fundamentally and primarily ethical."[3] Wondering whether businessmen would agree that government helps them to act ethically, I asked Project Three participants to comment on the relationship between government regulations and ethical behavior.[4]

From the replies I learned a phrase with an unethical connotation, *government work*—that is, work which a man does on company time solely for his personal benefit, for example, repairing his car. If he also uses company tools and parts for the job, it is *government work* par excellence. A phrase like this rarely becomes current unless it expresses some truth. This phrase apparently was coined to describe acts permitted by some managers only when their company had a government contract; for instance, charging a research project to a government contract with which the research was in no way connected. In any event, the phrase reflects the businessman's opinion about government's inefficiency, as well as his willingness to take advantage of the inefficiency.

Forty-two American managers offered opinions which are classifiable in terms of whether they think government regulation helps or hinders ethical behavior; 64 per cent said that it helps. In the light of the traditional business distrust and antipathy to government, this result is surprising. However, we should note the possible ambiguity in the term *government*. There are many government agencies interested in business behavior, and they have different policies and practices. The typical businessman deals with only a few of these agencies, which he will probably identify as the government.

One point was made independently by an insurance executive, a corporation attorney, and a production manager. They said that,

[3] Benjamin Masse, S.J., "The Functions of Government," in *The Concept of Business Ethics*, ed. Daniel N. DeLucca (Philadelphia: Council on Business Ethics, St. Joseph's College, 1964), p. 119.

[4] This question was asked only when the interviewee proved articulate about industry differences in ethical behavior. Slightly more than half commented.

on the whole, those industries which are regulated by government are those which showed a need for it, so that regulation almost inevitably improved what was a bad situation.

FEAR MOTIVATES

The reason most frequently given for the improvement of business behavior as a result of government activity was fear. Not surprisingly, a few interviewees objected strenuously to government involvement precisely because fear is utilized. When an improvement in public behavior is the principal goal of an action, fear can provide salutary motivation. As one company officer admitted, "Government regulation is a factor which intensifies disclosure, and the fear of apprehension which accompanies disclosure may well increase the amount of ethical behavior." Another manager spoke of a socially responsible action by his company which was motivated in part by fear of the Federal Trade Commission.

Opposition to the efficacy of fear as a motive was provided by a public relations counselor: "I don't think that government enforcement of laws or government regulations help ethics. They may increase the fear, but that doesn't help ethical behavior."[5] Interestingly, two other executives from the same company averred that government regulation improves behavior in certain industries.

The federal agency most frequently praised by interviewees was the Securities and Exchange Commission. As one veteran of Wall Street put it:

When I first ran into the SEC rules, I did not like them. I don't like any kind of regulation of my actions. However, the more familiar I became with them the more I could appreciate how worthwhile they are. They are good as long as everyone abides by them, and they also allow some flexibility.

However, even the SEC was criticized:

I'm a board member of a mutual fund. In fiduciary relationships there is usually a high standard set, but it can always be set down in greater detail. Now the SEC is investigating mutual funds. Spurred by the threat of investigation, the mutual funds are spelling out their obligations at ever greater length. I'm not sure that this is a good idea.

[5] The meaning which this speaker attaches to ethics is probably different from that which I am using.

Taxation is one activity of government which American businessmen seldom praise. "Since spending by government is unproductive, taxation is a diversion of resources from the hands of business and consumers, who can use them productively, into the hands of government, which cannot."[6] This view of taxes, with its curious concept of productivity, represents the outlook of a sizable segment of United States businessmen. It was predictable that none of our respondents would have a kind word for the Internal Revenue Service. Indeed, judging by the expletives used by businessmen in talking about taxation, the IRS should be renamed the Infernal Revenue Service. Taxation was said to promote unethical behavior in numerous ways, especially by rewarding dishonesty. For example, the president of a small sales agency exploded:

> Take income tax regulations, for instance. Every year the adjuster automatically cuts our expenses heavily. He assumes that we are guilty of cheating on our expense claims. . . . Conduct like that certainly leads to unethical behavior. We now increase our expense figures because we know about how much the adjuster will cut us back, but that's a heck of a way for the government to force us to act.

DIVIDED OPINION

The division of opinion between those who think that government activity helps business ethics, and those who think it harms, was reflected by two interviewees. Each cited both a harmful and helpful effect. The officer of several companies dealing in securities and the grain market said:

> The government's regulations have certainly helped: They discourage gambling and regulate selling and advertising when these tend to excesses. But the government's regulation of the grain business is entirely different; it's not helpful because it's poor economics. I'm talking about government edicts like the soil bank and the huge surpluses of grain stored around the country. These edicts may even encourage unethical practices. Sure, our company made money because of these government edicts; nevertheless I'm against them in the grain business.

The other interviewee, who manages an engineering department in a giant company, revealed how carelessness by some government employees made possible an overpriced contract, but the attempted injustice was thwarted by government auditors.

[6] Sutton *et al., op. cit.,* p. 196.

In Chapter 13, we saw that managers of transportation and public utilities companies said that their industries are relatively free of unethical practices. Did men in these industries credit government regulation with bringing this about? Yes, in part. One manager said: "Electrical utilities are ethical because we have large units, are subject to regulation and legislative inspection, and so, due to competitive problems, have discovered the necessity of being strictly honest and fair." More typical were the ambivalent views of two transportation executives:

Government regulation is necessary to keep balance, to keep reins on the money-hungry. But the government can be unfair. The ICC is certainly unfair to water-carriers by favoring railroads.

In my business we take ethics for granted and abide by them. Of course, we have a great deal of government control which makes this attitude necessary. . . . Some "fly-by-night" companies operate non-scheduled flights and do very well on performance and profits; we cannot do much about them until the government changes their rules.

Several railroad executives think a reduction of government control would help their industry:

I feel it is morally wrong to subsidize railroads, but it is not wrong to reduce taxes.

Everybody starts to look for loopholes once a law has been passed. The railroads were a monopoly problem once, and maybe there was good reason for the laws when they were passed. But now it would be good to get the government out of the railroad industry.

The search for legal loopholes mentioned in the last quotation is characteristic of many businessmen who regard a law as a challenge to their ability to circumvent it. A corporation counsel claimed:

Government regulation hurts. When it was decided to subsidize United States carriers, the outcome was for companies to make a deal here and to provide a rebate in some foreign bank. And the establishment of Robinson-Patman led to little but breaking of the law.[7]

One young president was quite frank: "I would regard any government regulation as a challenge."

To this laissez-faire attitude can be opposed the sentiments of an investment broker:

[7] The Robinson-Patman Act, passed in 1936, outlawed certain kinds of price discrimination in selling.

I approve of government action in connection with business. Often it is socially necessary. When businessmen blame government control for unethical business behavior, they are using the government as a scapegoat. I'm usually suspicious of men who do that sort of thing.

BUSINESSMEN FROM ABROAD THINK DIFFERENTLY

Eight foreign managers who commented on the topic were generally critical of American businessmen for refusing to admit that government has an important social role to play in the world today. These men from abroad felt that the relationship between government and business in their own land is more productive of socially responsible behavior than is the relationship between government and business in the United States. For instance, two men were shocked by American businessmen's attitudes toward government. A Canadian said: "I thought there would be more comment over the electrical industry incident, but the men I've talked to more or less thumbed their noses at the government." Similarly, a Japanese executive reported:

I was talking to an American businessman shortly after the electric industry antitrust suit. He told me that his industry and all other industries fixed prices just as the electrical manufacturing companies did, but that "we are smarter than they; they were stupid to let themselves get caught. There's nothing wrong in that; it's only laws and regulations." His words shocked me.

An English executive offered this comparison:

American business looks on government as an adversary rather than as a partner. Government is a dirty word here. But really, government needs business and vice versa. We look on government in our country as something of a nuisance, but a necessary nuisance. Government has a job to do. In the United States, radio stations want to make money and don't care what happens to children who are listening. Government should have the authority to influence what happens to the community, for example, on the radio.

Not very different was the outlook of an entrepreneur about to found a new company in Israel:

One of the norms I've set down about the operations of this company is that its activities must contribute to the welfare of the country. This condition is important, not for ethical reasons, but for selfish reasons. It happens to be the way to succeed in business in the long run.

You have to cooperate with the government. You may get into an area now where you can take advantage of government mistakes—there are enough of these—but the mistakes will be corrected in time and then where are you?

The attitude of most overseas businessmen toward government as a partner seems markedly different from the attitude of American businessmen. This difference was demonstrated in an academic discussion of France's economic planning. Professor Earl F. Cheit of the University of California said, "The Plan's objective is to bring economic power under political control."[8] Professor Gilbert M. Sauvage of France disagreed, saying that the primary purpose is "to help the businessman to expand his economic activity as a contribution to general economic development."[9]

Another example of this attitudinal difference was provided by a management consultant. He attended a meeting in Brazil at which leading businessmen agreed to work with the government in a program to expose unethical businessmen and force them to demonstrate more social responsibility. Contrast this agreement with the action of the Business Council, a group of top management representatives from the largest corporations in the United States. This group advises the President on business matters. In late 1961 the Secretary of Commerce asked the Business Council at one of its meetings to support a program for improving business ethics. The Secretary, Luther Hodges, said:

> Not a solitary soul stood up to support the proposed program or to endorse our view that the business community should get actively interested in this problem. . . . For whatever reason, our *Call for Action* got a very chilly reception from a blue ribbon panel of business leaders.[10]

One of the reasons for the hesitancy of United States businessmen to act in concert with government is the fact that various branches of the government march to different drummers. This will be illustrated in the discussion of industry codes of ethics, in the next chapter.

With international business increasing, cultural differences will cause some misunderstanding and tension. How significantly these differences will affect business behavior is not clear. The relatively

[8] Earl F. Cheit (ed.), *The Business Establishment* (New York: John Wiley & Sons, 1964), p. 181.

[9] "The French Businessman in His Milieu," in *ibid.*, p. 236.

[10] Luther H. Hodges, *The Business Conscience* (Englewood Cliffs, N.J.: Prentice-Hall, 1963), pp. 28–29.

common opinion held by foreigners about the lack of social responsibility shown by American businessmen will lead to requests for government intervention in more cases than United States executives would like. A French manager said:

Unless there is considerable government control and cooperation among free governments of the Western world, there is almost no hope for free enterprise to succeed in South America, Africa, and other undeveloped areas. The very nature of free enterprise and profits will cause mistreatment of natives, and this will naturally lead to reprisals.

It is noteworthy that strong actions by Presidents Kennedy and Johnson in dealing with price rises in major United States industries have won approval abroad.

At the outset of this chapter, it was asked, "Does the government help?" In summary, it can be answered that, historically, government regulation has helped many industries to more ethical behavior, especially to more human competition. The majority of the interviewees agreed that government intervention often helps business behavior. Nevertheless, United States businessmen generally oppose government action in this area as in most others. This is part of the American businessman's creed. Because of his low opinion of government servants, he resents their sitting in judgment on his actions.

The United States economy is performing well, as our national prosperity reveals. But the reasons why the economy is successful are complex, and the contributions of the various factors are debatable. Businessmen do not want to rock the boat lest a depression or recession set in and create problems for them. Consequently, changes in business behavior—even for ethical reasons—are feared. When these changes are championed by government, they are doubly feared. ·

A LOOK AHEAD

However, through international business and their role in achieving national objectives, large United States corporations are more and more frequently acting as instruments of national policy. One consequence is that "the position of the managers is getting closer and closer to that of the public administrators."[11] A public administrator is expected to promote the common good, and there

[11] Cheit (ed.), *op. cit.*, p. 182.

is a growing feeling that executives in corporations should strive for the same goal. As a result, these business leaders are going to be subject to more government regulations and to public demands for more responsible behavior. That some of the chief executives of large corporations are aware of this trend is evident from a 1966 *New York Times* survey. Howard Rambin, Jr., chairman of Texaco, Inc., said: "Business today is a partner of government and this cooperation is growing."[12] R. A. Peterson of the Bank of America agreed: "Business, whether it likes it or not, is a partner of government. The only operative question is whether it will choose to be a silent partner or an active partner . . . active partnership is the best route."[13] Edmund F. Martin of Republic Steel goes further: "We can function productively as businessmen only if we recognize that government and business must be partners . . . [Partners] must also both accept responsibility. To be blunt about it, we in business have not always been ready to accept ours."[14]

Some businessmen reluctantly accept the trend toward partnership between government and business as a fact of life. Other business leaders have a more positive attitude and reflect an awareness of the national need for this partnership. Men who have held positions in government and then returned to industry promote understanding between the two interest groups. So do businessmen who participate in committees advising government officials.

However, recognition of the need for cooperation comes largely from the ranks of big business, especially from companies which have contracts with the federal government. Small businessmen generally are skeptical and distrustful about direct involvement with the government. A possible outcome of these different attitudes could be alienation between large and small business, resulting in two different postures toward the social responsibilities of business.

[12] "Cooperation With Government an Aim," *New York Times*, July 3, 1966, p. 16F.

[13] *Ibid.*

[14] "Challenges of Modern Management," speech to the American Iron and Steel Institute, New York, May 25, 1966, p. 3.

Businessmen respondents, though they admitted distrust of competitors and the existence of accepted industry practices which are unethical, also indicated a desire to alter these practices and to build mutual trust. In this chapter we shall consider one way of implementing this desire, the use of codes or guidelines. These guidelines are commonly called by three different names: a code of ethical (or unethical) practices; a corporation creed; a policy statement. I shall use *code of ethics* to represent all three.

Ethical codes are not new to American industry and commerce. In 1924 Edgar L. Heermance compiled a handbook containing 133 different codes for companies or industries ranging from accounting firms to manufacturers of ice.[1] During 1933 and 1934, in accordance with the aims of the National Recovery Act, more than 500 industries adopted codes. They dealt with ethical issues like child labor, unfair competition, and restriction of production. In 1958 the American Management Association sponsored a study of 103 codes.[2] Some notion of the prevalence of such codes today may be gained from the fact that one-third of the Project Three participants work for companies possessing written codes.

Code content varies from general, brief statements to very specific and lengthy regulations. For example, here is the entire code of the Hartford Accident and Indemnity Company:

[1] Edgar L. Heermance, *Codes of Ethics: A Handbook* (Burlington, Vt.: Free Press Printing, 1924).

[2] Stewart Thompson, *Management Creeds and Philosophies* (New York: American Management Association, 1958).

The Hartford Policy—to deal fairly—to act courteously—to show a sincere desire to please at all times and under all circumstances is our creed.[3]

Here, at the other extreme, is a single sentence from the long and detailed Republic Aviation Corporation Code:

Employees are prohibited from transacting business with any individual formerly employed by this corporation who is acting in a sales or liaison capacity as an officer, employee, agent or representative of any supplier or prospective supplier—1) for a period of two years after the termination of his employment, or 2) with respect to any specific subject matter with which he was directly connected during the period of his employment.[4]

Probably the best-known code is the Four-Way Test promoted by Rotary, International. It is widely distributed on ornamental stamps and printed cards, usually in this form:

1. Is it the TRUTH?
2. Is it FAIR to all concerned?
3. Will it build GOOD WILL and BETTER FRIENDSHIPS?
4. Will it be BENEFICIAL to all concerned?

The content of guidelines for business behavior includes more than ethics; often it includes customs and etiquette, as well as exhortations to obey state and federal laws. The range of the content can be inferred from the four reasons for developing company codes given by executives in the American Management Association study:

1. To define the purpose of the company . . .
2. . . . To state the moral and ethical principles guiding its actions.
3. . . . To communicate the basic purposes and ethics of the company to all those in company ranks . . .
4. . . . To provide an over-all guide to those in decision-making positions so that they can act independently but within the framework of the firm's basic goals and principles.[5]

Codes can be composed for groups of various sizes and orientations: for a single department in a company, for the whole company, for an industry or trade association, for a professional or occu-

---

[3] *Ibid.*, p. 114.

[4] John W. Enell, "Business Ethics: A Collection of Documents Compiled by the American Management Association" (New York: American Management Association, 1962), p. 21.

[5] Thompson, *op. cit.*, p. 9.

pational group, for all businessmen in the United States or in the world. Codes for these different groups are not all equally feasible. For example, a 1961 news release concerning the Business Ethics Advisory Council of the Secretary of Commerce stated that one of the council's objectives was to design a code of ethics for business-men. However, discussions of the council's twenty-six members led to a consensus that it would be unwise to promulgate one code for *all* businessmen, and the pamphlet produced in January 1962 is titled, *A Statement on Business Ethics and a Call for Action, with Some Questions for Businessmen*.[6] In the pamphlet, the chairman of the council, William C. Decker, also chairman of the board of Corning Glass Works, writes: "To be meaningful a code of ethics must be written for an individual enterprise or particular industry."[7] The council advised President Kennedy that its future efforts "will involve working with key businessmen and association leaders in industry to encourage adoption, updating, and activation of com-pany and industry codes."[8]

RENEWED INTEREST

During the past dozen years, there has been a fresh interest in this country in codes to guide behavior. The federal government, as well as many state and city governments, has issued guidelines for some of its employees. So have many corporations and industries. For example, in 1964 the American Telephone and Telegraph Com-pany asked every employee to read and sign a nine-page pamphlet titled *Our Code of Business Conduct*. This is not the first period in our history when such action has taken place, but there has rarely been so much public support for it. Why?

One reason is the divergence in opinion over what constitutes ethical behavior in a specific situation. Because of the variety of value systems current in our pluralistic society, it is often impossible for men to achieve agreement on *principles*. It is somewhat easier to secure consensus on *practices*, or on guidelines for decisions. Decision-makers need some consensus concerning practices, and norms by which to judge whether a possible change will have good

[6] Business Ethics Advisory Council, *A Statement on Business Ethics* (Wash-ington, D.C.: Chamber of Commerce, 1962).

[7] *Ibid.*, p. 10.

[8] *Ibid.*, p. iv. The council did little to carry out this intention.

or bad social results. A code of ethical practices is a limited document, but it may be a step in the right direction.

BUSINESSMEN FAVOR CODES

Do businessmen welcome guidelines to help them make decisions in situations with an ethical dimension? To find out, and to
ascertain what kind of code they might approve, a number of questions were posed in Project Two. These queries all dealt with *industry* codes, which seem to have a greater potential for improving
business behavior than do *company* codes because of the many
temptations present in dealings between competitors and also because generally accepted practices which are unethical can rarely
be halted except by an industry-wide approach. The first question
asked was:

Recently, there has been discussion about constructing ethical codes
for business. In 1957, the AFL-CIO fashioned an Ethical Practices
Code, a measuring rod which organized labor has applied to abuses in
its ranks. How do you feel about an effort to develop a code of ethical
practices for your industry? How would you react if a group of experienced executives in your industry tried to draw up such a code?

The answer was a resounding "good idea!" Only one man in ten
opposed such an effort (Table 16.1).

Table 16.1
Would You Favor the Development of an Industry Code? (N = 1,471)

Favor strongly	50%
Favor somewhat	21
Neutral	19
Oppose somewhat	6
Oppose strongly	4

This general approval of industry-wide codes is not an isolated
phenomenon. It was corroborated by the findings of Stephen
Greyser.[9] Similarly, the Reverend John W. Clark, S.J., in a survey of

[9] Stephen A. Greyser, "Businessmen re Advertising: 'Yes, but . . .' " *Harvard
Business Review*, May–June, 1962, pp. 20ff. Further evidence of the need for a
code of ethics is given in the report of a survey of fifty-six managers in real estate
firms: Thomas P. Imse, *The Professionalization of Business Management* (New
York: Vantage Press, 1962), pp. 74–76.

West Coast businessmen, secured 86 per cent approval of the idea of introducing codes of ethical practices.[10]

Careful study of the written and interview replies which were received in Projects Two and Three indicates that doubt and some cynicism are mixed with the hope that is the prevailing note. A California manager wrote: "After 26 years in business, I think a code would be a triumph of optimism over experience." It is, after all, easy for businessmen to assent to the notion of a code; it is harder for them to live according to its contents.

I wanted to probe the reasons why managers favor or oppose an ethical code, hoping to learn whether a code could be made to work at all, and how it might operate. To find out, I posed the following hypothetical situation: "Assume, for the moment, that an ethical practices code has been drawn up for your industry by experienced executives. What do you think such a code and its reasonable enforcement would accomplish?" The opinions of businessmen about seven consequences of a code are listed in Table 16.2.

In summary, their replies indicate a striking ambivalence. They are optimistic about several consequences of an industry code; they are pessimistic about the rest, notably about the effectiveness of the code in times of severe competition or when code-breakers could avoid detection, and about the difficulty of enforcing the code.

The substantial agreement on the idea that a code would help executives to make certain decisions deserves additional discussion. Why would a code help? After all, a code is a form of restriction on business behavior. The following illustration aptly portrays why men are sometimes willing to impose restrictions on themselves. Suppose that you and your family live on a high hill, with a lovely, large back yard. The yard's only drawback is that it ends in a long, sheer drop on three sides. You have two choices: You can caution all who enter the yard about the danger of falling over the edge; consequently, no one will go within several feet of the edge, and you will often be anxious about how close you are to it. Or you can build a fence six inches from the edge, and eliminate anxiety at the same time that you gain more space for playing and gardening. Apparently there are many businessmen who are willing to fence themselves in with an ethical-practices code, provided that experienced executives in their industry have a hand in formulating it. They are willing because the fence will increase the area in which they can securely and ethically do business.

[10] *Religion and the Moral Standards of American Businessmen* (Cincinnati: South-Western Publishing Co., 1966), p. 125.

Table 16.2
What Consequences Do Businessmen Expect from Industry Codes?
(N = 1,460)

Possible Consequences of a Code	BUSINESSMEN GIVING THIS RATING TO EACH CONSEQUENCE				
	Agree	Partly Agree	Neutral	Partly Disagree	Disagree
Executives would welcome the code as useful aid when they wanted to refuse an unethical request impersonally.	59%	28%	5%	4%	4%
The code would help executives by defining clearly the limits of acceptable conduct.	48	33	7	5	7
The code would raise the ethical level of the industry.	36	35	12	7	10
People would violate the code whenever they thought they could avoid detection.	13	44	8	20	15
In situations of severe competition, the code would reduce sharp practices.	13	38	9	19	21
The code would protect inefficient firms and retard the dynamic growth of industry.	3	8	8	11	70
The code would be easy to enforce.	2	7	4	23	64

A code of ethics can help managers in several ways. For example, take situations in which it is difficult to refuse an unethical request, such as when it comes from a friend or associate. A direct refusal gives a holier-than-thou impression and may seriously jeopardize what otherwise is a pleasant interpersonal relationship. Faced with such a request, one looks for a way to refuse without offending. A specific code of ethics provides an impersonal and welcome way of refusing such a request. Of course a code can also be used (misused, really) as a screening device, to be cited when the amount of money involved is slight, to be ignored when the amount of money is large.

A code can serve as a good educational device for youthful newcomers to the business world. In view of their strong desires for business success, they can use some guidelines. As *Business Week* editorialized:

Businessmen, individually and collectively, should state their position on these ethical questions publicly and forcefully. Declarations of codes of ethics often sound hollow, but they can help guide the action of subordinates, for whom the corporation after all is responsible.[11]

This view coincides with the opinion of our respondents, recorded earlier in Table 6.1, that company policy—which includes ethical codes—is an important influence for responsible business behavior.

A code can discourage wrongdoers by making it easier to detect and punish unethical behavior. This is no small contribution. The president of Campbell Soup Company observed that business leaders "have not found a way to discourage the minority who by their actions provide the excuse for more and more government regulatory action."[12] A code might provide such a way.

Among the administrators most optimistic about a code of ethics for businessmen is John B. Shallenberger, research officer of the Comité International de l'Organisation Scientifique:

In my opinion, based on wide and intimate exposure to top managers, they are potentially a great force for good. All that is needed is a code, a delineation of parameters of performance, or a set of guidelines by which to steer one's course of management behavior, plus a general recognition by boards of directors and stockholders that managers desire to perform their duties on a high ethical plane and for the benefit of mankind. When the way is opened for free and socially accepted discussion of ethics and morals, managers will be the first to reveal deepseated desires that, in their fulfilling, would bring powerful forces to bear on the improvement of the lot of multitudes of people.

Two effective steps would go a long way toward unleashing this latent force, and I submit them as a proposal for action:

1. Codification of ethical standards of manager performance.

2. Establishment of a "Hippocratic Oath" to be administered by a suitable body of authority to all persons admitted to top management levels.[13]

Supporting this view is David Packard, president of the Hewlett-Packard Company, who wrote: "I hope we can continue to put more effort on the *why* of business, to work to develop a well-defined code of ethics for management."[14] Similarly, the editor of

[11] *Business Week*, February 18, 1961, p. 136.

[12] W. B. Murphy, quoted in *The Executive*, December 1961, p. 20.

[13] Mr. Shallenberger's views were stated in a personal letter to me dated February 23, 1961.

[14] "A Management Code of Ethics," *Supervisory Management*, June 1958, p. 33.

the *Bankers Monthly Magazine* writes of "the high desirability of formulating at the national level a Code of Ethics for Banking."[15]

SOME OBJECTIONS

What about opposition to industry codes? Some of it is rooted in the belief that "you can't legislate virtue." This objection confuses what is internal to man with what is external. No one believes that written rules change a man's heart. However, a written code may be desirable because it can make it easier for good men to conform their external behavior to their internal ideals. Written codes and laws are the ways that civilized societies have always employed to implement the will of the members of the society and to educate the young.

Another objection was urged in these terms: A code reduces the standards of some businessmen because the code becomes the maximum as well as the minimum for everybody in the industry. This objection supposes that, after the introduction of a code, a manager with high standards will lower them until they correspond to the minimum required by the code. If a manager would react in this way, it would suggest that his prior high standards were due less to personal conviction than to misunderstanding of company policy or industry practice.

Some contend that if a code is written, men will act on the assumption that whatever is not forbidden is permitted, with a resultant reduction in ethical practice. It seems more likely that businessmen with such an attitude will follow the same assumption whether there is a written code or not. For such men, more rules would be better than fewer.

A further objection was that many unethical actions are already prohibited by law, and there is little point in repeating the prohibition. Perhaps an apt reply is that it is good to wage this kind of battle on many fronts in order to assure success.

ACCENTUATE THE POSITIVE

A strong argument in favor of wording code contents positively is made by Professor Robert W. Austin, who also favors internal

[15] J. H. Peters, "Needed: A Written Code," *Bankers Monthly Magazine*, October 15, 1961, p. 2.

development of any code, i.e., it should be constructed by men who are experienced in the problem areas covered.[16] Austin believes that codes which emphasize "Thou shalt not" arouse public suspicion of the company or industry to which the code applies. He also says: "I am convinced that in this or any other area of conduct 'Thou shalt not's' imposed from above do not enlist support."[17] No doubt wording a regulation in a positive way is usually desirable, but any regulation involves restraint, however it be worded. A good code, which may be described as one in which restraint in one matter is accepted for the sake of freedom in another, will be observed by responsible businessmen precisely because of its wise realism. Its wording is subordinate in importance to its content. Perhaps the phrasing, "We will not," is a suitable compromise.

All these things are what a code *can* do. But will a code actually work? As noted in Table 16.2 our respondents have mixed feelings on this subject. Some observers, including representatives of the federal government, point to the inadequacy of the code of the General Electric Company in its price collusion difficulties as evidence to the contrary. Others recall the failure of the industry codes composed as a result of the National Recovery Act. Those codes were designed by the larger firms, which in some instances used them to protect monopoly positions. Whether a different outcome can be expected from codes today is disputed.

A major reason for pessimism about codes is the difficulty of effective enforcement. Our respondents saw enforcement as a big problem, and backed up their view with comments like "I would not think an enforcement agency is feasible," and "A code is impossible to police." In order to discover the most acceptable form of enforcement, I posed the following question: "Assume that an ethical practices code has been drawn up for your industry. Which of the following groups would you choose to enforce the code?" The results are shown in Table 16.3.

These statistics were substantiated by the Greyser survey which asked the same question.[18]

In view of the fact that the question concerned *industry* codes, it is noteworthy that two of every five respondents favored *company*

[16] "Code of Conduct for Executives," *Harvard Business Review*, September–October 1961, pp. 53ff.

[17] *Ibid.*, p. 59. To refute Austin's view, one might advert to 3,000 years of respect and sometime observance of the Ten Commandments.

[18] Greyser, *op. cit.*, p. 46.

Table 16.3
Who Would Businessmen Like to See Enforce a Code? (N = 1,469)

Management of each company, i.e., self-enforcement	40%
Group of executives selected from various companies	28
Group composed of executives from the industry, plus other members of the community	28
Government agency	4

self-enforcement.[19] As we saw in prior chapters, top management is often successful in promoting responsible intracompany behavior. Because of their proximity to other employees, executives have many opportunities for personal intramural influence.

When discussing industry behavior, however, there is reason for thinking company self-regulation inadequate. This probably explains why 60 per cent of our respondents preferred some form of regulation external to the company. Given the primacy of competition in our economic system, and acknowledging the degrading influence of some kinds of intercompany competition (as we saw in Chapter 13), it seems preferable for enforcement to come largely from outside the individual company. It is not that self-enforcement cannot work; but it has not been notably effective in solving industry problems in the past.

Between the extremes of company self-regulation and government enforcement (which is anathema, as we shall shortly see) is regulation by an industry or trade association. Some observers think that the community, because it is made up of consumers, also deserves a voice in many business issues with an ethical dimension.

As regards enforcement by a trade association or other industry-wide group, the history of antitrust cases indicates that such an approach allows the dominant firms to impose restrictions on smaller ones. This opportunity, sometimes exercised, tends to limit competitive activity under the guise of code enforcement.

Industry enforcement is not a panacea. Consider the "Standards of Practice" of the American Association of Advertising Agencies.

[19] Government agencies prefer company codes to industry codes because they fear that the latter might disguise anticompetitive behavior on the part of dominant firms.

A sizable number of our respondents identified dishonest advertising as the one unethical practice they would most like to see eliminated from their industry. This they did despite the existence of the broad standards of the AAAA opposing unethical practices. Consequently, one can hardly escape the conclusion that the Committee for Improvement of Advertising Content is not enforcing the Standards of Practice as rigorously as our respondents would like.

One flaw in the AAAA code is that all regulation takes place *after* an advertisement has done its work. This means, in effect, that one can get around the code. If, as the businessmen in our survey indicated, most people would violate a code when given the chance, then it is logical to conclude that spelling out in advance what the committee regards as wrong would be more effective as preventive regulation than general statements like "misleading exaggerations" and "misleading price claims." After years of operation and hundreds of decisions, the AAAA Committee ought to be able to formulate more detailed directives than the two just quoted, directives which will make it more difficult for corner-cutters to plead that they did not intend to mislead consumers.

In Stephen Greyser's thorough study of businessmen's views about advertising's role and performance, television received 57 per cent of the votes as the communication medium which has the most objectionable ads. What, then, is one to think about the *Interpretation of the AAAA Copy Code with respect to Television Commercials*, which begins: "The advertising agency should not recommend, and should discourage any advertiser from using, any advertising of an . . . objectionable character."[20] Dissatisfaction with enforcement of the television code was also evidenced during a class session at the Harvard Business School. Eighteen typical television commercials were shown to a group of fifty students. The majority of the students—hardly enemies of advertising—called most of the commercials misleading or in poor taste.

The AAAA problem is presented here not because it is unique or egregious, but simply because it aptly exemplifies the flaw in many existing codes: the failure to specify the practices industry members regard as unethical, and the absence of "teeth" to put these statements into effect.

[20] American Association of Advertising Agencies, *Interpretation of the AAAA Copy Code with Respect to Television Commercials* (New York: AAAA, April 21, 1960), p. 1.

WHAT THE AMERICAN
PSYCHOLOGICAL ASSOCIATION DID

How can the detailed norms needed for an effective code be formulated? The achievements of the American Psychological Association in formulating its *Ethical Standards of Psychologists* is a good model. The APA used an empirical approach, gathering data about the problems confronting psychologists. Members of the APA were asked to "describe a situation they knew of firsthand, in which a psychologist made a decision having ethical implications, and to indicate what the correspondents perceived as being the ethical issues involved."[21]

These descriptions were examined to discover patterns in the problems and thereby to provide a plan for organizing the information supplied. After the descriptions were categorized into six ethical areas, they were analyzed to obtain a number of specific problems in each of the six. Following this analysis, six committees were appointed, each concentrating on the problems of a single area. After much discussion and thoughtful study, these committees hammered out the code. With adaptation to its own circumstances, any industry could produce its own code in the same way.

There remains the question: Should the difficulties of enforcement or the likelihood of limited success deter efforts to construct industry codes? This answer can come only from top management which, as Adolf A. Berle, Jr., wrote, "has substantially absolute power. Thus the only real control which guides or limits [corporations'] economic and social action is the real, though undefined and tacit, philosophy of the men who compose them."[22]

KEEP GOVERNMENT OUT

One thing is clear from the data: Businessmen want to keep government out of code enforcement. Only 4 per cent in my survey and in Greyser's favored a government agency as code enforcer. This calls to mind the anti-government aspect of the businessman's creed which we examined in Chapter 15. Some respondents prob-

---

[21] American Psychological Association, *Ethical Standards of Psychologists* (Washington, D.C.: American Psychological Association, 1953), p. vi.

[22] *20th Century Capitalist Revolution* (New York: Harcourt, Brace & World, 1954), p. 180.

ably recalled the failure of the federal government to achieve worthwhile results through NRA-inspired industry codes in the 1930s. Business history reveals other, more dramatic, examples of unsuccessful attempts by government to enforce a code.[23] U.S. government officials, however, discount historical reasons as a major influence on business opposition to government involvement in codes.

Public officials experienced in reviewing codes adopted by trade associations think that businessmen tend to identify as unethical some practices which are merely competitive. These representatives of the federal government cite price advertising, the extension of credit terms, and the offering of discounts as matters which are frequently called unethical in industry codes, when in fact they serve as effective competitive weapons. Of course, these officials feel that the antitrust laws dealing with competition have an adequate, implicit standard of ethics, in the form of the "rule of reason." This rule of reason is supposed to buttress industry attempts to eliminate unethical practices. But corporate lawyers are leery of the rule of reason, are reluctant to advise top management to take any joint action lest the company's interpretation of what is reasonable not coincide with the government agency's interpretation. A corporate mistake in a judgment of this kind can be costly in both money and public opinion.

The disagreement between businessmen and government representatives about codes is rooted in the different goals of the two groups. Government agents are not much interested in the success of any one company. Neither do they regard industry stability as an important value in our free enterprise system. Instead they value, and try to promote, an atmosphere in which any budding entrepreneur has the opportunity to enter a market and compete. One way in which they promote this atmosphere is by prosecuting certain practices of established firms as illegal, although businessmen regard them as legal and ethical.

One point upon which the two groups agree is that it is the role

[23] A shocking instance of governmental ineptitude in attempting to enforce business codes was displayed in seventeenth century France. The rules for the French textile industry covered 2,200 pages and were intended to protect the interests of the established textile producers. When efforts were made to produce, import, or use printed calicoes, the government responded with incredible force. On one occasion in Valence, seventy-seven persons were hanged and fifty-eight more broken on the wheel. Cf. Eli F. Heckscher, *Mercantilism*, rev. ed., ed. E. F. Soderlund (New York: Macmillan, 1955), Vol. I, pp. 157–173.

of government to enforce law but not ethics. Both sides recognize that positive law is not always adequate and government resources not always sufficient to cope with all forms of business misbehavior. Some government agencies encourage voluntary, complementary programs to upgrade business practice, but always on condition that there be a prior understanding about the content and extent of the activities being proscribed. The doors of federal enforcement agencies are open to dialogues with trade associations and individual firms about cooperative programs, including codes. The Department of Justice has a "Business Review Procedure," under which businessmen can propose plans of action for the department's approval. Businessmen, however, bridle at the notion of asking government permission to act. Similarly, the Federal Trade Commission offers "advisory opinions" on proposed business conduct, as well as conducting trade practice conferences for certain industries.

SELF-REGULATION OR COLLUSION?

A code of ethical practices constructed and enforced by members of the industry is a form of voluntary self-regulation. So is collusion. How distinguish one from the other? This is a persistent problem of government agencies, as the following examples reveal.

A decade ago in Philadelphia, a group of broadcasting stations agreed to what seems a desirable practice, namely, to charge in fact what each station's published rate card said it would charge. The Justice Department instituted a lawsuit which ended in a consent decree restraining the stations from continuing this practice.[24] Apparently the Justice Department regarded the practice as price fixing.

In 1966 the Federal Trade Commission turned down the proposal of a group of businessmen and trade association representatives, who hoped to establish a review board to improve advertising practices in their community.[25] The FTC's advisory opinion safeguarded the individual's right to advertise and implied that a private

[24] Arthur Hull Hayes, "Codes of Ethics in Business," in *The Concept of Business Ethics*, ed. Daniel N. DeLucca (Philadelphia: Council on Business Ethics, St. Joseph's College, 1964), p. 34.

[25] Federal Trade Commission News Release, Advisory Opinion Digest No. 59, June 17, 1966.

group could not be trusted with the power to enforce advertising standards.

These two cases illustrate the role of the FTC and the Anti-Trust Division of the Justice Department as defenders of the business firm's right to compete. Their actions sometimes complicate the task of improving business ethics because, as Chapter 13 indicated, competition is at times a cause of unethical behavior in business. Businessmen say that they would like to improve industry practice (see Table 4.3), and that such improvement should take place on an industry-by-industry basis (see Chapter 13). But many businessmen are afraid to take action in their own industry. Mr. Theodore Thau, Assistant Secretary of Commerce, describes their fear in these words: "We don't dare do anything in the way of establishing industry codes that have any enforcement teeth in them; and without enforcement teeth they're meaningless in our industry. . . . We run the risk that the Federal Trade Commission or the Anti-Trust Division of the Department of Justice may get after us. . . ."[26] However, a government spokesman insisted that not all "enforcement teeth" are held in disfavor by his agency, which wants merely to be sure that the teeth are no sharper than is necessary to insure compliance with the code. Substantiating this assertion was the FTC's approval in May, 1967 of a self-policing code for subscription salesmen of four major magazines. Included in the approval was the power to fine members up to $5,000 for each violation of the code.[27]

Thau learned from government officials that what they regard as the necessary lifeblood of competition for newcomers in some industries is termed unethical by established members of those industries. By government norms, some trade association codes are devices to restrain trade. Thau observes that government's approach is interpreted by businessmen to mean that they may compete unethically until a specific action has been forbidden by positive law.

If Thau's analysis is correct, if the actions of government agencies encourage businessmen to think that under our laws they have a right to compete unethically until the law forbids it, something is wrong. Government agencies are useful public servants, but they should not be taking on tasks for which smaller, private groups are suited. What has happened to the idea that problems

---

[26] "The Business of Government and the Government of Business," in *The Concept of Business Ethics*, pp. 114–115.

[27] *Business Week*, June 3, 1967, p. 104.

should be solved as close to their origin as possible, and by the people most directly concerned? Do we want the actions of government agencies to foster the notion that businessmen should not be concerned with ethics, but only with positive law?

NATIONAL ASSOCIATION OF SECURITY DEALERS AND THE BETTER BUSINESS BUREAUS

There is in existence one group of businessmen with the right to regulate members cooperatively, at their own expense, for the public interest. This is the National Association of Security Dealers, to whom Congress granted a preferential antitrust exemption. There are 4,000 firms with membership in the NASD, and more than 80,000 registered representatives. The NASD regulates over-the-counter security transactions, i.e., those which do not take place on a stock exchange, and regularly exercises its power to expel, suspend, or fine members. So salutary has its influence been that it has been suggested by Reverend Benjamin Masse, S.J., as a model for other industries.[28]

Another private organization which has helped business to improve its behavior is the Association of Better Business Bureaus. The goal of BBB is to curb fraudulent and unethical practices in advertising and in selling. Besides working directly with companies which it suspects of false marketing or advertising, BBB also has a working relationship with communications media. When a company is guilty of false advertising, BBB presents the facts to newspaper, radio, and television officials, sometimes adding the opinion that the advertising is not in the public interest, and a recommendation that action of some kind be taken.

Both the NASD and BBB work closely with government agencies: the former with the Securities and Exchange Commission; the latter with the Federal Trade Commission. The existence and success of the NASD and BBB prove that government is willing, under certain conditions, to permit businessmen to construct and administer their own codes of ethics. It would be helpful if government agencies would agree among themselves to spell out what these conditions are, especially in the matter of code enforcement teeth. It would also be a step in the right direction if businessmen would be less suspicious of these agencies, better informed

[28] "NASD: Model for TV and Radio?" *America*, February 6, 1960, pp. 552–555.

about their practices and viewpoints, and more willing to submit industry codes for prior approval. There should be more cooperation between business and government in this matter of industry codes since both groups desire the same goal, an optimum of ethical competition.

ABOUT COMPANY CODES

Acknowledging the favorable opinion of codes held by Project Two respondents, it was decided to probe the matter in Project Three interviews. So they were asked: "Does your company have a formal or written code of ethics for the guidance of employees?" Thirty-two per cent answered affirmatively; these 32 were asked two more questions: (1) "Would you please describe very briefly the code; for example, does it cover all activities of all employees, or just some of them?" (2) "As far as you know, what has been the effect and influence of this code on employees' behavior?"

While the earlier written questions were aimed at *industry* codes, the interview questions focused on *company* codes. Why the switch? For two reasons: Most extant codes are companywide, and most managers know more about their company's code than about their industry's.

Descriptions of the codes reveal that they vary from generalizations apparently intended to impress stockholders ("like a pledge of allegiance," commented one executive) to detailed regulations about a host of activities. For instance, the board chairman of a giant corporation said:

We do have instructions for our purchasing department. And the top 400 executives have to sign a sworn statement concerning conflicts of interest, accepting gifts, and making special personal deals. We require this statement of the most vulnerable men in the company. These codes have proven salutary. On gifts we are pretty strict. We say that none are to be accepted. But if a man gets something worth less than ten dollars, the cost and trouble of reshipping will usually cost more than that, so we advise him to keep it and write a letter to the sender saying that he should cut out the gift-giving. If this doesn't work, we send a stronger letter saying that if it happens again, we will stop buying from the company.

Inability of a respondent to describe the company code—"We put a general code in our company newspaper once . . ."—probably indicated that it has little relevance for that man and, presumably, for his subordinates. This is not rare, if our interviewees were representative.

Attempting to judge the effect and influence of the code on employees' behavior, respondents were about equally divided; half affirmed that there have been good results in their company, and the other half were doubtful. Typical responses of the latter group were: "I'm in no position to judge," and "The code is too new for a valid judgment."

Men who affirmed that their experience with company codes has been satisfactory were realistic in their comments:

For our purchasing department, the code has a good effect because no one does better than the next guy.

When something is put in black and white, this is a lot different than mere talk from top management. A written code makes middle management less vulnerable.

A public relations consultant had an observation about a client's code:

We have helped a company which has an excellent code. And they really mean it. I went out interviewing their workers in the mines and I remember one worker told me: "No, the code doesn't work all the time. Management goofs or somebody gets away with something. But one thing I'll say, if you call it to your boss's attention that the code isn't being followed, everything grinds to a halt while management investigates the situation and sees what's going on."

At the conclusion of James M. Davis's research on "Codes of Ethics in Selected Business Associations in 1924 and 1963," he states:

A code of ethics should avoid the use of generalities, be derived empirically from the members of the association, and be enforced by committee action. If this procedure were pursued, the codes of ethics could provide useful guides to decision making and aid in the use of practical problem solving in the business situation.[29]

My research agrees with his finding. A code must provide rules of thumb close to the real business situation, and as specific as common sense permits. But it must not be overelaborated or descend to trifling details. Nor should it hope to offer a permanent solution

[29] Abstract of Educational Research Study (Graduate School, University of Tennessee, August 13, 1963).

to the ethical problems of business because the institutions and expectations of business change.

Every code must find reinforcement in the reason and conscience of the individuals whose conduct the code regulates. A written code can never be a substitute for individual integrity and character. It can only shed light on the businessman's decisions, not make them for him. Nevertheless, I share the respondents' strong support of reasonable ethical codes, which can be useful in strengthening the weak, identifying wrongdoers, educating the young, and keeping competition within reasonable limits.

At the very least, the discussions which precede the formulation of a code help men to clarify their thinking about the importance of responsible behavior, and about the proper role of profits and government in our society. Drawing up a code is an educational experience. Enforcing a code is more difficult, but it is necessary for really satisfactory results. The opposition to codes, including that of government agencies, can be overcome if the top management of leading companies in an industry want to do so.

17   What Does Education Accomplish?

To improve business ethics is a goal agreeable to businessmen and to those who do business with them. Education is an obvious means for achieving this goal.[1] But the relationship between the means and the goal is complex. Part of the complexity is semantic. "To improve business ethics" can mean two things: improving the behavior of businessmen, and increasing the body of knowledge about the rightness and wrongness of this behavior. In some circumstances, there seems to be a reciprocal relationship between increasing knowledge and improving behavior. But knowledge is not virtue, nor does it necessarily lead to virtuous behavior, as the lives of well-educated thieves prove.

Businessmen are decision-makers. To make a decision requires that there be something about which to decide. This something is provided by knowledge, but knowledge is not the only ingredient in the decision. The businessman's value system is another ingredient, which he applies to the facts and other relevant knowledge. What he decides depends on his values.

It is evident that knowledge can be taught; how values are acquired is less evident. One value which all men share is a built-in conviction that good is to be done and evil avoided, but individuals differ in the intensity with which they hold this conviction. Not all men have the same hierarchy of values. The difference stems from

[1] Two sources which I found useful in preparing this chapter were *Teaching and Morality* by Francis C. Wade, S.J. (Chicago: Loyola University Press, 1963); and "The Social and the Moral Sciences," by Herbert Johnston, reprinted from the *Catholic Educational Review*, October, November, December, 1957.

their education, both informal and formal. Educators disagree, in theory and in practice, about their responsibility for impressing students with the value of ethical behavior. Many educators are skeptical about the influence of formal education on value formation, though they concede that information and skills relevant to ethical decision-making can be imparted in the classroom.[2]

Aware of some of the difficulties and differences of opinion which complicate the relationship of education and business ethics, let us look at relevant data from my survey and from three other research projects.

WHAT OUR DATA REVEAL

In Chapter 8 we noted that a teacher had been the most important ethical influence on one in every twelve of our Project Three participants. This influence was personal, more the result of good example and inspiration than of knowledge handed on from teacher to pupil. Most of the teachers mentioned taught in elementary and high schools, during the years when students are most impressionable.

Of the respondents in Project Two, 35 per cent had taken a formal course in ethics or moral philosophy in college. The replies of these 514 managers to nine selected questions (cf. Appendix D) did not differ in any meaningful or consistent way from those of respondents who had not taken a course in college. This probably indicates that the courses had little influence on students' attitudes. There are several reasons why this similarity of response is not surprising. One reason is that the nine selected questions were not so complex as to require special training in ethics for a solution. A more important reason is the isolated manner in which ethics has usually been taught in colleges, with much emphasis on theory and abstract principles, and little attention to specific, concrete problems which involve the student.

[2] For example, cf. Andrew M. Greeley and Peter H. Rossi, *The Education of Catholic Americans* (Chicago: Aldine, 1966), p. 114. Lawyer-sociologist Jerome Carlin says: "Commitment to certain norms and values undoubtedly plays a role, and an important one, in the regulation of professional conduct. It is by no means certain, however, that such commitment can be instilled during professional training; indeed, data presented here and in other studies indicate that this is most unlikely" [*Lawyers' Ethics* (New York: Russell Sage Foundation, 1966), p. 6].

Did the amount of formal education of Project Two participants influence their replies? Very little. Employing the same nine questions used in analyzing other variables, I discovered no significant differences in the replies of businessmen who had attended college, regardless of the length of their attendance. Those who were in college for a year or two gave substantially the same answers as those who had attended graduate school. There was, however, a difference between those who had attended college and those whose education ended at high school. The replies of the less educated were more ethical in the questions dealing with expense account padding, using confidential information for private gain, hiring competitors' employees, and using status-symbol advertising. However, managers not educated beyond high school, who constituted only 5 per cent of our sample, were older men for the most part, more than half being over fifty. The more ethical answers of these men appear to be related to their age—Table 9.1 showed that the replies of respondents over fifty were more ethical than those of younger men—as well as to their education.

Even in a question which seems to be related closely to a person's knowledge, education made no difference. The question asked for agreement or disagreement with the statement, "It is more difficult to know what is right than it is to do it." The answers are presented in Table 17.1.

Table 17.1
More Difficult to Know Right than to Do It (N = 1,450)

Amount of Formal Education	Agree with Statement
High school	42%
Some college	40
College degree	45
Graduate school	42
Had taken course in ethics	45
Had not taken course in ethics	42

Replies to another question shed light obliquely on the value of college courses in ethics. The question was: "How often do you, as an executive, find yourself in the following situation: 'I had to make a decision so quickly that there was no time to consider its ethical implications.' " The similarity of replies, as listed in Table 17.2, indicates that taking an ethics course did not change the men's

Table 17.2
Impact of Ethics Course (N = 1,479)

How Often No Time for Ethics	Had Ethics Course	Had No Ethics Course
Never	23%	22%
Rarely	55	57
Occasionally	20	18
Regularly	1	2
Very frequently	1	1

attitude toward the importance of ethical problems. (Would one-fifth of these managers "occasionally" or "regularly" not take the time to consider the *financial* implications of a decision?)

In Project Two, neither a college course in ethics nor the amount of formal education made a significant difference in businessmen's replies. In a study of 103 managers, the Reverend John W. Clark, S.J., gathered data which indirectly support mine; his respondents think formal education is not a strong influence on ethical business behavior. He asked the participants to rank six factors "according to their importance in influencing ethical conduct in business generally."[3] "School and university training" was ranked *last*, following family training, conduct of superiors and peers, religious training, and industry practices.[4]

Data gathered during Project Three are more favorable to education as a help to businessmen. The data came from the interviewers, who, after all interviews were completed, named the twenty men with whom they would most like to be associated, insofar as business ethics is concerned. Of these twenty, 42 per cent had taken a course in ethics; of the other eighty men, only 22 per cent had taken a course. The interviewers also evaluated each manager, immediately after leaving him, on three items (Table 17.3): sensitivity to ethical issues; quality of thinking and reasoning; expression of ideas. In each instance, managers who had taken a course in ethics scored better than those who had not. Similarly, men with a college degree scored better on these three items than men who did not attend or complete college. These results suggest that a college education, and especially a course in ethics, improves a person's

[3] John W. Clark, S.J., *Religion and the Moral Standards of American Businessmen* (Cincinnati: South-Western Publishing Co., 1966), p. 190.

[4] *Ibid.*, p. 118.

Table 17.3
Education and Ethical Awareness **(N = 100)**

	Completed College	Did Not Complete College	Had Ethics Course	Had No Ethics Course
Sensitivity to ethical issues	3.0[a]	3.5	2.4	3.4
Quality of thinking about ethics	3.2	4.2	2.8	3.7
Expression of ideas	2.8	3.6	2.6	3.2

[a] The number used is a weighted arithmetic mean of the evaluations, which were made according to a 7-point scale, with 1 = excellent and 7 = very poor.

sensitivity to ethical problems, as well as his ability to think and speak about them. There is no implication that this improvement is related to acting more, or less, ethically.

Executive development programs have had an ethical impact on some participants. These programs, usually sponsored by universities and lasting from two to sixteen weeks, are attended by thousands of businessmen every year. Professor Kenneth Andrews, in his definitive study of 6,000 graduates of thirty-nine executive development programs, reports that 13 per cent of all responses in his survey referred to the programs' ethical impact.[5] There were wide variations in the influence of the programs; two had none of their graduates acknowledging ethical insights or growth, while one program had one-third of its graduates making such acknowledgments. According to Andrews, the principal reasons why some programs have a greater ethical impact than others are that they include ethical issues in the curriculum; provide the opportunity to discuss these issues, usually through cases; have vital and capable teachers; and are programs of longer duration.

The data from the Clark and Andrews surveys, as well as my own, hardly add up to an endorsement of formal education as the solution to the problem of business ethics. Since businessmen constitute the group most interested in the products of business education, let us now consider their thinking about the role of education in preparing young men to make ethical decisions.

[5] *The Effectiveness of University Management Development Programs* (Boston: Division of Research, Graduate School of Business Administration, Harvard University, 1966), p. 181.

BUSINESSMEN ARE CONCERNED

Business leaders have been much concerned of late about the decline of interest in business careers among talented collegians. Surveys of Harvard's senior classes, for example, showed that 39 per cent of the 1960 graduates planned a business career, whereas only 14 per cent of the class of 1965 planned such a career.[6] Philip Sporn, an executive of the American Electric Power Company, offered one reason for this decline:

> There is an important relationship between the inability of business to attract the most able students in adequate numbers and the widespread misunderstanding and even ignorance regarding the moral and intellectual climate in business . . . the judgment of some of our best young talent is affected by a sense of distrust of business as a way of life, particularly as it may not permit a concordance between the ethical standards of business and the ethics of living.[7]

Many businessmen feel that if this misunderstanding and ignorance were corrected, their recruiting problem would be simplified.

What do businessmen expect education to do? What do they want the student who joins their ranks to know and to believe about business ethics? The answer, and it is a complicating factor, is that businessmen do not speak with a single voice. Here, for example, are the views of two managers with different ideas about the goal of education:

> I would never send my son to that school. They are more interested in teaching ethics than in how to make a buck.

> I think that the business school from which I graduated is doing the world a disservice. In the classes you get the impression that it is all right to do illegal things, and wheeling and dealing is approved. Everybody wants to become a millionaire.

When businessmen envision the college graduate, what are their expectations about his knowledge and practice of business ethics? Fundamentally, they seem to want a person who makes decisions

[6] See Roger Ricklefs, "Scorning Business: More College Students Shun Corporate Jobs," *Wall Street Journal*, November 10, 1964, p. 1; Peter F. Drucker, "Is Business Letting Young People Down?" *Harvard Business Review*, November–December 1965, pp. 49–55; John S. Fielden, "The Right Young People for Business," March–April 1966, pp. 76–83.

[7] *Educating Tomorrow's Managers*, Committee for Economic Development, Policy Statement, October 1964, p. 41.

which satisfy the community, the opinion-makers, the communications media, and government representatives. In short, businessmen want pragmatic results. They want recruits who will not harm the image of business. Of course, most realize that this implies men who will know what is right, and will do it. But businessmen seem more interested in being thought well of than in being ethical. For many of them, being ethical means being regarded as ethical.

A CERTAIN AMBIVALENCE

Enthusiasm among businessmen for education in business ethics is more often for their colleagues and subordinates than for themselves. Those who attend meetings on business ethics are usually sent by their boss. A principal reason for reluctance to attend seems to be management's difficulty in linking ethical behavior with corporate profits or with improved personal effectiveness. In the revealing comment of one manager: "I should spend $150 to attend a series of meetings whose probable outcome is that I'll find out that some of the ways we are making money are unethical?" Sponsors of such meetings have learned not to use the word *ethics* in the title or in promotional literature. It is better to speak of *social responsibility* or *human challenges*. As Professor Michael Fogarty put it, "Ethics, unlike the rose, smells sweeter by almost any other name."[8]

Those managers who are eager for self-improvement in ethics typically are seeking some rules and tools for making decisions, and a problem-solving approach. Unfortunately, ethics is not the same kind of subject as marketing and production. It cannot be quantified, and is more abstract and complex than the regular business subjects, like accounting and finance. Consequently, it cannot be mastered quickly. A person must invest considerable time and mental energy before he reaches the level where he can appreciate the principles and problem-solving approach which he seeks.

Recently some businessmen have called for a course in business ethics to be taught in schools of business administration.[9] Perhaps one in every five business schools now offers such a course. This request prompts some reflection on the attitude and assumptions of

[8] "Wider Business Objectives," *Planning*, May 1966, p. 57.

[9] Besides speeches by business leaders, cf. Clark, *op. cit.*, p. 125, where 89 per cent of his respondents favored introduction of "courses in Business Ethics in business schools."

businessmen about collegiate education. Their feelings toward faculty members are mixed, often related to the subject taught and to a stereotype of the kind of person interested in teaching that subject. For example, philosophers and theologians, the men usually best equipped by training to deal with ethics, are regarded as fuzzy thinkers, persons who do not deal with hard facts, who probably could not succeed in the competitive world of business. Few managers make a distinction between a clergyman and a theologian, though the difference is of the same magnitude as that between a general practitioner of medicine and a specialist in internal medicine. In addition, many businessmen doubt that philosophers and theologians are really professional scholars.

Teachers of business subjects, though objects of the antipathy of businessmen toward men who have "never met a payroll," gain acceptance individually because businessmen value their advice. Many business school faculty members are consultants to industry, and some are on corporate boards of directors.

Despite a general lack of high regard for college teachers, businessmen have an optimistic faith in education. Knowledge is assumed to be a panacea. Many businessmen apparently believe that if a university decides to add a course in business ethics to its curriculum, a good teacher will be available to handle it, and that if a course in business ethics is offered, many students will take it. Replies in the Ruder study of business schools indicate that these two beliefs are seldom verified.[10] Several business schools do not offer a course in business ethics because they have been unable to find a qualified teacher. Five other schools dropped the course because of lack of student interest. Indeed, while it may be true that today's collegians have high ideals, attendance in college ethics courses is neither a manifestation nor a cause of these ideals.

Apparently businessmen have high expectations about the impact of a college-level ethics course on students. They should recall that for any learning to take place, the proper attitude is required.

[10] In 1962 William Ruder, Assistant Secretary of Commerce, sent a questionnaire to the deans of the 104 member schools of the American Association of Collegiate Schools of Business. Ruder's action was a follow-up of the activities of the Business Ethics Advisory Council. The questionnaire had ten parts and 33 questions, all in essay form. Seventy-four deans replied, with 43 of them attempting to answer most of the questions asked. No written summary of these replies has been prepared heretofore. The information in this chapter is garnered from the deans' answers, copies of which were loaned to me through the kindness of Theodore Thau and Philip Van Vlack.

Regardless of the subject, it is necessary that the student place a high value on learning it, else he will not be motivated sufficiently to study. As was said earlier, however, knowing what is good is not the same as doing good. If a man is to act ethically, he must place a premium on doing good. This conviction seems usually to be acquired in childhood, rarely later. So, a college course whose objective is to produce students who will make ethical business decisions —which seems to be businessmen's idea of the course's objective— may be attempting more than it can possibly achieve. Its success will depend in great measure on the moral character of the students before they enter the course.

VIEWS OF BUSINESS SCHOOL DEANS

Turning from businessmen's opinions and expectations about education, let us analyze the findings of the Ruder survey of business school deans. There is a wide variation in the understanding of ethics which these men brought to the survey. There are also vast differences in their interest in the subject, and in their opinions about its place in a curriculum. Here, for example, are three negative views:

I do not believe that the concept of "Business Ethics" has any very useful meaning.

As you know, there are many minds, and bents of minds, on this subject. It happens that my own interests are not so directed, and hence there has not been, in the last fifteen years or so, any leadership in this college directed to the study or promotion of study in business ethics, as such.

No course that we could offer would teach morals to any student. This is not our function.

More optimistic about the study of ethics is the dean who reported, "We have a formalized course in business ethics in the School of Commerce which has been taught without interruption since 1907."

Every one of the 74 deans who answered Ruder's questionnaire favored the inclusion of some of the subject matter of business ethics somewhere in the curriculum. Many deans felt that their school owed it to the students to expose them to problems which they would later face: "It seems that we have a deep-seated responsibility for the development of ethical consciousness among those students whom we are training for business and industry.

Replying to a series of open-end questions, most of the deans indicated a preference about the way business ethics should be included in the curriculum. As Table 17.4 shows, more than two-

Table 17.4
Place of Business Ethics in Curriculum (N = 70 deans)

	Number
Offer course in general ethics and integrate ethics into business courses.	7
Offer course in business ethics and integrate ethics into business courses.	14
Offer no separate course, but integrate ethics into business courses.	49

thirds favor integrating the subject matter into other business courses, without offering a separate course. For a better understanding of this table, it should be noted that the middle category includes courses with a variety of names (Business Ethics, Responsibilities of Business Leadership, Social Philosophy of Business, Business and Society, etc.) and that a few schools, which offer courses with the same names as these, do not regard them as courses on business ethics. Of the twenty-one schools offering courses in general or business ethics, twelve require student attendance; the remainder offer elective courses. These courses vary in length from one to three semester-hours, and most are aimed at senior students.

Of the 30 per cent of deans who favored a separate course in ethics, two-thirds preferred that the course be in business ethics; the remaining one-third preferred a more general course in ethics, for example, from the point of view of history or of comparative ethical systems.

WHY NOT A SEPARATE COURSE?

Why are not more business school leaders in favor of a separate course in ethics? Here are some of their reasons:

The reasons for not including it stem primarily from time pressures of covering other work.

The hesitation in including a course of ethics in the curriculum is the difficulty of defining and organizing what can be taught in this field.

I am not a believer in setting up special courses to cover particular ills or problems.

Most of the deans favored the integration of ethics into other business courses because they believe that this is better pedagogy. They feel that isolating business ethics for separate consideration can result in an ineffective learning situation.

Business ethics should be considered not in a vacuum but rather treated as a part of most, if not all, business courses so that the student thinks of it as an essential factor in business operations and as a part of the value systems which underlie all decisions made by businessmen.

Several deans mentioned that a major factor in the decision about how to incorporate ethics into the curriculum was the presence of a specially trained scholar on their faculty. One dean cited the ideal teacher for a separate course in ethics as "a philosopher with real management experience. Such people are rare." Another dean described the teacher qualifications for the integration of ethics in a regular business course: "For the purpose of reinforcing the importance of ethics in everyday life, the teacher who can teach techniques and strategies and at the same time debate the values which govern their use is especially good."

Having seen a cross-section of the deans' views, let us now take a critical look at them. While doing so, it will be good to keep in mind that decisions about curriculum are rarely made by the dean alone; in most schools, the faculty makes these decisions; in some schools, the dean has veto power.

A phrase that appears in a business school catalogue aptly describes the objective of many schools in the matter of business ethics:

> For future managerial growth and responsible citizenship, each man must develop the ability to reach conclusions *for himself* on a carefully reasoned basis. As a foundation, he must develop his own personal set of moral and ethical values. . . . Only such a set of personal and social values can provide the foundation for true independence of thought and maturity of judgment, in the conduct of business . . .[11]

When a school attempts to achieve this objective by integrating ethical considerations into business courses, without offering a sep-

[11] Catalog of Carnegie Institute of Technology Graduate School of Industrial Administration, 1962, p. 9.

arate and prior course in general or business ethics, a difficulty inevitably arises. Developing a "personal set of moral and ethical values" is a major undertaking. It is a rare student, indeed, who can fashion a set complete enough for his future business needs, especially if he is asked to do this in bits and pieces during courses whose main thrust is in learning something else, like marketing or accounting. To develop a set of ethical values, the typical student needs and deserves assistance, including the benefit of mankind's best thinking on this topic. If he is not exposed to this thinking in some systematic way, as in a course, it is doubtful that he will develop a set of personal values of sufficient breadth or depth for responsible decision-making.

WHO WILL TEACH THE FACULTY?

There is a further difficulty with the expectation that a student will learn much about ethics solely in courses like finance and production management. Most business school faculty members are unwilling or unable to give ethical problems more than superficial treatment. They have little confidence in their understanding of ethics and, consequently, seldom introduce it in class. When students bring up the subject, the faculty member rarely contributes much. In a classic case of confusion that I witnessed, one student found an ethical issue in a business policy case and took a strong affirmative stand; a second student took an equally strong negative stand; a third student said, "I disagree completely with both previous speakers." The teacher made no comment. Observation of subsequent classes made it evident that his silence stemmed more from ignorance than from a nondirective classroom attitude.

The majority of business schools are committed to the integrated approach without having a requirement that students take a course in general or business ethics. Consequently, teachers of business courses must be prepared to teach some ethics as background for answering students' questions. Before they can teach ethics, teachers must master it. It would be helpful if special arrangements could be made to enable present business school faculty to study ethics. Recent attempts at helping faculty learn more about business ethics, such as the Danforth Seminars at the Harvard Business School, were of limited success, perhaps because of their brevity and lack of a well-defined objective.

Existing doctoral programs in business administration typically do not require candidates to complete a course or pass an examination in ethics. So there is little reason to look for improvement in discussions of ethical issues in regular business courses unless doctoral students, who are the future teachers, are required to take ethics as part of their doctoral curriculum, or to pass an examination proving their knowledge of the subject.

Even in the unusual situation where a school has several faculty members capable of integrating ethics into business courses, there is a problem. As one dean phrased it, "The difficulty of approaching the matter in this informal way is that many concepts and issues may fall between stools." That is, the same idea may be treated in three different courses, while another idea is never covered.

THE COURSE-PLUS CONCEPT

I concur with the dean who wrote: "This subject should be approached on a formal course basis but, and this is very important, this course should be supplemented by discussion of ethical questions in all courses wherever these issues are relevant." But there are two difficulties in implementing this approach: The first involves course sequence, and the second involves student reaction to a required course in ethics.

It is obviously desirable that the course in general or business ethics should be completed prior to attempts to apply the knowledge acquired in this course to the material in other courses. But in most curriculums featuring this approach, the course in ethics is offered after or at the same time as the business courses. The reason is usually a desire of the curriculum planners that the students taking the ethics course be as mature as possible. This difficulty can be remedied by a change in the sequence of courses.

The second difficulty is not so easily solved. For this approach (course in ethics plus application in business courses) to be successful, all of the students should have taken the general ethics course before beginning to discuss ethical aspects of personnel management, for instance. But, as we said earlier, ethics is not a popular course among students. If it were, most collegians would be taking the ethics elective course offered by the philosophy department on practically every campus. So this approach must include a *required* course in general or business ethics. But students seem to resent anything that is mandatory. Consequently, the addition of a required course in ethics would hardly be a wise psychological move.

That leaves the difficult alternative of finding a competent, qualified faculty member who will offer an elective course in ethics so attractive that all the students will want to take it.

There seems to be agreement that future businessmen should learn ethics in a way that will make them knowledgeable as well as convinced of the need to act ethically. To find the educational approach that will accomplish this two-fold objective, systematic experimentation is needed in courses at both the undergraduate and graduate levels. Content, format, and methodology should be varied. The first step would be to gather complete information about all the courses that are now offered, and the experimenting that is now taking place in many classrooms.

In summary, our survey shows that the relationship between business ethics and education is complex. Awareness about ethical problems and the ability to think and speak about them is improved by college, especially if it includes a course in ethics. But there is no evidence that decision-making is more ethical as a result of college courses. Businessmen want the schools to produce recruits who will not harm the image of their company by unethical decisions, and many businessmen favor college courses in business ethics. However, few students show much interest in ethics courses, and academicians are not sure what to do to meet the business community's request for ethical managers.

The contribution of education to ethical decision-making in commerce and industry may be potentially great. But this potential will not be actualized until businessmen and educators together take practical steps to discover more precisely what must be learned, when it must be learned, and how best to help students to learn it.

The concept of religion usually includes three components: doctrine (beliefs), worship, and values governing behavior. The three —mnemonically known as creed, cult, and code—are logically interrelated, with cult and code dependent on creed. Communion, in the sense of a social bond among coreligionists, also can be regarded as a component of religion.

Ethics, concerned as it is with man's code of behavior, is related to religion in the minds of many businessmen who look to religion to provide content or objective standards for their personal code, as was shown in Chapter 2. Many also expect their church and clergymen to provide instruction and motivation for ethical behavior, as this chapter will demonstrate.

Early in this century Max Weber focused attention on the relationship between business and religion with his thesis that the spirit of capitalism was a by-product of "the Protestant ethic."[1] This thesis was an outgrowth of his assumption that each religion develops a distinctive outlook toward business and other major social institutions. Although Weber's assumption and thesis are disputed, there is general agreement that organized religion is a force for ethical behavior in business.

The various churches and denominations uniformly teach that a man's religious beliefs should strongly influence his actions. Indeed, the Second Vatican Council warned Catholics that "believers can have more than a little to do with the birth of atheism. To the

[1] Max Weber, *The Protestant Ethic and the Spirit of Capitalism* (New York: Charles Scribner's Sons, 1958).

extent that they . . . are deficient in their religious, moral, or social life, they must be said to conceal rather than reveal the authentic face of God and religion."[2] Persons who profess belief in God accept the Ten Commandments or other codes for human behavior, but the importance of religion's role, its relevance, is debatable; for example, a 1948 study found 54 per cent of a sample of Americans admitting that their religious beliefs had no effect on their ideas about business.[3]

Although not all believers are affiliated with a church, "not to identify oneself and be identified as either a Protestant, a Catholic, or a Jew is somehow not to be American."[4] Consequently, many who affiliate with a church (roughly synonymous with one's religious preference) do not regularly attend church services. Our data-gathering asked only about religious affiliation, as reported by survey participants. The answers were divided into categories as reported earlier in Tables 1.2 and 1.3.

Because religious affiliation was one among many variables present in our study, because the interviewers did not probe precisely what a respondent meant when he said he was, for example, Protestant, because there were many views about religion among our respondents, the findings of this chapter are lacking in precision. Also, the interpretation of any statistical data pertaining to religion is debatable because of the way in which ethnic and social groupings are interwoven with religious affiliations. To determine the influence of each of these three factors, which are principal ingredients of every culture, is a very difficult task, which I did not undertake.

The Jews present a special problem in interpretation. To be a Jew is not simply to belong to a religious denomination. Even when one adds the note of ethnic affiliation, mention must still be made of a sense of an historic community with a special reason for unity; to be an Irish Catholic, for example, does not suggest the same totality. Answering the question, "Do you have a religious preference?" one interviewee said, "Judaism," and then added the

[2] Walter M. Abbott, S.J. (ed.), *The Documents of Vatican II* (New York: Guild Press, 1966), p. 217.

[3] Lincoln Barnett, "God and the American People," *Ladies' Home Journal*, November 1948, p. 234.

[4] Will Herberg, *Protestant, Catholic, Jew*, rev. ed. (New York: Doubleday Anchor, 1960), p. 257.

qualification, "but this is more a matter of nationality than of religion." However, Professor Will Herberg's analysis revealed that "self-identification in religious terms [is] almost universal among American Jews."[5] That is, when asked "What is a Jew?", most United States Jews reply in religious rather than ethnic terms. They see themselves primarily as a religious grouping. To this view, however, sociologist Gerhard Lenski adds that "in the case of Judaism we are confronted with a group in which the religious associations have been seriously weakened."[6] At the same time, he acknowledges that the communal bond among American Jews is very strong. Lenski sees the factors which led to communal groups—interest in the synagogue and common religious beliefs—dwindling while the communal groups are flourishing. From the distinctions made by these informed observers, it is clear that it will be difficult to interpret the responses given by businessmen who said that their religious affiliation is Jewish.

Throughout this book, the analysis of Project Two data has involved answers to nine questions selected because they offered the most insight into respondents' attitudes and actions. Religious affiliation is the final variable whose influence I investigated in this manner, acknowledging that depth of meaning can hardly be elicited in this area by use of a questionnaire.[7] The results, contained in Table 18.1 indicate that the attitudes of the religiously affiliated are hardly distinguishable from the attitudes of the unaffiliated. The answers of the unaffiliated businessmen in Table 18.1 are more ethical by my norms—cf. Appendix D—than are the answers of the affiliated in the case of status-symbol advertising (question 5), and are equally ethical in the questions dealing with conflict of interest (8a) and profit maximization (1e). In only one of the questions to which the replies of the unaffiliated are less

[5] *Ibid.*, p. 190.

[6] Gerhard Lenski, *The Religious Factor* (New York: Doubleday, 1961), p. 33.

[7] Some readers may feel that it would have been more prudent not to report and analyze these data. After all, the findings are somewhat controversial, the sample leaves something to be desired, and the evidence is not conclusive. I pondered this course of action but decided that adopting it would suggest that ignorance is somehow better than knowledge, a patently untenable position for a researcher. So I report the findings despite their inadequacies, for they do shed light on a complex topic and help us to see why it is so difficult to put an end to the stereotype of the Jewish businessman as unethical.

Table 18.1
*Replies from the Religiously Affiliated and Unaffiliated*a

	Affiliated	Unaffiliated
1e. Agree that "For corporation executives to act in the interest of shareholders alone . . . is unethical."	83%	83%
1h. Agree that ". . . the spiritual and moral consequences of the businessman's actions are none of his concern."	5	6
2. Would use confidential corporate information for private financial gain.	43	45
3. Would probably hire personnel from a competitor to acquire scientific discovery.	49	54
4. Regard padding of expense account by $500 as unacceptable regardless of the circumstances.	86	83
5. See no ethical dimension in status-symbol advertising.	36	28
8a. Think it always ethical for executive to own stock in company with which his company regularly does business.	2	2
8b. Think that providing a call girl for a customer is always unethical.	90	78
8c. Think it always ethical for executive to exchange price information with other companies.	4	8

a For questions 1e, 1h, 8a, and 8c, $N = 1,501$ divided as follows: affiliated $=$ 1,373; unaffiliated $= 128$. For questions 2, 3, 4, and 5, $N = 804$ divided as follows: affiliated $= 739$; unaffiliated $= 65$.

ethical, the use of call girls (8b), is the difference large enough to be statistically significant.[8]

In Tables 18.3 and 18.4 also, as we shall see, the religiously unaffiliated businessmen's replies are neither notably nor consistently different from those of the affiliated. Perhaps this lack of difference between the views of the religiously unaffiliated minority and those of the affiliated majority in Project Two of our survey is not surprising in the melting pot of industrial America, in which the standards

[8] Statisticians speak of a result as *significant* if the difference discovered between the groups would not occur more than five times out of 100 by chance alone; a probability of .05. The test of significance used in calculations for this chapter was the chi-square.

and practices peculiar to any one group are gradually dissolved. Our data lend support to Lenski's observation that there is "a common core of morals" in this country, and to Herberg's contention that we are developing "a religion of America." One possible explanation of the similarity of answers is that the religiously unaffiliated are, perhaps unknowingly, living off religious capital bequeathed by their parents. But it is also likely that the beliefs of businessmen who identified themselves with organized religion do not make a significant difference in their economic attitudes.

INTER-RELIGION COMPARISON

Having considered the answers of religiously affiliated and unaffiliated businessmen, we turn to the replies given by members of the three major religious groups. The first and most important thing to be said is that most of the replies in projects Two and Three revealed a similarity among Protestants, Catholics, and Jews. There was more agreement in their attitudes than there was disagreement. However, the answers did reveal some differences, and I shall analyze these.

Before doing so, however, it will be helpful to advert to several of the conclusions of earlier chapters. Competition was seen to be the factor of greatest influence on ethical behavior in business. Probably because it is the functional area in which competition is most prevalent, marketing seems to bring more pressure for unethical behavior than do other areas. For example, comparing the answers of respondents experienced in marketing with those whose background was not marketing, in seven of the nine questions a larger percentage of marketing men gave answers indicating a less ethical attitude than did nonmarketing men. A similar conclusion follows from a comparison of the answers of "all other respondents" with the replies of (1) men in retail and wholesale businesses; (2) men in small companies; (3) men under forty years of age. In other words, each of the following factors correlated to some degree with less ethical replies to nine questions in Project Two: working for a small company, experience in marketing, working in retail or wholesale business, and youth.

With these findings in mind, we turn to the career profiles of the Protestant, Catholic, and Jewish businessman in our Project Two sample. These profiles differ, as Table 18.2 shows, and there is reason for thinking that these career differences influenced the

Table 18.2
Background of Businessmen by Religious Affiliation[a]

	Protestant (N = 1,047)	Catholic (N = 223)	Jewish (N = 103)	Unaffiliated (N = 128)
Less than 40 years of age	31%	46%	42%	46%
Experience in marketing area	28	31	37	30
Member of top management	46	38	56	44
Company employs less than 500	40	38	69	48

[a] Cf. Table 1.2 for complete profile, and Appendix A for wording of questions.

replies of our respondents. The Protestants are notably older than the non-Protestants. Fewer Catholics belong to the ranks of top management, perhaps because more of them work for large companies. The Jews, more than the others, have worked in marketing (rather than manufacturing, engineering, construction, etc.), are employed in small companies and in retailing or wholesaling, and occupy top management positions. That many of the Jewish respondents work for small firms is probably, in part, a result of Gentile discrimination.[9] The comparatively large number of Jews in top management is presumably related to their employment by small companies, in which capable managers rise to the top more quickly than they do in large companies.

In the light of the data in Table 18.2, it is useful to recall the prejudiced stereotype of the Jewish businessman which has been present in our culture. In this stereotype the Jewish businessman is seen as eager to compete for business success, willing to use all available means to reach this goal, especially adept at marketing, desirous of economic power, and somewhat tricky and shrewd. As Charles Stember indicates, the stereotype is a combination of an "economic man" and a "Shylock image."[10] Obviously, the stereotype is unfavorable to the Jewish businessman's ethics. In 1961 Lenski found that Jews were perceived as less fair in their business

[9] Lenski, *op. cit.*, pp. 63, 92; also see Lewis B. Ward, "The Ethnics of Executive Selection," *Harvard Business Review*, March–April 1965, pp. 6ff.

[10] The content of the stereotype of the Jewish businessman is thoroughly discussed in Charles Herbert Stember *et al.*, *Jews in the Mind of America* (New York: Basic Books, 1966). Stember's careful and exhaustive study of empirical data leads him to conclude: "One fact consistently emerges from our analyses: Anti-Semitism in all its forms massively declined in the United States between the prewar or war years and the early 1960's" (p. 208).

dealings than were Christians. Of his respondents, 70 per cent expressed a *favorable* image of Protestants' fairness in business; 68 per cent, of Catholics' fairness; and 40 per cent, of Jews' fairness.[11] His finding undoubtedly reveals some judgment by stereotype on the part of Christian respondents. Stember has recently produced convincing evidence that the stereotype is gradually disappearing, but it still exists in some quarters.

Table 18.2 reveals that the Jews in our Project Two sample have followed a career pattern somewhat different from that followed by other respondents. This pattern—employment in a small company, often starting in the marketing department, with a relatively rapid rise to top management—is sufficiently similar to the stereotype to prompt superficial observers to regard the stereotype as accurate. Because there is some truth to the stereotype—someone has said that every stereotype is a half-truth—it is perpetuated. However, the half-falsehood is also perpetuated. Some Jews are in small companies because the doors of large companies are closed to them; others are in family wholesale and retail firms in which marketing is the essential operation. Their jobs subject them, and others in those companies and that kind of work, to comparatively heavy pressures for unethical conduct. Where competition is severe, unethical behavior is more common than it is elsewhere. Jews, for a variety of reasons, are in industries, companies, and jobs where competition is often severe. So the stereotype of the Jewish businessman as unethical goes on.

In the light of the career patterns of the Jewish businessmen in our sample, it would be expected that their replies will reflect their business experience and be less ethical than the replies of other respondents. As Table 18.3 shows, this is the case.

There are marked differences in the replies of businessmen of different religious affiliations. The answers of Protestants are typically more ethical than those of the other groups, and the Jewish responses are generally less ethical than those of the other groups. On all nine questions the differences are in the same direction, i.e., the Jewish responses reveal a less ethical attitude, or a lower threshold of ethical sensitivity, than do the responses of the Protestants or the Catholics. In seven of the nine questions, the differences are statistically significant.

Let us look at additional data which seem to shed light on our topic. Recall that questions 2, 3, 4, and 5 in Project Two were

[11] Lenski, *op. cit.*, pp. 58ff.

asked in two ways: Approximately half of the respondents were asked what *they* would do in the situation described, while the other half were asked what the *average businessman* would do. Table 18.3 shows the answers to these questions of the managers who said what they would do. Table 18.4 contains the replies of those who gave opinions about the average businessman.

Table 18.3
Responses According to Religious Affiliation[a]

	Protestant	Catholic	Jewish
1e. Agree that "For corporation executives to act in the interest of shareholders alone . . . is unethical."	83%	82%	78%
1h. Agree that ". . . the spiritual and moral consequences of the businessman's actions are none of his concern."	4	4	10
2. Would use confidential corporate information for private financial gain.	41	43	60
3. Would probably hire personnel from a competitor to acquire scientific discovery.	47	50	67
4. Regard padding of expense account by $500 as unacceptable regardless of the circumstances.	89	77	74
5. See no ethical dimension in status-symbol advertising.	34	35	53
8a. Think it always ethical for executive to own stock in company with which his company regularly does business.	2	2	5
8b. Think that providing a call girl for a customer is always unethical.	90	91	80
8c. Think it always ethical for executive to exchange price information with other companies.	4	4	5

[a] For questions 1e, 1h, 8a, 8b, and 8c, N = 1,373 divided as follows: Protestant = 1,047; Catholic = 223; Jewish = 103. For questions 2, 3, 4, and 5, N = 739 divided as follows: Protestant = 564; Catholic = 122; Jewish = 53.

The differences, which are statistically significant for items 2, 3, and 4, suggest that Protestant managers were less pessimistic than the others about the behavior of the average businessman, and that the Catholics and Jews saw the business world as less ethical than the other groups saw it. Certainly related to this viewpoint are the

Table 18.4
What Respondents Think Average Businessman Would Do

	Protestant (N = 483)	Catholic (N = 101)	Jewish (N = 50)	Unaffiliated (N = 63)
2. He probably would use confidential corporate information for private financial gain.	59%	61%	86%	60%
3. He probably would hire personnel from a competitor to acquire a scientific discovery.	67	70	92	67
4. He regards padding of expense account by $500 as unacceptable regardless of the circumstances.	67	54	42	48
5. He probably sees no ethical dimension in status-symbol advertising.	47	55	45	47

answers given to four other questions that deal with attitudes about competition and selling. These data are included in Table 18.5.

For all four items in Table 18.5, the Jews perceived the business world as more competitive or less ethical than any other group did. As in Table 18.4, the Catholics and Jews saw business somewhat differently than did the Protestants. The Protestants regarded business competition as less severe than did the Catholics and Jews, and were more optimistic about current industry practices and the utility of written codes of ethics. One wonders whether the tendency of these Jewish and Catholic businessmen to see their environment as more hostile than do Protestants is a kind of minority-group defensiveness.

One other difference shows up in comparing answers by religious affiliation. When questioned about using confidential information for personal gain, none of the Jews and 2 per cent of the other respondents replied that they would tell their broker about the confidential news, but 40 per cent of the Jews—compared to 13 per cent of the non-Jews—said that they would tell a good friend.

From Project Three interviews, we have one other small indication that some ideas of Jewish businessmen about ethics are different from those of non-Jews. In commenting on the statement, ". . . it is ethical for a businessman, in time of financial distress

Table 18.5
Attitudes About Competition and Selling

	Protestant (N = 1,047)	Catholic (N = 223)	Jewish (N = 103)	Unaffiliated (N = 128)
1b. Agree with statement, "Let the buyer beware."	19%	23%	31%	28%
1g. Agree that "competition today is stiffer than ever . . ."	38	44	58	41
11. There are many generally accepted practices in my industry which are unethical	9	12	18	10
13c. Agree that "in situations of severe competition, the code would reduce the use of sharp practices."	52	51	36	52

or severe competition, to make decisions directly opposed to those which his conscience dictates," one of every twelve non-Jews agreed with the statement, while four of nine Jews agreed.

In interpreting this data, the reader must judge for himself the adequacy of the sample, which is described in Chapter 1, and the reasonableness of what I regard as ethical answers to the relevant questions (cf. Appendix D). The fact is that the Jewish businessmen answered some of the questions in a way notably different from the Christians. The question is: Why?

One way of explaining the differences in our data is that the Jewish respondents were more honest and realistic in their replies than were Christians. That is, the answers of the Jewish respondents more accurately reflect their attitudes and actions than do the answers of the Protestants and Catholics.

The explanation I have advanced is that the careers chosen by the Jews, in part because some other careers were closed to them by prejudiced employers, were those in which competition was relatively severe and in which there exist more than ordinary pressures for unethical behavior. Competition being a most important influence on business behavior, the Jews in our survey developed attitudes and ways of acting which are ethically somewhat different from the other respondents. If these other respondents had career patterns similar to the Jews, it is probable that their replies would have been much the same. This explanation parallels that of Jerome E. Carlin about the lawyers in his survey: "Jewish and Catholic lawyers have a lower ethics rating than Protestant lawyers because they are more likely to be exposed to pressures to violate ethical norms. Under similar conditions of practice, Jewish and Catholic lawyers are no more likely to violate norms than Protestant lawyers."[12]

The different answers in Table 18.3 are, of course, related to the type of questions asked. They emphasize *personal* ethics, as distinguished from what is usually referred to as *social* responsibility in business. There are, for example, no questions about racial integration or air and water pollution. The reasons for this emphasis are discussed in Appendix C. It is generally conceded that, in matters of social responsibility, American Jews have demonstrated more concern and sensitivity than have Christians. So it may be that the questions used in Project Two unintentionally discriminate against Jews by failing to secure information about important matters in which Jewish answers would probably have been more ethical than those of Christians. However, this leaves the possibility of interpreting some of the data in this survey to mean that Jews lag behind Christians in matters of personal ethics in business. It will require a more comprehensive study, with a larger sample of businessmen, to test this hypothesis.

To obtain a vantage point for looking at the hypothesis that Jewish businessmen are more socially responsible than Christian businessmen, I obtained the raw data of the only empirical study about which I had heard that dealt with these matters. It was a questionnaire administered to 103 West Coast businessmen by the Reverend John W. Clark, S.J.[13] Nine men in Clark's sample identified their religion as Jewish. Clark classified seven of his case situations as problems of social responsibility. These cases involved racial integration, discharge of older workers, corporate contributions to colleges, etc. Respondents were asked to indicate approval or disapproval of the action. In a cumulative score index, which Clark called a social responsibility scale, six of the nine Jews scored above the median for the 103 respondents.

The results of Clark's survey, though based on a very small

[12] *Lawyer's Ethics* (New York: Russell Sage Foundation, 1966), p. 169.
[13] *Religion and the Moral Standards of American Businessmen* (Cincinnati: South-Western Publishing Co., 1966).

sample, indicate that the hypothesis that Jewish businessmen are more socially responsible than their Christian counterparts is worth investigating.

Concluding this interreligion comparison, I reiterate that there was more similarity among the answers provided by Protestant, Catholic, and Jewish businessmen than there was dissimilarity. The quality of the answers indicates that these major religious groups can hardly claim much influence on the business behavior of their members. Let us look at some of the reasons for this seeming lack of success.

THE GAP BETWEEN BUSINESSMEN AND CLERGY

Religious institutions and clergymen are generally respected by businessmen, but have they any real influence on their decisions? Religion provides elevating ideas, but do they in fact provide much uplift for managers? Only an optimist could say that the data which are the basis for the remainder of this chapter offer grounds for an affirmative answer. One Project Three query provided information directly relevant to these two questions. The participants, after their interview, were asked to answer the question in Exhibit 18.1.

Exhibit 18.1

By marking an "X" somewhere on the line below, please indicate to what extent your religious beliefs influence your business decisions.

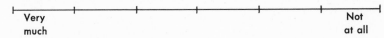

Very   Not
much   at all

Two-thirds of the businessmen put their "X" closer to "Very much" than to "Not at all." However, many of these men were unable to speak meaningfully about the role of religious beliefs in their business lives. Our results seem to corroborate the conclusion of the authors of *The American Business Creed:* "The place of religion in the business creed is an honored, but ill-defined one. The creed bows to the importance of religion, admits seeking religious guidance, but continues to be a predominantly secular ideology."[14]

A major reason for the lack of influence of religion on business

[14] Francis X. Sutton *et al.*, *The American Business Creed* (Cambridge, Mass.: Harvard University Press, 1956), p. 269.

decisions is the gap in understanding between clergymen and businessmen. The gap is due partly to semantic and communication problems. It is also related to a continuing inability to reconcile some of the teachings of revealed religion with certain aspects of American culture. How, for example, can the Sermon on the Mount be adequately reconciled with the competitive, acquisitive spirit that epitomizes our capitalistic economy? And the Gospel's insistence on the dangers of riches clashes with the prevalent American attitude that wealth is a value in itself.

Another reason for the gap between businessmen and the clergy is a difference of opinion over whether the church should take a position (and whether the clergyman should preach that position) on social issues. This is related to the divided opinion about the amount of freedom in secular affairs which should be accorded the clergyman as a *citizen*. Many laymen doubt that it is possible for a clergyman to disassociate his words and actions from his position in the church; they feel that what he says, especially if he is a leader, is interpreted as the position of the church. J. Howard Pew, a board member of the Sun Oil Company and for forty years a member also of the board of the United Presbyterian Foundation, told the National Council of United Presbyterian Men:

> Many of these men [businessmen and professional men in the Presbyterian Church] could afford to give far more than they do . . . but the great majority are strongly opposed to much of what the corporate Church is doing. They cannot understand how our corporate Church could tolerate such statements and pronouncements on social issues [civil rights, right-to-work laws, collective bargaining, etc.] as they have seen in the press. They feel that the corporate Church should not go into politics; that it has no mandate to meddle in secular affairs.[15]

Pew found articulate supporters like General Robert E. Wood, former president of Sears, Roebuck and Company. But most clergymen, including Presbyterians, disagree with Pew's views. Indeed, many of them feel that they have a right and duty to support measures which seem to them to promote the common good, and to oppose measures which seem harmful. Recently clergymen have criticized and picketed businessmen on policies and practices involving manufacturing weapons for war, hiring the disadvantaged, and investing funds in South African firms. And in May, 1967 the United Presbyterian Church in the U.S. adopted a new confession

[15] J. Howard Pew, speech delivered at Palmer House, Chicago, March 19, 1960.

which incorporates and emphasizes the social dimensions of Christian faith.

This problem is a thorny one. Some clergymen charge that business leaders like Pew and Wood are upholding an antiquated "business is business" viewpoint, and that the churches and synagogues cannot be relevant unless they do get involved in social issues. J. Irwin Miller, chairman of the board of Cummins Engine Company, replies that if the churches are to discharge the responsibility which they have assumed, "they must be a great deal more competent, better informed, and far-sighted than they have shown themselves to be up to now."[16]

We asked survey respondents to agree or disagree with a paraphrase of the Pew opinion: "Clergymen should not meddle in the social problems of business." Pretesting revealed that *meddle* was an ambiguous word. The ambiguity is more evident when one looks at the contradictory proposition: Clergymen should meddle in the social problems of business. Nevertheless, the ambiguous word was included because of some interesting correlations in the pretesting. The 1,506 replies are divided as follows: 37 per cent agreed, 15 per cent were neutral, 48 per cent disagreed. The Pew viewpoint was upheld by three of every eight businessmen. Religious affiliation made no statistically significant difference in the responses. Since *meddle* denotes unnecessary or impertinent assistance, its use probably reduced the number of men who would have disagreed had the statement been less ambiguous, e.g., "Clergymen should not speak about the social problems of business."

It is interesting to examine some other answers of the 556 men who agreed that clergymen should not meddle in the social problems of business. Just as these men oppose statements by the clergy, so they are not enthusiastic about written codes of ethics for their industry, and take a dim view of a company policy on gifts. In general, these men regard ethical problems as personal matters; they want no help in coping with them. Shortly we shall see other evidence of this highly individualistic attitude on the part of a sizable minority of our respondents.

Becoming more specific in our investigation, we asked: "In your opinion, how much guidance was provided by your church and clergymen for the ethical problems you and your business acquaint-

[16] Remarks made before the Fiftieth Anniversary World Convocation of the National Industrial Conference Board, September 19–21, 1966, at the Waldorf-Astoria, New York.

ances faced in the last five years?" The replies are presented in Table 18.6.

Table 18.6
Amount of Guidance Provided by Church for Businessmen
(N = 1,505)

None	35%
Some, but not enough	24
About the right amount	17
Too much	1
Can't really say	23

Why did 23 per cent refuse an opinion? Some were men who had no religious affiliation and therefore felt that the question was not addressed to them. Perhaps others preferred not to criticize the clergy. Probably the principal reason was the lack of communication between businessmen and clergy.

A more arresting fact, however, is that only one in every five of these educated men who gave an opinion thought that his church and clergy have provided adequate guidance for the businessman's ethical problems. This should be sobering to clergymen, many of whom have warned members of their congregation about practicing their religion on only one day a week. Many Catholic priests have quoted Ed Willock's verse:

> Mr. Business went to Mass,
> He never missed a Sunday;
> Mr. Business went to hell
> For what he did on Monday!

Our statistics show that Mr. Business feels that he has not had adequate help in solving the problems and overcoming the temptations he faces from Monday to Friday. In Project Three, this feeling was explored. One vice-president opened his interview with me by saying: "I'm glad that your profession is finally taking notice of the problems which we businessmen face." An eastern executive leveled stinging criticism at the intellectual leaders of his church:

I feel that the theology faculty at X is weak and out of tune with the problems of today. They seem to be trying to make life comfortable for Protestants, and this leads them into all sorts of undesirable compromises.

A board chairman charged that the church is failing the businessman indirectly:

I don't think that the cure for bad business ethics can come from the top down. I'm convinced that it must come from the bottom up, that is, it must start with the family. The church may be failing society by not concentrating on the family as the basic unit.

Comparing the responses according to religious affiliation, in Table 18.7 we see that the majority of all three religious groups are dissatisfied.

Table 18.7
Satisfaction With Church-Provided Guidance

	Protestant (N = 1,044)	Catholic (N = 228)	Jewish (N = 102)
None	33%	24%	53%
Some, but not enough	26	31	13
About the right amount	16	27	13
Too much	1	0	0
Can't really say	24	18	21

Although our data indicate that most Catholic businessmen are not satisfied with the guidance provided by their church, few bring their ethical problems to priests. This is evident from a survey of 5,500 midwestern priests. Replying to the question, "What are the principal moral problems among the people you encounter in your apostolic work?" only 9 per cent included "business ethics."[17]

It would be erroneous to conclude that managers who answered "None" to our query thereby signified readiness to accept help from the church. Replying to another question, almost one-fifth (268) of our respondents said they wanted no help from the church. They proffered a variety of reasons, some of which resemble the Pew view:

A New York stockbroker: "The average clergyman has such a scant understanding of the U.S. economy that his intervention in this area would be a mistake."

The president of a small bank: "If the clergy would stick to their business of preaching the gospel, they and business would be better off. The clergy admits the weakness of their faith when they turn from the

[17] Cletus Wessels, O.P., "The Human Dimension of the Apostolate," *Ave Maria*, March 11, 1967, p. 12.

gospel and try to get into other fields of influence and preach a doctrine of social gospel."

The view that the Church's efforts to assist business have been adequate was supported by a minority of respondents. The chief executive of a large corporation blamed businessmen for not hearing the church's message: "Too few men understand or listen."

Most managers who criticized organized religion's past lack of guidance in business ethics hope for help in the future. They indicated the kind of assistance they would welcome through their answers to two questions. The first question was:

Listed below are three kinds of guidance for ethical business behavior which clergymen might offer to businessmen, largely through sermons and writing. How helpful would they be to you? To tell us, please rank the three by placing the number "1" after the activity which would be *most* helpful, "2" after the next most helpful, and "3" after the *least* helpful.

    a. Emphasize motives for doing good and avoiding evil
    b. Explain ethical principles clearly
    c. Apply ethical principles to typical business situations

Table 18.8
Clergy Guidance Desired by Businessmen (N = 1,403)

	First Choice	Second Choice	Third Choice
b. Explain principles	47%	40%	13%
c. Apply principles	30	39	31
a. Emphasize motives	23	21	56

The answers are presented in Table 18.8. It seems surprising that application of principles, being the most pragmatic of the choices, was not favored by businessmen. Why was explanation of principles favored over application? Here are two representative reasons:

A personnel director: "I don't think the average clergyman knows enough about business to be specific."

A president: "The question of competency enters here. The personality and ability of the preacher or padre makes all the difference."

Such reservations about the level of business knowledge possessed by the average clergyman were common in our replies. Presumably they were born during a sermon when an ill-informed cleric ventured into economic waters over his head. Efforts at educating clergymen in the realities of business and economics have been undertaken in recent years by the American Management Association, the National Association of Manufacturers, the Danforth Foundation, and the Clergy Economic Education Foundation.

An interesting comment on the subject of clergymen applying principles to specific situations came from the Second Vatican Council: "Let the layman not imagine that his pastors are always such experts, that to every problem which arises, however complicated, they can readily give him a concrete solution, or even that such is their mission."[18]

The second question asked was (Table 18.9):

Listed below are three kinds of assistance which clergymen might offer to businessmen. What would be the value of such assistance? To tell us, please rank the three by placing the number "1" after that kind of behavior which would be *most* helpful, "2" after the next most helpful, and "3" after the *least* helpful.

   a. Be easily available at church, synagogue, or rectory for individual consultation

   b. Meet regularly with small groups of businessmen to discuss their problems.

   c. Be available regularly at factory or company office for individual consultation.

Table 18.9
Kind of Clergy Help Welcomed by Businessmen (N = 1,376)

	First Choice	Second Choice	Third Choice
b. Meet with small groups	63%	31%	6%
a. Be available at church	31	41	28
c. Be available at factory	6	28	66

Apparently many businessmen welcome the idea of small group discussions with a single clergyman present. The idea is receiving a thorough trial from the Laymen's Movement in Rye, New York, from the National Conference of Christian Employers and Managers in Chicago, St. Paul, and elsewhere, and from Industrial Mission groups in Detroit, Chicago, Boston, and elsewhere.

There was little enthusiasm for the regular presence of a clergyman at the office or plant for individual consultation. Reynolds Tobacco, Texas Aluminum, LeTourneau Incorporated, D-X Sunray

18 Abbott (ed.), *op. cit.*, p. 244.

Oil, and other companies, most of them in the South, have employed "plant pastors." Apart from practical difficulties with the idea, respondents preferred consultation of this type to take place at the rectory, synagogue, or parsonage. There was a suspicion that the plant pastor, who is usually on the company payroll, would be regarded by hourly paid workers as a representative of management. The president of a company with a plant pastor gives eloquent evidence that the wishes of top management are respected by the pastor:

What does he "preach" about? Almost anything he pleases, so long as he avoids controversial subjects and is careful not to offend any Christian's viewpoint . . . In the nineteen years since we have had a chaplain, no personal offense has been given by his preaching.[19]

This statement strikes a discordant note for those who believe in the prophetic role of the clergyman, and who recall that speaking unpopular truths was the hallmark of the Old Testament prophets.

In general, then, our respondents would welcome more guidance from their clergymen. Why has such guidance not been forthcoming? There are three obvious reasons: lack of time; lack of preparation in the seminary courses; lack of authoritative writing to which clergymen can refer for information and direction. Businessmen especially welcome assistance if the cleric is well educated in business, economics, or other social sciences. There is a small but growing number of so-called "delayed vocations" to the ministry. These include men with years of business experience. And it is rare for the better graduate schools of business not to have at least one clergyman in attendance. So there will be more clergymen knowledgeable about business in the near future.

Businessmen, trying to cope with new gray-area problems, could use the assistance of competent moral theologians. One form which this aid might take is the construction of medial norms to provide guidance for the solution of everyday problems in business. Such medial norms are needed. There is, in this country, widespread acceptance among businessmen of the handful of general ethical principles which are the foundation of our Judaeo-Christian civilization. But between these general principles (such as "Thou shalt not steal") and the concrete problems of the businessman (such as whether or not price-fixing is stealing from customers) there is a void. If theologians cooperate with businessmen, this void can be

[19] John E. Mitchell, *The Christian in Business* (Westwood, N.J.: Fleming H. Revell Company), 1962, p. 129.

filled by medial norms, i.e., refinements and applications of the general principles. Some of these norms would apply to an occupational area, like selling; others to an industry, like steel; and others to a kind of activity, like pricing. These norms would shed light not only on daily business decisions but also on the possible content of industry codes. Naturally, because business problems change, ample provisions would have to be made for regular re-examination of medial norms.

Beginnings have been made in acquainting moral theologians with the ethical dilemmas of managers. The Viatorian Seminary in Washington, D.C., has sponsored special seminars for these groups. The Catholic Theological Society of America has devoted sessions at its annual meetings. The Chicago Theological Seminary and the Religion and Labor Council of America have provided students of theology with opportunities for intellectual interaction with businessmen. Other seminaries are including more business problems in their courses in moral theology in recent years, and the same interest is reflected in theological journals.

How can this goal of cooperation between theologians and businessmen be pursued most effectively? The best answer can come only from experimentation. Different avenues of approach should be tried. The businessman should initiate the cooperative venture because he faces the ethical problems and will presumably benefit more from their solution than will the theologian. There is another reason for suggesting that the businessman take the lead in promoting the meetings. Some clergymen are skeptical that the businessman really wants to learn ethical solutions to his problems. Such skeptics will be convinced of the businessman's sincerity when he asks for assistance.

19   Synthesis and Suggestions

Two broad impressions strike me as I attempt to summarize and synthesize my findings. The first is that business ethics is a vast topic, covering a multitude of business decisions, practices, and policies. Because the topic is so large, one must be careful in generalizing about it. Making generalization more hazardous is the ambiguity of the terms *business* and *ethical*. The second impression is that the image of businessmen's ethics which emerges from our data is somewhat different from the image which the public apparently holds. The popular image seems unfair to the typical participant in our survey, who appears to be a member of what President Johnson called "the overwhelming majority of honest businessmen."[1] The evidence presented should prompt the reader to re-examine his image of the businessman, and to ask whether the image does justice to the businessmen he knows.

Part of our data centered around the question: How important is ethics to businessmen? To answer this query about any individual, we must ask two other questions: Is he convinced that it is important to act ethically? Does he know much about what constitutes ethical behavior? Let us see how our survey participants fare by these norms.

Perhaps the best criterion for judging how important ethics is to a person is how much he sacrifices—in terms of position, money, time, and energy—in order to act ethically. Measured by this criterion, our Project Three interviewees deserve praise. Eighty-three per cent provided examples of decisions they made for ethical

[1] Lyndon B. Johnson, "Message to Congress on Consumer Interests," *New York Times*, March 22, 1966, p. 22.

reasons despite personal disadvantage. Four of every five managers recalled rewarding or disciplining employees for ethical reasons. And 20 per cent quit a job because of corporate or individual behavior that they felt was irreconcilable with their personal standards. These are encouraging signs. So is the desire demonstrated by Project Two respondents to improve the ethical climate in their industry by eliminating certain common practices and by the reasonable use of codes of ethical conduct.

However, a sizable minority of respondents in Projects Two and Three displayed insensitivity to ethical issues: 32 per cent could not recall ever having faced a conflict between what was expected of them as efficient businessmen and what was expected of them as ethical persons; 16 per cent failed to recall *ever* having made a decision in which ethical reasons were more important than the motives of profit or personal advantage; and 21 per cent admitted that they occasionally or regularly failed to take time to consider the ethical implications of a decision. Another facet of this insensitivity is the way that some businessmen identified as ethical problems only those situations involving large sums of money. In the words of one manager, "Our company has no ethical problems. The last one we had was five years ago when the treasurer absconded with $50,000."

Another way of asking the second question posed above is: With what insight and clarity does the person speak about ethics? Usually this is related to the efforts he has made to understand this complex topic. Our survey participants did not provide many insights about business ethics. Of course, few attempted to defend an obviously unjust act on the grounds that it was really acceptable behavior, or took refuge behind the claim that lower standards are permissible in business than elsewhere. And most respondents revealed an awareness of their social responsibilities in *general* terms. Rarely, however, were the reasons they gave for *specific* ethical decisions impressive. Perhaps one-fifth of our 100 interviewees demonstrated the vocabulary, ideas, and power to reason about ethics that we associate with *excellence* in professions like law or medicine. At least an equal number did not demonstrate possession of these qualities to the extent that is usually associated with professional *competence.*

How important is ethics to businessmen? Probably the best answer is: No more important than it is to the average American. The main reason for the similarity of attitudes is that both the conviction of the importance of ethical behavior and much of the knowledge about ethics ordinarily are acquired before a person enters the business world. After a man begins to work, it takes an unusual occurrence to change his mind about the relevance of ethics, or to prompt him to increase his knowledge about it.

The *study* of ethics is not of major significance at any level in American education. The typical view about learning business ethics seems to be pragmatic: "When I need it, I'll learn it." Most persons get interested in it only after they feel they have been victimized. Few university faculties regard an ethics course of sufficient value to require it of all students. Not many students think the course useful enough to choose it as an elective. Ethics shares in the low esteem in which all philosophy courses are currently held. This view reflects the claim of the natural sciences that empirical verification and quantitative measurement are necessary hallmarks of a science. This claim limits, unnecessarily in my opinion, the meaning of science to a single methodology. Since other methodologies also enable man to reason his way to new knowledge and truth, they also deserve the name of science. Ethics is a science because ethical reasoning can reach conclusions that are universally, necessarily, and demonstrably true.[2]

The academic respectability of ethics is suspect also because its subject matter, the rightness and wrongness of human acts, is closely associated with religion. Religions of the Judaeo-Christian-Islamic tradition require faith of their adherents and depend on divine revelation. In this tradition, faith and revelation transcend rational categories. As a consequence, many people assume that ethics, which covers much of the same subject matter as religion, is not rational. This is a mistaken assumption. The science of ethics, which is based on the insights of human reason aided by empirical data, is rational. Faith may lead to the same conclusions as ethics in many cases, but that is also true of other sciences.

THE ETHICAL BUSINESSMAN

Throughout this study, I have tried to maintain a positive approach to our topic. Now I shall draw together strands from previous chapters and sketch the characteristics of the ethical businessman. The sketch is idealistic rather than realistic. It may provide a useful

[2] Cf. Herbert Johnston, *Business Ethics*, 2nd ed. (New York: Pitman, 1961), pp. 19–22; Thomas M. Garrett, S.J., *Business Ethics* (New York: Appleton-Century-Crofts, 1966), p. 4.

standard of measurement for anyone interested in making a personal comparison.

As a youth, aided by the words and example of his parents and teachers, the ethical businessman gradually developed the conviction that it was important to act ethically. He has carried this conviction through life. In college he studied and discussed ethics, especially as it applied to business situations.

He has a single standard of behavior at home and at work, but has more trouble applying it at work because of the competition and questionable practices he faces there. He tries to follow his conscience, which is not always easy because the most profitable course of action sometimes clashes with his personal values. He is socially sensitive in his decisions, especially those directly affecting coworkers.

He works for an ethical boss in a company with a deserved reputation for integrity, perhaps after leaving a boss or company with whose standards he was dissatisfied. Both within the company and without, he encounters enough competition to call forth his best efforts and keep him on his toes, without being pressured into almost irresistible temptations. He works in an industry which is well-established, has a code of ethical practices, and has its competitive activities scanned occasionally by a governmental agency.

His belief that good ethics is good business in the long run, as well as his developing self-confidence, help him to become more ethical as he grows older. His wife, with whom he discusses his work, is helpful through her insights into his personnel problems, and by being moderate in her ambitions for him and their family. He welcomes guidance from clergymen and scholars, but the more specific it is, the more he insists that it come from men who really understand business.

HOW IMPROVE BUSINESS ETHICS?

The improvement of business ethics is a goal with which few persons will find fault. Our survey respondents strongly favored it. They recommended written codes for companies and industries, more and better college courses in ethics, and knowledgeable guidance from clergymen as means for improving business behavior. However, achieving agreement on fundamental notions of ethics is an obstacle to improvement of business behavior. The Reverend John J. Lynch, S.J., has forcefully argued that there is no foundation for even a simple code of ethical practices unless agreement can be reached on an objectively sound *norm* of morality.

Whether ultimate appeal is made to common decency, professional integrity, a sense of social responsibility, or the brotherhood of man, the essential first step toward the formulation of an ethics for businessmen would seem to be the proposal and universal acceptance of a basic norm of business morality which will dictate and properly sustain the specific imperatives of a practical code. Without such a point of reference individual directives will for many be meaningful only if and while their observance remains personally advantageous.[3]

Agreement on a norm of ethics is surely a goal to be worked for. But in the meantime, since there is substantial agreement about what is not ethical in many specific business situations, businessmen can rely on this consensus when they need to make a decision but are unable to provide a complete and logical explanation for their opinion. Deeper analysis of this consensus might reveal that its origins are commonly accepted ideas of justice, fair practice, and human rights. Businessmen, scholars, and clergymen should work together for agreement on these fundamental concepts. While doing so, however, they must be alert to the possibility that the present consensus does not reflect all the values that are applicable to certain business situations.

To improve business ethics, experimentation would be useful. Here are three examples of experiments suggested by the needs and and comments of our respondents: one concerned with boards of directors, another with management consultants, and the third with a corporate social audit.

Since a plant is part of a community, and since most businessmen desire to make decisions in accord with the community's best interests, corporate boards of directors should include a public representative. An intelligent person who is not dependent on the corporation for his job, and who is charged with the responsibility of representing the common good, would be likely to provide an unbiased view of the community's best interests. It is interesting that, in the past, businessmen were critical about the lack of businessmen on church boards of trustees. Most churches now have businessmen acting as advisers on all major administrative decisions. Only one major United States corporation, to the best of my knowledge, has a clergyman on its board of directors.[4] In view of the occasional

---

[3] "Notes on Moral Theology," *Theological Studies*, June 1962, pp. 250–251.

[4] The Reverend John B. Coburn is a director of Corning Glass Works. In

criticism of corporations for unethical or irresponsible behavior, it seems that a clergyman with a knowledge of business would make a useful addition to some boards.

Just as managers now use consultants for problems in marketing, production, and personnel, they might begin to utilize ethical consultants. These should be men possessing degrees in business administration and theology, or philosophy, plus some experience in business. Chief Justice Earl Warren has urged "the development of the profession of the counselor in ethics, having the same relation to interpersonal conduct beyond the Law, that the lawyer has to conduct that is subject to the review in the courts."[5] For such a development, it would be necessary that combined degree programs be available to students. To my knowledge, no United States university offers a doctorate that combines business administration, theology, and philosophy. There are, however, men with degrees in these fields, and these men could be used to try out the feasibility of the role of ethical consultant to industry.

good

Howard R. Bowen's excellent proposal of the social audit of a corporation has never been tried. He suggested that:

Just as businesses subject themselves to audits of their accounts by independent public-accountant firms, they might also subject themselves to periodic examination by independent outside experts who would evaluate the performance of the business from the *social* point of view. The social auditors would make an independent and disinterested appraisal of a company's policies regarding prices, wages, research and development, advertising, public relations, human relations, community relations, employment stabilization, etc. They would then submit a comprehensive report to the directors and to the management with evaluation and recommendations. Such a report would be for the information of responsible officials and not a public document.[6]

This idea deserves a trial. A social audit would provide management with an independent evaluation of the manner in which the company is fulfilling its social obligations, and would assure the community of the company's interest in the common good. To do the job properly would require a team of auditors, including persons

---

1957, American Motors formed a clergymen's panel of ten men to advise management on the ethical aspects of collective bargaining. The panel met until 1960.

[5] "Proposed: A Counselor in Ethics," *Phi Psi Quarterly*, Spring 1963, p. 12.

[6] *Social Responsibilities of the Businessman* (New York: Harper & Row, 1953), p. 155.

with a broad knowledge of the industry in which the company competes and of the community in which it is located. Probably men who have retired from top management positions could make important contributions to such audits. The success of a social audit would depend principally on the company's top management. With their cooperation in securing the facts, and their determination to implement reasonable recommendations, a social audit would produce results. The crucial question is whether the board of trustees, management, and the shareholders would consider money spent on a social audit well invested. It would rarely be possible to point to additional profits as a result of the audit.

MODERATING COMPETITION

The shortcomings of competition from an ethical standpoint have long been discussed by economists and clergymen alike.[7] Throughout this study, we have noted that our economic system, with its emphasis on competition, produces some results that are ethically and socially undesirable. Chapters 4, 8, 11, 13, and 14 provide illustrations of the link between competition and unethical business behavior, e.g., in seeking promotion, in intra-industry practices, and in international business. If the ethical optimum is to be achieved in business behavior, competition of certain kinds must be moderated. Managers are responsible for attaining the goals of the corporation. These goals are becoming increasingly social. For example, some institutional stockholders are insisting that companies in which they hold stock make special efforts to hire members of minority groups, and to favor suppliers who are known as "equal opportunity" employers. This trend, stimulated by social activists as well as by university thinkers, will continue. Increased productivity, once acceptable as a reason for enduring the asocial effects of economic competition, is less acceptable as each year sees a new record for gross national product. Competition will be moderated. Who will set the limits: the company, the industry, the local community, or some branch of government?

Partly because cooperation usually produces more humane results than does competition, the trend in American industry will be

[7] For some views of the conflict between ethics and competition, cf. Leo Brown, S.J., *et al.*, *Social Orientations* (Chicago: Loyola University Press, 1954), pp. 153–189; Frank H. Knight, *The Ethics of Competition* (New York: Harper & Row, 1935) pp. 40–75.

to more cooperation. A continuing problem of the future will be to find the appropriate blend of competition and cooperation, a blend which will vary with the needs of the times. One area in which experimentation in cooperation should take place is labor-management relations, perhaps through some form of comanagement. Comanagement, which involves a sharing of decision-making by wage earners, is practiced in several European countries.[8] For example, in the German steel industry a corporate board of directors normally has eleven members; five are selected by the stockholders and five by labor, while the eleventh member is usually chosen by the other ten. If the United States adopts comanagement as a supplement to collective bargaining, the American version will be different from the European because the role of our labor unions is different, e.g., less politically involved. It is noteworthy that the social philosophy underlying comanagement is akin to that which is producing a grass roots movement toward greater solidarity in many small social units. This movement, whose description usually includes the word *community*, is especially strong in religious-oriented groups.

SUGGESTIONS FOR RESEARCH

For improvement of business ethics, in addition to experimentation, more research is needed. Many of the findings of this survey require further investigation and support before they deserve to be accepted as guides for action. In the course of this survey, it became obvious that many other aspects of business ethics deserve investigation. Here are five ideas worthy of further study:

1. *The expectations and attitudes of shareholders about managerial decisions which reflect a sense of social responsibility.* Managers regularly explain or defend their decisions with words about long-run profits, even when the decision is based on noneconomic reasons. Why is this? Presumably managers assume that the shareholders are not as socially enlightened as they. Is this so? If shareholders oppose management's plans, e.g., to improve working conditions or to make donations to charitable enterprises, does man-

---

[8] Harvard's Professor James J. Healy predicts that "we are likely to achieve a form of co-management through the bargaining table within the next decade to fifteen years," in "Are Unions Coming of Age?" *Harvard Business School Bulletin*, June 1959, p. 24.

agement have the right to ignore the shareholders' wishes? Perhaps research on this topic would lead to insights about the nature of the corporation and about the shareholder's relationship to management and to the board of directors, which is supposed to represent the shareholders.

2. *A comparison of collegians' ethics with their opinions of businessmen's ethics.* With so many collegians admitting that they cheat on examinations, for the stated reason of competing for grades, why is it that students have so little empathy with the businessmen who act unethically because of competitive pressures? Research might help the collegian to understand the businessman and his difficulties, and might help businessmen to understand why students are showing so little enthusiasm for business as a career.

3. *Empirical studies of the broad impact of business practices which indirectly affect large numbers of people.* Examples of such practices are collective bargaining, corporate mergers, stock options, and tax laws on personal property. Each of these practices has a complex and far-reaching impact, of which the ethical aspect is an important part. Perhaps the command of economics, ethics, and law required for such studies is responsible for the disparity between the importance of these practices in our society and the attention which researchers have devoted to them. Without a mass of data, it is foolhardy to attempt macro-ethical evaluation of topics like the four mentioned.

4. *The ethics of consumers.* Some business behavior is a reaction to the practices of consumers, e.g., the increased prices in supermarkets due to thefts by consumers, and the high cost of automobile accident insurance because of padded claims. This topic could be studied via the businessman's image of the consumer. Probably there will be differences in this image according to the consumer's age, affluence, or neighborhood. Such a study would help people to realize the interdependence of buyer and seller, and the illogic of thinking that no individual is harmed when a large company is cheated.

5. *What consumers expect of businessmen.* Most business transactions depend in large measure on public confidence in businessmen. The first requirement for a high level of confidence is that the businessman's behavior be predictably ethical. For the businessman habitually to act ethically, and so earn public confidence, he cannot be vague about what is required of him. Like an athlete hurling a discus, the businessman needs to know the boundaries within which he may exert all his energies—to set records for efficient service, quality products, and profits—and beyond which his

actions will be judged unfair. So it would be helpful to discover the consumer consensus about a topic like interest rates on installment purchases.

THE BIG PICTURE

In conclusion, here are impressions of three significant trends in business ethics. There is progress in *knowledge* about business behavior in our culture, about the motivation of businessmen, and about the application of ethical principles to industrial situations.[9] Many of these principles have been known for a long time, but have never before been applied to current business practice.[10] The rise of new problems due to technological change has prevented the increase in knowledge of business ethics from appearing as noteworthy as it really is. Research is being done by theologians, philosophers, and business scholars.[11]

There are clear signs of increased *interest* in business ethics, especially among faculty members and administrators in collegiate schools of business. The number of courses with titles like The Social Environment of Business, Business and Society, and Managerial Ethics is growing. Textbooks for marketing, management, and accounting are now appearing, for the first time, with a chapter devoted to ethics. During the last decade several organizations of managers devoted to improving the social awareness of their members have been founded. That clergymen and seminarians might better understand the problems of their businessmen parishioners,

[9] One indication of the vast amount that has been written about business ethics in recent years is the publication of a bibliography of 103 pages, through the efforts of Philip W. Van Vlack, Charles L. Sewrey, and Charles E. Nielsen: *Economic Ethics Bibliography*, Bulletin 524, December 1964, Economics Department, Agricultural Experiment Station, South Dakota State University, Brookings, South Dakota.

[10] An excellent illustration of a theologian applying moral principles to a current problem is Richard A. McCormick, S.J., "The Polygraph in Business and Industry," *Theological Studies*, September 1966, pp. 421–433.

[11] Among the research projects that have been completed are Donald C. Jackson, "An Axiological Analysis of the Quality of Fairness in a Business Environment" (unpublished dissertation, School of Government, Business and International Affairs, George Washington University, June 1965); Thomas F. Schutte, "An Exploratory Analysis of Executives' Perceptions Towards Business Ethics" (unpublished dissertation, School of Business, University of Colorado, 1963); and Opinion Research Corporation of Princeton, New Jersey, published a research report titled *The Ethics of American Business* in August 1964.

seminars are being sponsored.[12] Foundation funds are occasionally available for such meetings, as well as for others aimed at helping business school faculty to update their understanding of the social responsibilities of managers.[13] The praiseworthy actions and opinions of the high-ranking businessmen quoted in this book assure a continuation of this interest in business ethics.

Looking back over the years of this century, one can clearly discern a gradual improvement in businessmen's *behavior*. This upward curve is really a sequence of crests and troughs, but few troughs fall as low as the previous one, and most crests climb higher than their predecessor. The ratchet effect is usually present in the improvement of standards of business conduct, i.e., the improvement is generally accepted. This is due in part to voluntary codes of ethics and to governmental regulations, which provide motivation and support for decision-makers.

Some observers have suggested that a kind of moral Darwinism prevails in United States business, with the less ethical companies dying in the long run. This may be true in industries in which product quality can be identified by the average purchaser, or in which frequent repeat sales are the pattern. But it is utopian to think that moral Darwinism is *dominant* in industries in which economic competition is a major force. This is not to deny that good ethics is *usually* good business in the long run.

Other observers have concluded that the moral equivalent of Gresham's Law is operative, with unethical business practices driving the ethical ones out of the market place. This is another way of saying that the lowest common denominator of behavior tends to prevail in a highly competitive situation. This view downgrades the influence of the professional managers and well-intentioned executives who make key decisions. But the view must be taken seriously. Organized crime has moved into key positions in some respectable businesses.[14] If criminals are able to run an economically efficient operation, are they not liable to pull the ethical standards of the industry down to their own level? Or, to consider a more likely possibility, in the event of a severe economic recession in this country, e.g., during the industrial change-over period after the Vietnam

[12] "Operation Dialogue" of the Presidents Association, American Management Association, is the best planned and financed of these efforts.

[13] The Clergy Economic Education Foundation sponsors packaged three-day meetings for clergymen.

[14] Thomas C. Schelling, "Economics and the Underworld," *Harvard Today*, Spring 1967, pp. 27–30.

cease-fire, will businessmen be sufficiently motivated to withstand the temptation to compete unethically? Or will Gresham's Law prevail, at least for a time in some industries?

On the one hand, it is discouraging to see how far we must still go in this country to have a reasonably ethical and human economic system. On the other hand, it is encouraging to see how far we have advanced toward this goal in this century.

The challenge which faces businessmen is to improve the upward trends in interest, knowledge, and behavior with respect to business ethics. One of the major obstacles to this improvement is a selfish and unethical minority of businessmen. This group exercises a bad influence which is disproportionate to the number of men involved. The reason is, once again, competition. Although few businesses operate in a perfectly competitive market, many businessmen react to unethical competition as though their only option were to duplicate their opponent's every action. Their assumption seems to be that the best way to fight economic fire is with fire. Not enough businessmen are willing to take a reduced profit rather than lower themselves to the ethical levels of competitors. Perhaps one reason is that few customers are willing to pay extra for ethical behavior by the seller unless it is accompanied by economic advantage. It is good to hear public spokesmen insist that the corporation is a social, as well as an economic, entity, that it is a miniature society with social goals. But if the corporation is really to become a socio-economic entity, the public must help to pay the social costs, for example, by paying higher prices or by accepting lower returns on investment.

In the present climate of business, the material needs of millions in this country are satisfied through behavior that is usually ethical. Achieving a higher level of business behavior will require the habitual practice of justice and charity by businessmen. By reading and reflection, they must upgrade their knowledge of business ethics. By financing research, they must deepen what is known about this complex field. Improvement will require cooperation among businessmen and representatives of other sectors of the community. But basically, though improvement can be aided and hastened by external means like voluntary codes of ethics and governmental agencies, business behavior must be improved from within, man by man. A businessman is a man before he is a manager, and the more ethical, reasonable, and human he is, the better man and manager he will be.

Appendix A   Project Two Questionnaire

This appendix contains the questionnaire used in Project Two. There are two versions of questions two through seven of the questionnaire, for reasons which are explained in Chapter 2. Because the questionnaire employed in Project Two is similar to the one used in Project One, the latter is not reproduced here.

Harvard Business Review
Survey on Ethical Problems and Attitudes

1.   Listed below are a number of statements that have been made by observers of the business scene. How do you feel about these statements? Please *circle* the number which best corresponds to your feeling about each statement. (Please do not circle more than one number per statement.)

	Agree	Partly agree	Neutral	Partly disagree	Disagree
a. "Sound ethics is good business in the long run."	1	2	3	4	5
b. "Let the buyer beware."	1	2	3	4	5
c. "The American business executive tends to ignore the great ethical laws as they apply immediately to his work. He is preoccupied chiefly with gain."	1	2	3	4	5
d. "Whatever is good business is good ethics."	1	2	3	4	5
e. "For corporation executives to act in the interest					

of shareholders alone,
and not also in the interest of employees and
consumers, is unethical." 　1　　2　　3　　4　　5

f. "Clergymen should not
meddle in the social
problems of business." 　1　　2　　3　　4　　5

g. "Competition today is
stiffer than ever. As a result, many businessmen
find themselves forced to
resort to practices which
are considered shady,
but which appear neces-
sary to survive." 　1　　2　　3　　4　　5

h. "The businessman exists
for only one purpose: to
create and deliver value
satisfactions at a profit to
himself. If what is offered
can be sold at a profit,
then it is legitimate. The
spiritual and moral con-
sequences of the busi-
nessman's actions are
none of his concern." 　1　　2　　3　　4　　5

2. Imagine that you are a member of the board of directors of a large corporation. At a board meeting, you learn of an impending merger with a smaller
company which has had an unprofitable year, and whose stock is presently
selling at a price so low that you are certain that it will rise when news of the
merger becomes public knowledge. What would you do? (Please check as
many as are applicable.)

a. I would buy some shares for myself ☐
b. I would tell my broker about the forthcoming merger ☐
c. I would tell a good friend about the merger ☐
d. I would do none of the above ☐

3. Imagine that you are the president of a company in a highly competitive
industry. You learn that a competitor has made an important scientific discovery which will give him an advantage that will substantially reduce, but
not eliminate, the profits of your company for about a year. If there were
some hope of hiring one of the competitor's employees who knew the details
of the discovery, would you try to hire him? (Please check *one* only.)

I probably would ☐
I probably would not ☐

4. An executive earning $10,000 a year has been padding his expense account by about $500 a year. What do you think? (Please check *as many* as are applicable.)

    a. Acceptable if other executives in the company do the same thing ☐
    b. Acceptable if the executive's superior knows about it and says
       nothing ☐
    c. Unacceptable regardless of the circumstances ☐

5. As president of a company manufacturing consumer goods, you are considering new ideas for increasing sales. Your marketing department has presented two programs, each of which would achieve the desired increase in sales. PROGRAM A employs an advertising theme portraying ownership of your product as a symbol of the purchaser's superiority. PROGRAM B uses an advertising theme emphasizing the quality of your product. Which program would you choose? (Please check *one* only.)

    I would probably choose PROGRAM A ☐
    I see no reason to choose one program over the other ☐
    I would probably choose PROGRAM B ☐

6. Some businessmen give gifts to buyers, managers, or other executives with whom they regularly do business. What do you think? (Please check *as many* as are applicable.)

    a. This practice is unethical ☐
    b. A company should have a written policy about gifts ☐
    c. No gift worth more than $100 should be offered or accepted ☐
    d. This practice is unwise ☐

7. Many factors can influence a businessman's decisions. From your experience, how would you rank each of the factors listed below according to the influence it exerts on an executive to make decisions which are *ethical?* (Indicate the *most* influential by placing a "1" beside it, the next most influential by a "2," and so on to "5" for the *least* influential.)

                                                          RANK (1, 2, 3, 4, or 5)

    a. Formal company policy   _____
    b. A man's personal code of behavior   _____
    c. The behavior of a man's equals in the company   _____
    d. Ethical climate of the industry   _____
    e. The behavior of a man's superiors in the company _____

The following is an alternate version of questions 2 through 7, sent to a random half of the respondents in Project Two.

2. At a board meeting, a member of the board of directors of a large corporation learns of an impending merger with a smaller company. The smaller company has had an unprofitable year, and the company's stock is presently

selling at a price so low that the director is certain that it will rise when news of the merger becomes public knowledge. What do you think the *average* director would do in this situation? (Please check *as many* as are applicable.)

a. He would probably buy some shares for himself ☐
b. He would probably tell his broker about the forthcoming merger ☐
c. He would probably tell a good friend about the merger ☐
d. He would probably do none of the above ☐

3. The president of a company in a highly competitive industry learns that a competitor has made an important scientific discovery that will substantially reduce, but not eliminate, the profits of the president's own company for about a year. If there were some hope of hiring one of the competitor's employees who knew the details of the discovery, would the *average* company president try to hire him? (Please check *one* only.)

He probably would ☐
He probably would not ☐

4. An executive earning $10,000 a year has been padding his expense account by about $500 a year. How do you think the average businessman would feel about this? (Please check *as many* as are applicable.)

a. Acceptable if other executives in the company do the same thing ☐
b. Acceptable if the executive's superior knows about it and says nothing ☐
c. Unacceptable regardless of the circumstances ☐

5. The president of a company manufacturing consumer goods is considering new ideas for increasing sales. His marketing department has presented two programs, each of which would achieve the desired increase in sales. PROGRAM A employs an advertising theme portraying ownership of the product as a symbol of the purchaser's superiority. PROGRAM B uses an advertising theme emphasizing the quality of the product. Which program do you think that the *average* executive would choose? (Please check *one* only.)

He would probably choose PROGRAM A ☐
He would see no reason to choose one program over the other ☐
He would probably choose PROGRAM B ☐

6. Some businessmen give gifts to buyers, managers, or other executives with whom they regularly do business. How do you think the *average* executive feels about this? (Please check *as many* as are applicable.)

a. This practice is unethical ☐
b. A company should have a written policy about gifts ☐
c. No gift worth more than $100 should be offered or accepted ☐
d. This practice is unwise ☐

7. Many factors can influence a businessman's decisions. From your experience, how would you rank each of the factors listed below according to the influence it exerts on an executive to make decisions which are *unethical*? (Indicate the *most* influential by placing a "1" beside it, the next most influential by a "2," and so on to "5" for the *least* influential.)

RANK (1, 2, 3, 4, or 5)

a. Lack of formal company policy   _____

b. A man's personal financial needs   _____

c. The behavior of a man's equals in the company   _____

d. Ethical climate of the industry   _____

e. The behavior of a man's superiors in the company   _____

8. Listed below are a number of business practices that occur from time to time. Please *circle* the number which best approximates your opinion about each of these practices. (Please do not circle more than *one* number for each practice.)

	Always ethical	Depends on the circumstances	Always unethical
a. An executive owns stock in a company with which his own company does business regularly	1	2	3
b. An executive arranges for a "call girl" at the request of a purchasing agent with whom he regularly does business	1	2	3
c. An executive exchanges price information with his counterpart in other companies in his industry	1	2	3

9. Which of the following two statements better describes your feelings about the ethical problems you have had to face as an executive? (Please check *one* only.)

"It is easier to know what is right than it is to do it." ☐

"It is more difficult to know what is right than it is to do it." ☐

10. How often do you, as an executive, find yourself in the following situation: "I had to make a decision so quickly that there was no time to consider its ethical implications." (Please check *one* only.)

Never ☐

Rarely ☐

Occasionally ☐

Regularly ☐

Very frequently ☐

11. In every industry there are some generally accepted business practices. In your industry, are there any such practices which you regard as unethical? (Please check *one* only.)

         No   ☐
         Yes, a few   ☐
         Yes, many   ☐
         I don't know   ☐

If yes, please describe the *one* unethical practice you would *most* like to see eliminated:

_____

_____

_____

_____

_____

_____

12. Recently, there has been discussion about constructing ethical codes for business. In 1957, the AFL-CIO fashioned an Ethical Practices Code, a measuring rod which organized labor has applied to abuses in its ranks. How do you feel about an effort to develop a code of ethical practices for your industry? How would you react if a group of experienced executives in your industry tried to draw up such a code? (Please check *one* only.)

         I would favor strongly   ☐
         I would favor somewhat   ☐
         I am neutral on this topic   ☐
         I would oppose somewhat   ☐
         I would oppose strongly   ☐

13. Assume, for the moment, that an ethical practices code has been drawn up for your industry by experienced executives. What do you think such a code and its reasonable enforcement would accomplish? To tell us, please circle the number which best corresponds to your opinion of each of the possible consequences listed below. (Please do not circle more than *one* number for each possible consequence.)

	Agree	Partly agree	Neutral	Partly disagree	Disagree
a. The code would raise the ethical level of the industry	1	2	3	4	5
b. The code would be easy to enforce	1	2	3	4	5
c. In situations of severe					

	Agree	Partly agree	Neutral	Partly disagree	Disagree
competition, the code would reduce the use of sharp practices	1	2	3	4	5
d. Executives would welcome the code as a useful aid when they wanted to refuse an unethical request impersonally	1	2	3	4	5
e. The code would protect inefficient firms and retard the dynamic growth of the industry	1	2	3	4	5
f. The code would help executives by defining clearly the limits of acceptable conduct	1	2	3	4	5
g. People would violate the code whenever they thought they could avoid detection	1	2	3	4	5

14. Assume, for the moment, that an ethical practices code has been drawn up for your industry. Which one of the following groups would you choose to enforce the code? (Please check *one* only.)

A group of executives selected from various companies ☐
A government agency ☐
The management of each company, i.e., self-enforcement ☐
A group composed of executives from the industry plus other members of the community ☐

15. In your opinion, how much guidance was provided by your Church and clergymen for the ethical problems you and your business acquaintances faced in the last five years? (Please check *one* only.)

None ☐
Some, but not enough ☐
About the right amount ☐
Too much ☐
Can't really say ☐

16. Listed below are three kinds of guidance for ethical business behavior which clergymen might offer to businessmen, largely through sermons and writing. How helpful would they be to you? To tell us, please rank the three by placing the number "1" after the activity which would be *most* helpful, "2" after the next most helpful, and "3" after the *least* helpful.

RANK *(1, 2, or 3)*

a. Emphasize motives for doing good and avoiding evil _____
b. Explain ethical principles clearly _____
c. Apply ethical principles to typical business situations _____

17. Listed below are three kinds of assistance which clergymen might offer to businessmen. What would be the value of such assistance? To tell us, please rank the three by placing the number "1" after that kind of behavior which would be most helpful, "2" after the next most helpful, and "3" after the *least* helpful.

RANK *(1, 2, or 3)*

a. Be easily available at church, synagogue, or rectory for individual consultation _____
b. Meet regularly with small groups of businessmen to discuss their problems _____
c. Be available regularly at factory or company office for individual consultation _____

18. In effect, questions 16 and 17 discuss two different types of help that a clergyman can offer a businessman. Which of these two types would you prefer? (Please check *one* only.)

a. The three items mentioned in question 16 ☐
b. The three items mentioned in question 17 ☐
c. No help of these types wanted ☐
d. Don't know ☐

19. Probably there have been times when you have experienced a conflict between what was expected of you as an efficient, profit-conscious businessman, and what was expected of you as an ethical person. Please describe below the business situation which has been for you the source of deepest concern because of such a conflict:

_____
_____
_____
_____
_____

FOR STATISTICAL PURPOSES ONLY

20. Which of the following describes the functional areas in which you are most experienced? (Please check *one* only.)

Accounting ☐   Personnel or Labor Relations ☐
Engineering ☐   Production ☐
Finance ☐   Public Relations ☐
Marketing ☐   Other (Specify) _____ ☐

21. What type of business are you in? (Please check *one most important* only.)

Manufacturing consumer goods ☐   Construction   ☐
Manufacturing industrial goods ☐   Mining, extraction, oil   ☐
Engineering, research and de-   Retail or wholesale trade   ☐
velopment   ☐   Transportation or public utilities ☐
Management consulting and   Advertising, media, publishing ☐
business services   ☐   Consumer services   ☐
Banking, investment, insurance ☐   Other (Specify) _____ ☐

22. Your present title or position: _____

23. Age nearest birthday: _____   24. State of residence: _____

26. Size of company (by number of
employees):

25. Your income group:

Under $10,000   ☐   1–49   ☐
$10,000–$19,999   ☐   50–99   ☐
$20,000–$29,999   ☐   100–249   ☐
$30,000–$39,999   ☐   250–499   ☐
$40,000–$49,999   ☐   500–999   ☐
$50,000–$74,999   ☐   1,000–9,999   ☐
$75,000–$99,999   ☐   10,000–19,999   ☐
$100,000 or more   ☐   20,000 or more   ☐

27. Your formal education ended at:

High School   ☐   Bachelor's Degree ☐
Some College   ☐   Graduate School   ☐

28. Did you ever take a formal course in ethics or moral philosophy in college:

Yes ☐
No   ☐

29. What is your religious affiliation:

Protestant   ☐   Please specify Protestant
Catholic   ☐   denomination: _____
Jewish   ☐
Unaffiliated   ☐
Other (Specify) _____ ☐

Appendix B   Project Three Interview Questions

This appendix contains the schedule of questions used in the structured interviews of Project Three. All the questions were asked in the same order of each of 100 interviewees. The interviewers took notes during the interviews and transcribed them immediately afterward.

1. A. Do you agree that good ethics is good business in the long run?
   B. Would you mind telling me why you think that this is so (is not so)?
      (*If "Yes" to A*)
   C. You agree, don't you, that a single decision made for ethical reasons can be costly or unprofitable?
      (*If "Yes" to C*)
   D. How do you explain this apparent difference between a single decision (or the short run) and the long run?
2. A. (*Hand Respondent Card*)

   Please try to recall a business decision which you made for ethical reasons despite your belief, at the time, that it would be less profitable for your company or for yourself than would an alternative decision. In other words, can you recall an occasion when you chose ethical behavior in preference to financial gain, or when you acted on moral principle even though you felt that your action would be criticized or might endanger your job?

   B. (*Ask for Details of this One Decision, E.G.*)
      How many people were directly involved? How much money? How was the decision made, by committee, or with support from above and/or below, or by the man alone? Why was the decision made, i.e., what were the principles or criteria that were applied?

3. A. If a company has a reputation for ethical behavior, do you think that this is a significant factor in attracting young men who possess high ethical standards? In other words, does like attract like?
   B. Why?
4. A. Do you think that some industries are more ethical in their decisions and actions than are other industries?
      (*If* "*Yes*" *to* A)
   B. Would you please name one industry that you think is very ethical, or one that you think is unethical?
   C. Why is that industry so ethical (unethical)?
      (*Inquire Whether Any of the Following Are Significant Factors*)
      Amount of government regulation; size of companies; kind of competition; industry code of ethical practices.
5. A. Do you think that executives in certain occupations or doing certain kinds of work act more ethically than executives doing other kinds of work?
      (*If* "*Yes*"*to* A)
   B. Would you please name one kind of work that you think is very ethical, or one that you think is unethical?
   C. Why is that kind of work so ethical (unethical)?
6. A. What do you think of the common opinion that the typical businessman has two sets of ethical standards, one of which he applies to his business activities, the other he applies to his private life?
      (*If* "*Agree*" *To* A)
   B. Why do you think this is so?
   C. Thinking for a moment of the three most ethical businessmen you know, do you think that there is a difference between their private morality and their business morality?
7. A. (*Hand Respondent Card*)

   "The first responsibility of a businessman is to keep his business solvent, for if his business is bankrupt it will no longer provide a living for himself and jobs for others. Therefore, it is ethical for a businessman, in time of financial distress or severe competition, to make decisions directly opposed to those which his conscience dictates." Do you agree or disagree?

   B. Would you care to elaborate your answer?
8. A. In a *Harvard Business Review* survey, in which 1,600 businessmen were asked what they would do in certain situations, or what they thought about certain statements, the responses of the older executives were more ethical than those of the younger executives. Does this surprise you?
   B. Why?

(*To Prompt More Thinking, Ask Questions Like*) Do you think that there has been a general moral decline in our nation during the last decade? Do you think that business ethics has improved in recent years?

9. A. Let's talk for a moment about the person who makes the most important decisions in your company. Obviously, his words and actions imply certain views about the place of ethics in business, and about what constitutes unethical behavior. Would you say that his views have had a significant influence on yours?

B. Would you mind explaining or illustrating what you mean?

C. Now I'd like to ask the same question about your immediate superior. Have his views on ethics had a significant influence on yours?

D. Would you mind explaining or illustrating what you mean?

E. Who, would you say, has been the most important single influence on your acting ethically in business?

F. What, would you say, is the most important motive for your acting ethically in business?

G. Is there one piece of advice, or principle, or rule of thumb which you have found most helpful, or used most frequently, in making ethical business decisions? (*If "Yes"*) What is it?

10. A. (*Hand Respondent Card*)

Please try to recall an occasion when you rewarded some person in your company for ethical behavior (for instance, by promotion, pay raise, or congratulations), or when you penalized someone for unethical behavior (for instance, by dismissal, demotion, or reprimand). Would you mind describing the occasion?

B. (*If Not Clear, Ask*) Was the person rewarded (penalized) a subordinate, an equal, or a superior?

11. A. Most men have worked for more than one company. Have you ever left a company for ethical reasons, for instance, because of pressure to do what you thought was wrong, or because of a difference of opinion as to what constituted ethical behavior? (*If "Yes" to A*)

B. Would you mind describing the situation?

12. A. Does your company have a formal or written code of ethics for the guidance of employees? (*If "Yes" to A*)

B. Would you please describe very briefly the code, for example, does it cover all activities of all employees, or just some of them?

C. As far as you know, what has been the effect and influence of this code on employees' behavior?

13. A. Would you mind talking a bit about the meaning of your reli-

gious beliefs for your actions as a businessman? In other words, how would you describe the influence of your religious beliefs on your business decisions?

B. Do you believe that your ethical business decisions are rewarded by God (the Supreme Being) in this life? (*If "Yes"*) How?

C. . . . will be rewarded by God after your death? (*If "Yes"*) How?

D. Do you believe that your unethical business decisions are punished by God in this life? (*If "Yes"*) How?

E. . . . will be punished by God after your death? (*If "Yes"*) How?

14. A. Will you please try to tell me what you mean when you say that an action is ethical? In other words, what does *ethical* mean to you?

B. (*Hand Respondent Card*)

Here are nine descriptions or definitions of *ethical*. Please select the one which comes closest to what you usually mean when you say that an action is ethical.

1. About the same as what is legal.
2. Corresponds to my self-interest.
3. What my feelings tell me is right.
4. Customary behavior in our society.
5. Whatever does the most good for the most people.
6. In accord with my religious beliefs.
7. Contributes most to personal liberty.
8. Conforms to "the golden rule."
9. What I want in that particular situation.

Interview Answer Sheet

1. A. Yes _____ (1-1). No _____ (1-2). Don't know _____ (1-3).
2. A. Quick recall _____ (2-1). Slow recall _____ (2-2). No recall _____ (2-3).
3. A. Yes _____ (3-1). No _____ (3-2). Don't know _____ (3-3).
4. A. Yes _____ (4-1). No _____ (4-2). Don't know _____ (4-3).
   B. Ethical _____ (5-1). Unethical _____ (5-2).
      Name of industry _____ (6).
5. A. Yes _____ (7-1). No _____ (7-2). Don't know _____ (7-3).
   B. Ethical _____ (8-1). Unethical _____ (8-2).
      Name of occupation _____ (9).
6. A. Agree _____ (10-1). Disagree _____ (10-2). Don't know _____ (10-3).
   C. Yes _____ (11-1). No _____ (11-2). Don't know _____ (11-3).
7. A. Agree _____ (12-1). Disagree _____ (12-2). Don't know _____ (12-3).
8. A. Yes _____ (13-1). No _____ (13-2). Don't know _____ (13-3).
9. A. Yes _____ (14-1). No _____ (14-2). Don't know _____ (14-3).
   C. Yes _____ (15-1). No _____ (15-2). Don't know _____ (15-3).

10. A. Quick recall _____ (16-1).   Slow recall _____ (16-2).   No recall (16-3).
   Rewarded _____ (17-1).   Penalized _____ (17-2).
   B. Subordinate _____ (18-1).   Equal _____ (18.2).   Superior _____ (18.3).
11. A. Yes _____ (19-1).   No _____ (19-2).   Don't know _____ (19-3).
12. A. Yes _____ (20-1).   No _____ (20-2).   Don't know _____ (20-3).
13. A. Influence of religious beliefs (scale: 7 = very much influence, 1 = no influence) _____ (21).
   B. Yes _____ (22-1).   No _____ (22-2).   Don't know _____ (22-3).
   C. Yes _____ (23-1).   No _____ (23-2).   Don't know _____ (23-3).
   D. Yes _____ (24-1).   No _____ (24-2).   Don't know _____ (24-3).
   E. Yes _____ (25-1).   No _____ (25-2).   Don't know _____ (25-3).
14. B. Definition number _____ (26).
   Other numbers mentioned _____ .

Respondent's name _____ .
Respondent's number _____ (27, 28, 29).

To Be Answered by Respondent at End of Interview

15. What is your title or position? _____ (30)
16. What industry (or type of business) is your company in? _____
   _____ (31)
17. By marking an "X" somewhere on the line below, please rate the ethical climate of your industry.

   Absolutely   Absolutely   (32)
   unethical   ethical
18. Approximately how many people does your company employ? _____ (33)
19. Approximately how large are the assets (book value) of your company?
   _____ (34)
20. By marking an "X" somewhere on the line below, please rate the ethical practices of your company.

   Absolutely   Absolutely   (35)
   unethical   ethical
21. Your age at nearest birthday? _____ (36)
22. Have you ever written a book, magazine article, or letter to an editor about business ethics? _____ (37)
23. (If "yes" to 22)   Where did the writing appear in print? _____
   _____
24. Are you a member of an organization which actively promotes business ethics? _____ (38)
25. (If "yes" to 24)   What is the organization's name? _____
   _____
26. Have you or your company received any awards for responsible (ethical) business behavior in the last decade? _____ (39)

27. (If "yes" to 26)   Please identify the award. _____

_____

28. By marking an "X" somewhere on the line below, please indicate to what extent your religious beliefs influence your business decisions.

●————+————+————+————+————+————● (40)
Very   Not
much   at all

Interviewer's Sheet

29. Respondent's name: _____
30. His company's name: _____
31. Company address: _____

_____

32. Date of interview: _____
33. Place of interview: _____
34. Interviewer: _____
35. How was this respondent contacted? _____

_____

36. (If president or chairman of board)   Who was the founder of your company? _____ (41)
37. At what level did your formal education end? _____ (42)
38. Did you ever take a formal course in ethics or moral philosophy in college?

_____ (43)

39. Do you have a religious preference, i.e., are you Protestant, Jewish, Catholic, or something else? _____ (44)
40. (If Protestant)   What denomination? _____ (45)

Interviewer's Post-interview Impression Of Respondent
(Score each of these four items on a seven-point scale)

41. His *attitude* toward being interviewed about this subject by me.
(1 = very cooperative, 7 = very uncooperative)   _____ (46)
42. His *sensitivity* to ethical issues.
(1 = very acute, 7 = very obtuse)   _____ (47)
43. His *ideas and reasoning* about ethics.
(1 = profound, 7 = shallow)   _____ (48)
44. The *expression* of his ideas.
(1 = eloquent, 7 = inarticulate)   _____ (49)

Appendix C About the Questions, Answers, and Interviewers

The approach to businessmen's ethics was empirical, with data systematically secured from a cross section of 1,712 managers. They were asked about specific practices like gift-giving and pirating personnel; the interviewers—a layman and I—also inquired about general matters like the influence of competition, governmental regulation, and religion on ethical decision. The emphasis was on common problems, the kind that disturb the average manager because he must make decisions about them. We did not ordinarily inquire into decisions about the broad, social responsibilities of business, partly because the typical manager has little acquaintance with them, e.g., air and water pollution. We emphasized individual ethics more than social ethics. Some observers feel that this approach neglects important social issues. While I agree that it is important to know whether businessmen's decisions foster broad human values and serve national purposes, I think that it is also important to learn how a person has reacted or thinks he would react to specific case situations, like the ones that we asked about. I think that specific questions are more likely to produce meaningful data than are more general questions. For example, from a person's reaction to the use of confidential information for personal gain or toward expense account padding, one can reasonably extrapolate to his probable reaction to ethical problems of broader scope. In other words, I think that man's ethical behavior is relatively consistent, that the man who habitually tries to be just to his neighbor is likely also to practice justice toward the community.

Care was exercised in wording the questions so that their meaning would be clear and unambiguous. Every item was pretested. Each project eliminated the mistakes and unproductive inquiries of its predecessor. To insure comparability of responses, each interviewee in Project Three was asked the same questions in the same order. Some flexibility was allowed to the interviewer: He could choose to ask certain fixed secondary questions, or to follow a new line of inquiry when he thought the interviewee would provide useful information. Four of the interview questions were typed on cards and handed to the interviewee. Use of these cards helped to insure understanding of long or complex questions. Because of the danger of wishful thinking in any discussion of ethics, the questions stressed past actions, decisions, and experiences of the interviewee, rather than his verbalized ideals. Immediately after each interview, notes taken during the conversation were transcribed.

What assurance had the interviewers that the men tried to tell the truth? This is a difficult question. Anyone experienced in writing cases about business knows how few executives will let company faults or weaknesses be put in print.[1] I tried to remove reasons which might prompt interviewees not to tell the truth; for example, the written questionnaires were anonymous, and none of the survey participants are identified in this book. Anonymity helps those who wish to reveal ethical shortcomings—their own, their company's, or their industry's—and also removes a motive from those who might use the situation as an occasion for self-serving remarks. Granted the natural tendency to be self-serving, which can be distinct from truth-serving, it should be noted that the two need not be opposed. Often, telling the truth happens also to benefit the teller. Careful designing of questions minimizes the likelihood of getting self-serving answers.

It is usually good interviewing technique to avoid asking a man questions about which he has a reason—especially a legitimate reason, like his right to secrecy about personal faults under certain circumstances—for concealing the truth. As far as possible my colleague and I refrained from asking about men's faults or failings. Instead we emphasized a positive approach.

I acknowledge the tendency of interviewees to give answers that are expected and to say what they think the researcher would like to hear. These difficulties we tried to counteract by challenging inconsistent or sanctimonious replies.

[1] This is not uniquely true of business; educational institutions and hospitals are also reluctant to release information that is not edifying. So prevalent is this inclination to cover up or conceal faults that the Harvard Business School includes, in any agreement to write a company history, stipulations that nothing may be withheld from the historian and that he must be able to publish whatever he finds.

What of our competency as interviewers? Before the survey, our work had provided extensive practice in interviewing. Beforehand, we talked at length about the objectives of the research and the interview questions, and conducted practice interviews using the final version of the questions. Each of us interviewed a businessman in the presence of the other, and discussed the performance and evaluated the replies together afterward. This helped to guarantee uniformity of performance.

I wore clerical garb during the interviews I conducted. The other interviewer wore the usual business suit. Use of a skilled layman-interviewer enabled me to compare answers, and so learn what bias or modifications were attributable to the fact that I am a priest. I concluded that differences in replies which may be related to the calling of the interviewer did not significantly influence any of the major findings of this study. The 1,612 respondents to the questionnaires were unaware that a clergyman had formulated the questions and would analyze the answers, so there is no possibility of bias from this source in Projects One and Two.

Summing up, I accept the likelihood that I did not get the whole truth from some respondents and interviewees. To a query whether my data are of high quality, I would reply by asking: Are there any other data of comparable quality? I believe that the statistics, experiences, and opinions included in this book provide evidence that cannot be ignored, evidence that is reliable and useful for thinking about the American businessman. Here are reasons for this belief:

1. There seems no adequate reason, except the respondent's wish to tell the truth, for some of the answers, e.g., 70 per cent think that there are generally accepted business practices in their industry which are unethical. When 70 per cent anonymously admit something that is a discredit to their group, they probably are telling the truth.

2. The consistency of answers to questions which were substantially identical in two different projects; e.g., 57 per cent of the respondents in Project One and 56.4 per cent of the respondents in Project Two said that they would not take advantage of secret information to make a personal gain. More significant is the fact that some questions from Project Two were used in later studies by two other researchers, and their results are virtually the same as mine.[2]

3. Some interviewees' frank criticism of me and of my profes-

[2] Stephen Greyser, "Businessmen re Advertising: 'Yes, but . . .'" *Harvard Business Review* (May–June, 1962); James H. Kennedy, "Ethics in the Textile Industry," *Phi Psi Quarterly* (Spring, 1963).

sion, e.g., "theologians are the laziest men in the world"; "your profession is finally taking notice of the problems we face"; "your article in the *Harvard Business Review* had a bad title, and I have many objections to its contents."

4. An obvious, strong desire on the part of many interviewees to have us understand business as it actually is, e.g., one merchant opened the interview with a twenty-minute history of his company because he felt that its attitude toward ethics was unique and that hearing its history would enable the interviewer to appreciate this. Several men provided confidential information about prominent companies and executives, asking that it not be published for their own protection but wanting the interviewer to know about it "so that you see the whole picture of business ethics."

5. The other interviewer and I have academic degrees in business administration and experience in industry, and we feel that what we were told generally had the ring of reality.

6. The replies of a control group of fourteen interviewees, selected for their honesty and understanding of the purposes of Project Three, do not differ markedly from the replies of the other eighty-six men.

Besides the limitations imposed by using data provided by men who are personally involved in the topic being studied, I also acknowledge the shortcomings of quantitative techniques as tools for learning about man's behavior. The tabulated responses to a questionnaire about ethics are not guaranteed to yield objective truth. So I have taken pains to qualify my conclusions. To accomplish my purpose, I had to secure a wealth of data. To handle all this information, it was necessary to employ a statistical approach. Information received through the questionnaires and interviews which could be coded was punched on data processing cards. All the statistics used were machine-tabulated.

Appendix D Answers to Nine Questions

In Chapters 9, 11, 12, 17, and 18 the analysis depends in part on an evaluation of answers given by businessmen to nine questions. These questions are contained in the Project Two questionnaire, which can be found in Appendix A. Here is the reasoning by which I decided that certain of these answers were more or less ethical than others, with the questions identified by the number under which they are listed in Appendix A.

ANSWER TO QUESTION 1e

To disagree with this statement is to imply either that employees and consumers have no rights or that, whenever their rights conflict with the rights of stockholders, the latter prevail. This assigns to capital, and to property rights in general, a priority over the right of workers and consumers to justice. Such priority implies that managers, when weighing the claims of workers, customers, and stockholders, should always give preference to the latter, an implication that is ethically repugnant, especially in a democratic society.

ANSWER TO QUESTION 1h

Actions have consequences, many of which are foreseeable. All peoples and the laws of many nations have insisted that man must exercise reasonable foresight, and that he is responsible for the foreseeable results of his actions. There is no reason for exempting business decisions from these demands for mature behavior. Consequently, to agree with the quotation given is to reveal an attitude lacking in ethical concern for one's fellow man.

ANSWER TO QUESTION 2

The use of "insider information" is the issue. As a board member, the man learns a fact which he thinks will certainly increase the value of the common stock. May he use that information? Since the man is *certain* about what will happen, his buying stock would be like betting on a sure thing. Since the seller of the stock presumably would not have access to the confidential information, the buyer would be taking unfair advantage of him. Furthermore, the use of insider information, were it known, would hurt the public confidence necessary for the orderly conduct of the stock market. Therefore it would be unethical for the board member to use the confidential information for the benefit of himself or others.

Because the 1934 Securities Exchange Act forbids the use of such information, its use would also be unethical because it would break the civil law.[1]

ANSWER TO QUESTION 3

Learning a competitor's trade secret by hiring one of his employees is the ethical problem. While it is true that the individual worker must be allowed job mobility so that he can better himself, it is also true that he owes loyalty to his current employer. More importantly, if the employee—because of his job—knows a production secret of his employer, it seems clear that the secret belongs to the company. Just because the employee can carry the secret away in his head does not make it his. A competitor has no right to the secret unless he can secure it by ethical means. By virtue of the work contract, the employee is obliged not to reveal secrets of his company to a competitor when that revelation would be harmful to his company. Consequently, the man who would not try to hire a competitor's employee for this purpose is more ethical than the man who would try it.

[1] Cf. Securities Exchange Act Release No. 6668 (November 8, 1961) and William L. Cary, "The Case for Higher Corporate Standards," *Harvard Business Review*, September–October 1962, p. 57.

ANSWER TO QUESTION 4

Padding an expense account increases the amount of money claimed by asking reimbursement for expenditures not actually made. It involves lying in order to steal. Nor can padding ordinarily be defended on the ground that it is really a supplement to the man's salary. It is not treated as a salary supplement on the company's books, and so leads to deceiving the stockholders and others about employees' salaries. And it almost inevitably leads to falsification of the report to the Internal Revenue Service.

That others are doing the same kind of padding does not alter its objective morality or immorality.

Because a boss says nothing about an employee's action does not necessarily indicate tacit approval of the action. The boss's silence may mean only that he needs the executive so badly that he is afraid to rebuke him. Therefore, the ethical answer is "Unacceptable regardless of the circumstances."

ANSWER TO QUESTION 5

Status-symbol advertising is not per se unethical. However, it has features which raise ethical doubts. It emphasizes the symbol in preference to the reality; it fosters the consumer's desire to seem to be what he is not; it appeals to the consumer's snobbishness; at times it implies that more or better material possessions make one a better person.

Since the financial reason for choosing one type of advertising has been eliminated in the case, the choice was between an appeal to reason, stressing product quality, and an appeal to weakness in the consumers' character. The former is more in keeping with man's dignity, more ennobling, and hence more ethical.

Those who saw no reason to choose the advertising of quality in preference to the advertising of status seem to lack a degree of sensitivity to ethical values.

ANSWER TO QUESTION 8a

A conflict of interest exists when a man's self-interest clashes with the best interest of the company which employs him. Every employee has certain contractual obligations to his company. The man who owns only a few shares of stock in a company for which he does not work is in no position to influence decisions in that company. Owning stock is a morally neutral act. A situation such as that described in question 8a is a potential conflict of interest. It becomes a real conflict only when the person puts himself in a position where there is a likelihood that he will favor himself at the company's expense. By seriously weakening his independence of judgment and action, he leads himself into temptation. So the action described would sometimes but not always be unethical, depending on the circumstances.

Some state laws and company rules prohibit a company officer from owning a substantial (not trivial) amount of stock in another company. There are also laws which require full disclosure of stock transactions in such situations. But no law prohibits a businessman from any or all ownership of stock in another company.

ANSWER TO QUESTION 8b

Since use of call girls means committing a type of adultery or fornication which is always harmful to the fabric of family life, the ethos of marriage, or respect for human dignity, procuring a call girl constitutes formal cooperation in an evil act and is unethical. Civil law also forbids it.

ANSWER TO QUESTION 8c

The exchange of price information between companies in the same industry is ethically and legally neutral. Depending on the type of information as well as the purpose and the effect of the exchange, a specific action might be unethical and/or illegal. Therefore, "always ethical" is too lenient, ignoring the possibility of collusion and its usual companion, unfair pricing, while "always unethical" is too strict, implying that the casual interchange of even a single price is wrong.[2]

[2] For further consideration of the ethical aspects of these nine questions, cf. Thomas M. Garrett, S.J., *Business Ethics* (New York: Appleton-Century-Crofts, 1966); Thomas M. Garrett, S.J., *Ethics in Business* (New York: Sheed and Ward, 1963); Herbert Johnston, *Business Ethics* (New York: Pitman, 1961); Henry Wirtenberger, S.J., *Morality and Business* (Chicago: Loyola University Press, 1962).

Index

AAAA, *see* American Association of Advertising Agencies
Accountant, 99–100
Advancement, competition for, 94–96, 212
Advertising industry, 115–116; and ethical-practices code, 163; and Better Business Bureaus, 168
Aerospace industry, 121
AFL-CIO, ethical practices code, 156
Africa, 151. *See also* South Africa
Age, 48; and ethical attitude, 4, 74–80, 90, 174
Allport-Vernon-Lindzey Values Test, 19
Ambition, relation to ethics, 78, 80
American Association of Advertising Agencies, "Standards of Practice," 162–163
American Association of Collegiate Schools of Business, 179n
American Business Creed, The, 144, 197
American Electric Power Company, 177
American Iron and Steel Institute, 139
American Management Association, 2–3, 153, 203; and ethical codes, 154
American Motors, 211n
American Psychological Association, 164
American Stock Exchange, 2
American Telephone and Telegraph Company, 155

Americans in international business, 128–134
Andrews, Kenneth, 176
Anthony, Robert N., 64
Antitrust laws, U.S., 143, 165, 166–167; and NASD, 168. *See also* Electrical industry, antitrust suits
Aquinas, St. Thomas, 43–44
Arab Nations, 141
Audit, social, of corporation, 211–212
Austin, Robert W., 160–161
Automobile industry, 1, 2, 133

Bank of America, 152
Bankers Monthly Magazine, 160
Banking, 32, 116; overseas branches, 133
Bankruptcy, 59, 61, 64–66. *See also* Solvency
Behavior, ethical: parental influence on, 5, 67–69, 209; disparity with standards, 15–16, 70–73, 155, 209; and sanctions for unethical behavior, 33–34, 57–59; off-the-job, 34–36; motivating factors for, 46–54; boss's influence, 48, 81–88, 209; influence of conscience, 48, 55–66, 67, 209; occupational differences in, 96–98; influence of custom on, 135–138, 142; and government regulation, 145–147; effect of ethical code on, 157–160, 169–170
Beis, Richard, 137
Berle, Adolf A., Jr., 164

7